Dear Dean:

Thanks so [much for]
all your help a[nd your]
support. It's really appreciated.

God bless,

Pat

To Dean:
So good to have fellowship
with old friends. May the
Lord continue to bless your
ministry. With love,

Margaret Troutt

Phil 4:13

July 1980

The General was a Lady

The General was a Lady

The Story
of Evangeline Booth

by Margaret Troutt

A. J. Holman Co.
Nashville

Printed in the United States of America

U.S. Library of Congress Cataloging in Publication Data

The Salvation Army
The general was a lady

ISBN 0-87981-139-0 (Paper Back)
ISBN 0-87981-141-2 (Hard Back)

Contents

Foreword vii

Preface ix

1. ALL FLAGS WAVING 11

2. GOD'S CHRISTMAS GIFT 15

3. A GOODLY HERITAGE 18

4. HALLELUJAHS AND AMENS 24

5. GROWING PAINS 33

6. ANGEL OF THE SLUMS 41

7. SEND EVA 55

8. DOUBLE DUTY 64

9. LOVE STORY 74

10. CRISIS IN THE U.S.A. 81

11. MUSTERED TO CANADA 89

12. THE GAMBLER AND THE LADY 103

13. MARCH ON 115

Contents

14. AT HOME 132

15. A NEW ERA 144

16. DOUGHBOYS AND DOUGHNUTS 152

17. MUSIC MAKER 165

18. THE WORLD'S GREATEST ROMANCE .. 179

19. FULL STEAM AHEAD 190

20. STORMY WEATHER 203

21. THE GREAT DEPRESSION 217

22. OUT OF THE CLOUD 225

23. GENERAL EVANGELINE 237

24. THE WORLD FOR GOD 248

25. GRUELING SCHEDULES 260

26. AFTERGLOW 273

27. BATTLE'S END 284

Notes 288

Bibliography 307

The Booth Family 312

Index 316

Foreword

There could hardly be a more appropriate time for the appearance of this biography, issued as it is in the Centenary Year of The Salvation Army in the United States of America.

For thirty years, Evangeline Cory Booth charted and commanded the work and the witness of the Movement in "the home of the brave and the land of the free." Gifted daughter of the Founders, William and Catherine Booth, and herself the fourth General (1934-1939), her occupancy of that high office validated for all time the assertion that for women and men officers alike there are within The Salvation Army equal opportunities for service and responsibility.

A world figure of amazing talent, dramatic presence, and immense platform power, she was a leader of people who was herself willingly led by the Christ to whom she had early declared (as one of her several inspired songs puts it), "I bring Thee all."

Therein lies the true secret of Evangeline Booth's accomplishments, as the reader perusing this chronicle will quickly and unforgettably come to realize.

London   —GENERAL ARNOLD BROWN
1979

Preface

The day Evangeline Booth arrived to lecture the cadets at the Chicago school for officers' training, I was the young cadet chosen to open the door for her.

A compassionate leader, a strict disciplinarian, and a dynamic speaker, this sometimes unpredictable woman swept regally through the door, followed by two or three high-ranking officers. But she didn't pass me as if I were a piece of furniture. She stopped for a moment, appraised me with her piercing brown eyes, then smiled approval. That day I was convinced she wore a halo, and I never forgot this first glimpse of her.

Through the years our paths crossed on several occasions. Whether listening to her preach to great crowds of people in public meetings or to officers in private councils, I sat enthralled. She made a tremendous impact upon my life. I never dreamed as I opened the door for her that one day I would be asked to open the door of her life to readers.

The purpose of this book is to acquaint people with one of the greatest women of her era—perhaps *the* greatest woman. She continues to live through the people who knew and loved her, through the on-going outreach of her extensive ministry, and through her history-making accomplishments. Her human frailties were part of her complex personality and charisma.

Under her innovative leadership—thirty years in the United States and eight years in Canada—the Salvation Army's many-faceted program became a part of America's religious and sociological life. She retired as General of the worldwide organization, the only woman to date to hold that rank.

I acknowledge with deep gratitude those who helped me in the preparation of this book:

General Arnold Brown, who wrote the Foreword.

Commissioner Norman S. Marshall, now international secretary for the Americas, who asked me three years ago on behalf of the Salvation Army's literary board to write a new biography of Evangeline Booth.

Colonel Albert Scott, who succeeded Commissioner Marshall as chief secretary in the eastern U.S.A. territory and sustained high interest in the progress of the book.

Members of the Salvation Army's international literary department, who assisted greatly in research and in evaluation of the manuscript.

Major Dorothy Breen, literary secretary of the eastern U.S.A. territory, for her patience, understanding cooperation, and helpfulness throughout the time of research and writing.

Brigadier Christine McMillan, for her continual source of historical information, personal encouragement, and chapter evaluations.

Colonel Dorothy Phillips, for her sincere interest from the beginning and for editorial suggestions that improved many chapters.

The many people who granted me interviews, and my non-Salvation Army writer friends of The Robin who evaluated several chapters.

Dr. Russell T. Hitt, of the A. J. Holman Company, for his sympathetic editing of the manuscript.

My husband, John, whom I can never adequately thank for his concerned care, heartening stimulus, and constant support.

—MARGARET TROUTT

1

All Flags Waving

September 14, 1934.

New York City wore an air of expectancy. A tremendous crowd had gathered at City Hall, where the steps were a riot of color. Flags, bunting, and the suppressed excitement engendered by last-minute checkups on microphones meant something special was going to happen.

Old-timers passed the word along that Mayor Fiorello H. LaGuardia had promised this would be the city's greatest welcome-home to a citizen since Lindbergh's reception after his "Lone Eagle" ocean flight, and to this end he had enlisted the aid of the United States Army and Navy and both city and state governments. What was the occasion? Commander Evangeline Booth was returning to America as General-Elect of The Salvation Army.

When the mammoth ship *Leviathan* that was bringing the new General and her party back to America neared quarantine, a flotilla of gaily beflagged boats, with conspicuous signs proclaiming WELCOME HOME, GENERAL EVANGELINE BOOTH, sailed out under the Salvation Army tricolor flag to greet her.

The city's official launch, the *Riverside,* led the way.

Jammed on it were newsmen, photographers, sound cameramen, Salvation Army administrative personnel, the New York Staff Band, and representatives of the Mayor's 250-member welcoming committee, with Salvation Army Brigadier John Allen as admiral for the day and also chief megaphone man. The launch *Seagate* followed, its decks crowded with uniformed Salvationists and the Boston band. Next came three tugs, representing the Central, Western, and Southern territories of The Salvation Army, all crowded with Salvationists, many of them shouting "hallelujah" through megaphones.

As the mighty *Leviathan* and the flotilla met, cheers filled the air. Whistles blew double forte. The bands outdid each other as they played "There's a Welcome Home, a Soldier's Welcome Home." From the clouds, two airplanes swooped down. Noted aviator Ruth Nichols piloting one of them, unloaded five bushels of roses onto the ship, a fragrant token from one woman to another, each a leader in her field.

The enthusiastic greeters were thrilled when they caught their first glimpse of Evangeline Booth. She lifted her right arm in characteristic fashion and smiled; some thought she wiped a tear from her eye. (Later she admitted, "I was almost overcome with this manifestation of love for the Army and me. How my father would have rejoiced over it.") Then she boarded the *Riverside,* where everybody wanted to hug her, kiss her, or shake her hand. Photographers' cameras clicked, reporters hurled questions, broadcasters insisted on a speech.

As the Salvation Army flotilla approached Castle Gardens, famous in Army history as the spot where Commissioner George Scott Railton and his pioneer party of seven lassies held their first open-air meeting on American soil more than fifty years before, the city fireboats streamed their glittering salute in a thousand cascading, watery jets. Sirens screeched, whistles blew, horns tooted, pennants whipped in the breeze, and when General Evangeline disembarked, another great band and a large crowd roared their welcome to her.

A cordon of motorcycle and mounted police took their place at the head of the parade planned for the occasion. Members of the U.S. Army and Navy and the New York police and fire departments marched with Salvationists up the "Grand Canyon" of Broadway to City Hall, carrying the Stars and Stripes, the Salvation Army flag, and the flags of many nations. The band of the Sixteenth Infantry augmented three large Salvation Army bands. Hundreds of policemen lined the curbs, keeping the milling crowds in line.

Ringing cheers echoed and re-echoed as the Salvation Army's fourth General, standing erect in an open car, acknowledged the greetings of fellow New Yorkers. Ticker tape cascaded from a thousand windows crowded with people. Never in her lifetime of welcomes and farewells had Evangeline Booth been acclaimed with such enthusiasm and affection.

Evangeline returned to the City Hall steps for the formal civic welcome where more than 8,000 people heard Mayor LaGuardia congratulate her on her appointment as General of the "greatest and most useful army in the whole world." In response, the new General said she was "overwhelmed by this marvelous welcome from the City of New York" and appealed to her listeners to accompany her with their goodwill and prayers as she went forth to "carry the gospel to a world that—as we all know—is in desperate need of Christ."

What kind of person was Evangeline Booth, hailed by historians as one of the greatest women of her era? She was a woman, dedicated, determined, devoted:

- who led thousands to her Lord through her preaching;
- who stirred the emotions of untold numbers with her great oratory and dramatic lectures;
- who had a keen mind, was charming and witty, and drew people with her personal magnetism;
- who had the style of a prima donna, though often insecure and in need of reassurance;
- who was a strict disciplinarian, but never harbored a grudge;
- who was an able administrator and inspired love, devotion, and loyalty because she herself sincerely loved all kinds of people, whatever their circumstances.

But in addition, Evangeline could be demanding, unpredictable, willful, impulsive, and mercurial.

Her story begins on Christmas Day, 1865, in Victorian England.

2
God's Christmas Gift

On Christmas Eve, 1865, the tall, rangy general superintendent of the East London Christian Mission cut his fiery sermon short and locked the door early.

"W'at's 'e doin' that fer?" complained one of the newly converted toughs from the Whitechapel district.

"Don'tcha know? Yer ain't seen the Missus lately, 'ave yer? Well. . . ."

William Booth absentmindedly touched his top hat in a farewell gesture and hurried down Whitechapel Road. As he walked through the swirling snow, he remembered how, less than six months before, he had been invited to lead a revival mission here in the East End. He had preached in a tent on the old Quaker burial ground, just a stone's throw from the slums of Whitechapel Road.

Booth knew that few people knew how great was the degradation of this cesspool of human misery in London's East End. It surpassed anything he had seen when he had worked with the poor as a Methodist circuit minister or, during the past four years, when he had preached to the unchurched masses. The poverty and pain of the East End, where cats fared better than people, was an unknown world to most people in Victorian England. The irony was that just a short distance from this stinking blight was the fashionable West End, the seat of the British world's money and power.

Booth looked toward the Blind Beggar public house. He often preached in front of it, passionately "banging a Bible and waving an umbrella to attract attention."[1] He had become adroit at fending off dead cats, rotten garbage, and other refuse thrown at him by drunken rowdies. Starved children, with wolfish faces, were scrounging through piles of discarded rubbish in the street and gobbling up pieces of decayed food, but to-night he did not stop. Catherine, his wife, might need him, so he pushed on against the wintry blast that whipped his long black coat around his legs.

Once at home, he closed the front door softly behind him, although he was sure the three oldest of their six children were still awake upstairs. They had been speculating about the new baby, whether it would be a boy or a girl; more especially, whether it would be born on Christmas Day. He hurried up to Catherine. "Don't worry, William," she told him.

During the long, sleepless night Booth sat or walked the floor in the room adjacent to hers. Every time the midwife came to the door, he bounded over to ask, "Is everything going well?" until finally, the next morning, he knelt beside Catherine and looked tearfully at the small bundle of new life nestled against her breast.

"She's going to be like you, William," Catherine said.

He was deeply touched, as any father would be, and not only because this little one resembled him. Wasn't there something special about this child, conceived the same year he responded to God's call to minister to the poverty-stricken East Enders and now born on Christmas Day? Surely this babe was a token of God's covenant, a Christmas gift assuring him and Catherine of God's blessing upon this new venture to which He had called them.

The two watched the child and reflected upon God's goodness to them. Catherine Booth had been reading *Uncle Tom's Cabin* and wanted a "Little Eva" in her home. "Born like the Holy Evangel, on Christ's birthday," she said, breaking the silence. "Shall we call her Evangeline?"[2]

For some reason William Booth registered the child as Eveline Cory,[3] but she was never called anything but Eva until after she came to the United States in 1904 as Commander.

Carefully lifting the baby from Catherine's arms, Booth placed her in her first cradle, a basket lined with straw, and took her downstairs. The other six children, all high-spirited youngsters, were eating breakfast. They looked up expectantly as their father, still in his long frock coat, with a big smile on his black-bearded face, held the basket out to them.

"Here," he said, "is God's Christmas gift."[4]

They crowded around to see the baby. Emma, the sister who later was especially close to Eva, said, "Look at her beautiful hair. It's almost red, and so much of it."

"Papa, does she look like you or Mama?" Bramwell, the oldest child, wanted to know.

"She looks like a real Booth," his father said proudly.

3

A Goodly Heritage

Evangeline Booth became proud of her heritage—spiritual as well as physical. She and the other Booth children never tired of hearing their mother tell about the night in July 1865, before she was born, when William Booth had burst into the room, his eyes shining, and said to Catherine, "Darling, I've found my destiny!"

One can imagine Catherine Booth sitting before a glowing fire with her children around her as she recalled that unforgettable night. "Your father came home from meeting near midnight as usual. I was already home because I wasn't feeling well. I was carrying you at the time, Eva." (Years later Evangeline said, "I was there when the Army was born.") "I can still hear his exact words: 'Oh, Kate, as I passed by the doors of the flaming gin palaces tonight, I seemed to hear a voice sounding in my ears, "Where can you go and find such heathen as these, and where is there so great a need for your labors?" And I felt as though I ought at every cost to stop and preach to these East End multitudes.' "

Catherine Booth stopped and sat gazing into the flames. "We had a fire that night, too, but I felt a cold chill as I thought about what this would mean—another move, another beginning again. It wasn't easy, even now with the collections. We couldn't expect the poverty-stricken East Enders to support us.

"Your father and I sat there thinking about this. I was praying; I'm sure he was, too. Then I said, 'William, if you feel you ought to stay, stay. We have trusted the Lord *once* for our support and we can trust Him *again*.'

"We had no idea then of the marvellous work to come."[1]

Preaching was not a new venture for William Booth, although until his conversion at fifteen, he had been just a nominal Christian—one in name only. His biographer describes him as "Willful Will"—a child of fiery temper, impetuous, passionate, and a ringleader among his peers.[2] This could also be a description of Evangeline as a child. She had inherited her father's long nose, too. Booth's mother, Mary Moss Booth, as her name suggests, was probably Jewish.[3] His father, Samuel Booth, suffered financial losses and at thirteen William was taken out of school and apprenticed to a pawnbroker in the poorest part of Nottingham.[4]

Walking one evening to a Bible class at the Broad Street Wesleyan Methodist Chapel, William thought about his shortcomings. That night he knelt at a plain wooden table where others knelt and pledged, "God shall have all there is of William Booth."[5]

Now filled with evangelistic fervor, he became the spearhead of a group of teenagers which nightly preached on street corners of the Nottingham slums and often knelt to pray with repentant sinners. When he attempted to bring the converts within the Methodist fold, William had his first confrontation with an organized church's unwillingness to associate with have-nots.[6] Years later he would respond to the need for a church home for the poor who knelt at his altars (later termed penitent-forms).

Meanwhile, growing up in Ashbourne, Derbyshire, was a small girl named Catherine Mumford who would one day fall in love with William Booth. Catherine's parents encouraged her to study the Bible, and by the time she was twelve, she had read the Bible aloud eight times.[7] The frail girl was confined to her room one winter with symptoms of consumption, and serious curvature of the spine forced her to spend another year in bed. During these years she concentrated on books of religious history and theology, acquiring useful knowledge for later years.[8]

For his part, at the end of his six-year apprenticeship, William Booth also moved to London and became well known as a lay preacher in the pulpit of Methodist reformers' chapels. Catherine first heard him speak at Binfield House Chapel and thought he preached one of the best sermons she had heard there.[9]

With William and Catherine, friendship soon ripened into love. Since William was in and out of London as a lay evangelist, their romance was sustained by letters.

A letter from Catherine instigated their one lovers' quarrel. Catherine Mumford was ahead of her time on women's rights. She wrote a burning retort to her minister who had dismissed women as the weaker sex mentally, and sent Booth a copy.

To her dismay, William agreed with the minister, arguing that while woman was superior in her affection, "my honest conviction is that man is her superior in intellect." Catherine challenged him to prove women's inferiority from the Word of God.

Finally, William said, "I am for the world's salvation; I will quarrel with no means that promises help."[10] Years later Booth placed his own daughters and other women in vital roles of The Salvation Army. On his first visit to the capitol building in Washington, the Army's Founder was waylaid by reporters, who asked why he had permitted women to take leadership positions hitherto held exclusively by men. In humorous vein, he replied, "Why, some of my best men are women!"[11]

William was always conscious of his lack of formal religious training. In 1854 he joined the Methodist New Connexion and studied in London for six months under the supervision of Dr. William Cooke.[12]

William Booth and Catherine Mumford, both 26, were married by the Reverend Dr. Thomas at the Stockwell New Chapel, South London, on June 16, 1855.[13]

By 1861 Catherine's name began to appear in newspapers as a "woman preacher."[14] In Victorian England, any woman who spoke in public faced censure. Catherine's acceptance by congregations did not extend to many of the clergy. When the Methodist Conference met in May, a large number of members felt that these unpredictable Booths needed curbing.

Before the conference, William had written to Dr. Henry Crofts, the president, reminding him that he had been waiting four years to be reassigned to full-time evangelistic work.[15] When his appointment was considered, it set off a heated debate. Catherine, sitting in the gallery, got more upset every minute. How dare these men try to thwart God's purpose for her William!

When Dr. Crofts asked observers in the gallery to leave, Catherine left her seat but remained at the door at the head of the stairs. Dr. Cooke, Booth's old principal, proposed a compromise. Let Booth's appointment as superintendent to the Newcastle circuit, one of the most important in the Connexion, stand but allow him to arrange with its officers for time away from pastoral work to do evangelistic work elsewhere.

William was horrified. How could he leave the responsibility for the Connexion's toughest circuit with junior officers and go off to hold evangelistic meetings? If William was horrified, Catherine was downright indignant. While she loved the Methodists, she knew that the suggested compromise would bring only frustration. Unable to restrain herself, she exclaimed, "No, never!"

When Dr. Cooke's compromise became a substantive resolution and was passed by a large majority, William Booth left the chapel. Catherine met him, and they walked away together. Eight weeks later William sent in his resignation to Dr. Crofts.[16] Although he left the Methodist New Connexion, William Booth never lost his love for the Methodist Church.

During the next four years invitations poured in for the Booths to conduct revivals. This, along with the thousands who professed conversion in his meetings, convinced William of divine approval.

In 1865 the Booths moved to Hammersmith, West London. William began preaching to the poor East Enders, walking eight miles there and back each Sunday, while Catherine attracted large crowds to her meetings in London's affluent West End.

When they decided in July that William should devote his entire efforts to the salvation of the East Enders, they realized that they would be on their own financially. Since William Booth, along with the apostle Paul, believed that "I can do all things through Christ which strengtheneth me" (Philippians 4:13) he didn't sit around and worry about his lack of money. Every night the lean, hawk-nosed man took his stand in front of the Blind Begger or the Vine public house.[17]

Mrs. Booth continued preaching in the West End until the end of October when her overtaxed body rebelled. Evangeline would be born in less than two months. In November Booth moved Catherine, their six children and Mary Kirkton to No. 1 Cambridge Lodge Villas, Hackney, East London, where Eva and later the eighth child, Lucy Milward, were born.[18]

When Evangeline was six weeks old, her mother began a ten-week series of meetings.[19] Soon after this, Catherine became so ill with dysentery which resisted treatment that her family became alarmed.[20] It was almost two years before she was well enough to do public work.

None of the Booths ever did anything by halves. Throughout her life Evangeline worked until she collapsed and had to rest, often resuming activities against doctor's orders.

Her mother's poor health and the fact that William Booth was now concentrating his efforts on the nearby East Enders rather than going away from home for long periods of revival meetings, meant that Evangeline received more attention from her father than had the previous six children.

4

Hallelujahs and Amens

Auburn-haired Evangeline, to be known by everyone as Eva for the next thirty-nine years, never knew a lonely moment as a child. With the exception of Marian, a semi-invalid as the result of smallpox, all the Booth children were extroverts, some of them too lively for their stream of governesses.

For Catherine and William were agreed that their children must have a good education. They had tried day schools for Bramwell, but because they moved around so often, Catherine felt that no one paid enough attention to him.[1] So they decided that, by practicing self-denial, they would hire a governess. The year before Eva was born, the last one of a series walked out, but William wrote Catherine reassuringly that a governess "with some heart and conscience" would show up. As he reminded her, "We have not regretted parting with any of the lot yet."[2] Sure enough, a short time later, a Miss MacBean, who had heard of the Booths, offered to be the governess to the children.[3]

Baby Eva was the pet of the family. Eighteen years later Bramwell, who was nine when she was born, wrote to her, "I feel today about you as though you were grown little again . . . and I want to lift you in my arms and sing to you till you rest."[4] (This was probably when Eva was taking an enforced rest before going to the Great Western Hall in London.)

Acknowledged by the family as "Papa's favorite," and with his Hebraic features, Eva also resembled him in temperament. This pleased them both. Eva grew accustomed to the concessions made to her by the rest of the family. Not only the family but also William's followers catered to her whims, and she soon accepted as a matter of course that she was special. Naturally outgoing and uninhibited, and never shy, she tended to dramatize everything that happened to her. Along with the other Booth children, she had a severe case of whooping cough. While the others whooped in a normal way, Eva spun around like a top when she coughed.

But Eva was not the only enthusiast and live wire among the Booth children. As someone once asked, "How could they be otherwise with such a father and such a mother, and in an environment of hallelujahs and amens ever since they were born?"[5]

As a small child, Eva was part of the audience when eleven-year-old Ballington set up an impromptu meeting in the nursery and preached. Kate, age ten, and Emma, eight, sometimes had trouble keeping their dolls quiet. When this happened, Ballington demanded, "Take those babies out of the meeting." But his sisters refused to go, reminding him, "Papa would not have told us to leave; Papa would have kept on preaching."[6]

Eva watched Ballington shape a pillow as though it were a convert, thrusting it down at a makeshift penitent-form William used as an altar, and urging, "Give up the drink, brother."[7]

The two-story Cambridge Villas house proved comfortable and adequate for the growing family, and the large garden provided space for the children's birds, dogs, guinea pigs, rabbits, and white mice.[8] But Catherine Booth thought it a nerve-racking place to live. After the birth of her eighth and last child, Lucy Milward, she almost suffered a nervous breakdown. William was so busy he seemed not to notice her condition. The sound of a dog barking in the street, the rattle of carriage wheels on the road, even the chirping of sparrows outside her window prevented Catherine from sleeping.

Then, while out walking with the children one morning, she noticed a house at No. 3 Gore Road, opposite Victoria Park. It stood by itself on a quiet street. She suggested to William that they move there, but he said the house was too expensive.

"We must move, William. I'll take in another lodger in addition to Miss Jane Short to help with the rent, even though it means more housework." She was able to convince a still-dubious William only when she told him, "Unless quiet can be secured for me, I will soon be beyond the need of any house at all."[9]

In December 1868 the Booth family, with faithful Mary Kirkton and Miss Jane Short, moved to No. 3 Gore Road, where they were joined by Miss Mary Coutts Billups, daughter of a wealthy friend of the Booths.[10]

The Gore Road house was a three-storied, double-fronted one, with large plate-glass windows and big living rooms, plus a half basement.[11] Catherine thoroughly enjoyed the relief from noise. But a Booth home was never really quiet. William established an office headquarters for administrative purposes as soon as he could afford one, but much of the mission's business was still discussed at home.

Shortly before Eva's seventh birthday, George Scott Railton, who later became William Booth's first lieutenant, moved into the Booth home. He remained there for the next eleven years.[12]

Miss Jane Short, soon known as Sister Jane, became a member of the family, sometimes even sharing her bedroom with one of the Booth children, and worked herself nearly to death in the service of the mission.[13] She had worried about going to live with them. How could the Booths in their home life live up to what they were in their preaching? She loved them and did not want to be disillusioned. However, Miss Short was not disappointed. She was impressed by William's great love for his wife and thought the children were delightful.[14]

The Booths insisted on plain, serviceable clothes for their children, reminding them that they must set an example for London's poor. When her mother sent beautiful outfits to the children, Catherine would remove the fancy lace or trimming and urge her mother to send only simple, unadorned clothes. One day Miss Short heard William tell the children, "When I get you all to heaven, I'll deck you; it will be safe there."[15] The plain clothes Eva had to wear as a child may have been one of the reasons she sent a dress or outfit that was serviceable but attractive to every officer's child for Christmas when she was Commander in the United States.

The first Christmas Sister Jane spent with the Booths, they made great preparations the week ahead for a happy, joyful holiday. The General entered into the excitement with the children. But when he returned from preaching in Whitechapel on Christmas morning, everyone knew something was wrong. His face was pale, his gray eyes haunted. Although he tried to enter into the children's fun, he finally gave up and strode around the room like a caged lion. At last he cried out, "I'll never have a Christmas Day like this again!" In the dead silence that followed, he said, "The poor have nothing but the public house—nothing but the public house."[16]

That was the last Christmas the Booth family ever

spent together. The following year, they scattered among the slums distributing 150 plum puddings, many of them made in their own kitchen.[17] As soon as she was old enough, Eva helped distribute "Christmas cheer," and ever after it was her habit to spend Christmas Day visiting the lonely, the shut-in, the sick, or those in straitened circumstances.

Polly, a young girl waiting on table in the Booth household, never forgot the day Eva saw a hungry man loitering outside the house on Gore Road. Eva jumped from her chair and asked, "Mama, may I take my dinner to that man outside?"

"Yes, Eva."

She ran outside, and a few minutes later Polly saw the man wolfing down the food.[18]

Sometimes Eva's impulsiveness got her into trouble, such as the time she defended Marian (Marie, to the family). Catherine had asked Eva to help Marie with her lessons. One day when their parents were away, Marie, slow at grasping a French lesson, provoked the governess until she grabbed Marie by the hair and shook her. Whereupon Eva slapped the governess and was ordered to bed with nothing but dry bread and a glass of milk until she apologized.

For two days she refused to say she was sorry. When her mother returned, she told Eva, "Even when we have the highest motives, a Christian must practice restraint. Come now, Eva, aren't you sorry for the *way* you defended Marie?"

Eva still wanted to say no, but looking into her mother's pleading eyes, she finally said, "I'm *nearly* sorry." Nearly was the best she could do.[19]

The children were always aware of the world around them, but Catherine Booth encouraged them to enjoy

life to the full. Some noisy arguments centered around
Eva. She was an outstanding cricket player and both
teams wanted her on their side. Catherine rarely inter-
fered and gave them free rein in their third-floor playroom. Above the ceiling in the room where she usually
worked was a double floor, packed with sawdust, which
deadened the sounds of commotion upstairs. Unless William came home too tired and distraught, he romped
with his children. Games usually included their favorite,
"Fox and Geese," with Father always the fox.[20]

William or Catherine read aloud from the Bible in
family devotions, and Bible characters became familiar
friends to the youngsters. In their playroom, they acted
out scenes: Abraham giving proof of his faith and obedience to God by his willingness to sacrifice his son, Isaac;
David slaying Goliath; Daniel in the lions' den; and, upon
Eva's insistence, Queen Esther going before the king to
intercede for her people. Noah's Ark and his biblical
menagerie were among their props. The animals were
used so often that their limbs and bodies broke down.
They then became burnt offerings (albeit not perfect) as
commanded in the Book of Leviticus. The sacrificial
table soon showed a deep black circle from the charcoal
used in these ceremonies. They also had their own revival
meetings, patterned after those conducted by their
father, with resounding "hallelujahs" and "amens."[21] Eva
would offer to set up the chairs for meetings, provided
her brothers and sisters would let her do the talking.[22]

And Eva never forgot that, when she was a small
child, her mother took her into the garden and said to
her, "Eva, the world is full of sin, full of wickedness. I
want the world to be a better place because you, Eva, have
lived in it."[23]

Although she kept a cook to help with meals for the
increasingly large number of people at their table,

Catherine Booth did much of the baking herself. Eva tried to be on hand when her mother was at the big wooden kitchen table, mixing the dough.[24] More often than not, her father would dash excitedly into the kitchen to share a new plan for the Christian Mission or to try out a new sermon on his wife.[25] Eva would run over and stand at his knee, listening to every word. William Booth could not speak without enthusiasm and gestures. An indelible impression stayed with Eva all her life. "I would quiver with excitement as I heard him preaching about Moses, Abraham, Daniel, dramatizing their lives and applying them to practical, everyday Christianity. He would forget that only Mama and I were there. My mother was a great speaker. She had a special ministry with intellectuals and influential people. With her logical and philosophical arguments, she confounded agnostics and unbelievers. But as a child, my unspoken prayer was always, 'Oh, God, help me some day to preach like Papa.' "[26]

The family's redhaired cook, Emma Westbrook, encouraged and applauded Eva in any new venture she tackled.[27] She was part of the group who listened the day five-year-old Eva climbed up on the kitchen table, between the butter and the bacon, and preached her first sermon.[28] Her text was the nursery rhyme beginning, "Hey diddle, diddle, the cat and the fiddle." Her father heard about the episode and decided to keep his eye on this impetuous child.[29]

A few years later, he sat on the stairs and made notes when Eva, again in the kitchen, stood on a chair and preached. This time she used "God Is Love" for her text. Booth was amazed at the impassioned appeal she made to her improvised audience of dolls, reminding them that Christ's love was all that stood between them and hellfire. He told himself, "Truly, she is a child of great promise.

God will use her to draw thousands of sinners to the Saviour's Cross."[30]

Like her father, Eva Booth would never give great theological discourses. Her sermons would center upon God's love for sinners, urging them to seek salvation through Jesus Christ. She would then show them how to apply this love to their everyday life in times of crisis, when they were discouraged, downhearted, and floundering, and would teach them how to become strong, mature Christians.

As she watched her older brothers and sisters helping in the meetings her parents conducted, Eva could hardly wait to get started herself. But was she good enough? She settled that question on her seventh birthday. Years later she wrote:

> Our parents had prayed with us and kissed us goodnight. But I couldn't sleep because I knew I wasn't as good as my mother and father wanted me to be.
>
> I slipped out of bed and in my bare feet ran to their room. Kneeling by the bed, I cried, "Mama, I want to be converted like you and Papa, and Katie and Emma and . . ." I can still feel the warmth of her arms as I knelt by her side, and feel my father's hand upon my head. Kneeling there with the simple trust of a little girl, I gave my heart to the children's Saviour."[31]

Then one night Eva made her debut at one of her father's meetings. He had preached with his usual fervor, and amid cries of "hallelujah," "praise the Lord," and "amen," the penitent-form had been lined again and again with sinners seeking forgiveness. At last William Booth raised his hand for silence and announced, "My little Eva will sing for us." Eva stood up, looking very small in her brown dress and inverted saucer hat. She did not seem at all nervous as she sang, every word distinct and easily understood, the way her father liked. "God bless her," people in the great crowd murmured.[32]

Although Booth often featured Eva after that as a singer or musician, she had to wait until she was fifteen to wear the uniform of a sergeant and put on the Salvation Army bonnet designed by her mother.[33]

5
Growing Pains

By 1878 some of the missioners were already using military terms. Elijah Cadman, a converted chimney sweep, declared "War! War in Whitby!" to be waged by "Captain Cadman, evangelist of the Christian Mission." Six-foot James Dowdle, the "Happy Fiddler," talked about "mustering his forces" and "opening fire" on communities.[1]

Many of the field evangelists were getting impatient with the slowness of policy decisions from the thirty-four-member committee that governed the Christian Mission. George Scott Railton told William Booth, "We gave up our lives to work under *you* and those you should appoint, rather than under one another."[2]

In May, recovering from the grippe, William summoned Bramwell and Railton to his bedroom. When Bramwell arrived, his father was walking up and down in a yellow dressing gown, dictating to Railton. Bramwell looked at the proofs of the Christian Mission's annual report. When he read "We are a volunteer army," he said, "Volunteer! I'm not a volunteer. I'm a regular or nothing."

His father stopped walking, leaned over Railton's shoulder, took his pen from his hand, scratched out the word volunteer, and wrote in its place the word salvation. "Thank God for that,"[3] said Bramwell and Railton.

The new name, The Salvation Army, first appeared in the September 1878 issue of the *Christian Mission Magazine*.[4] Some of the missioners were not too enthusiastic about becoming an army. But after William's War Congress in August, they fell in line and marched to battle against sin under the "Blood and Fire" banner of The Salvation Army. He changed the name of the Mission's magazine to *The Salvationist* (changed to *The War Cry* in December 1879),[5] and kept his soldiers informed of changes in terminology.

Evangelists became officers who worked in a local corps hall or barracks rather than a mission house; members were soldiers whose tithe became a cartridge to be fired each week. Soldiers did not die, they were "promoted to glory." But in an era when uniforms were seen everywhere, it was two years before Salvationists' uniforms were standardized. Then the men wore dark blue serge patrol jackets over red guernseys (slip-over knit shirts); the women plain long dresses with black straw bonnets.

This self-named Salvation Army, which encouraged semiliterate converts to tell the gospel story, was an affront to the intellectual Anglican clergy.[6] Even Queen Victoria, temporarily annoyed when William Booth became General of The Salvation Army, asserted, "Mine should be the only Army in the British Empire; mine the only one with Generals."[7] But Eva, just coming into her teens, was an enthusiastic soldier. She drilled the cook and anyone else she could round up in marching, countermarching, and standing at attention. Herbert complained to their father that Eva, as usual, was going to extremes and asked, "Can't you stop her from saluting every time she meets one of us?" William just chuckled and, with a twinkle in his eye, continued to return Eva's snappy salutes.[8]

One of Eva's pets, a monkey named Jeannie, irritated visitors by grimacing at them, leaping upon their hats, and snatching at their feather trimmings. With the help of the cook, Eva made a Salvation Army uniform for the monkey, hoping this would improve her pet's behavior. But when Eva added the red ribbon on which was embroidered The Salvation Army, her mother felt she had gone too far and undressed the monkey, answering her daughter's question with "Eva, she doesn't live the life." Evangeline always remembered the importance of "living the life."[9]

In 1880, the General moved his family from Gore Road to Clapton Common, East London, fitted up the Gore Road house as a training home to accommodate thirty women cadets, and appointed Eva's sister Emma to take charge. A few months later, the General acquired another house in Hackney and adapted it as a training home for men, putting his second son, Ballington, in charge.[10]

A short time before this, William Booth had received an appeal from Salvationists who had moved from England to the United States, begging him to send officers to America. Amos Shirley, his wife, Anna, and their sixteen-year-old daughter, Eliza (who had served a short time as a lieutenant in England), soon after arriving in Philadelphia, "opened fire" with a religious open-air meeting on a street corner. They held indoor services, patterned after Army meetings in England, in an old chair factory Amos Shirley had rented. Scarlet posters invited the public to come and hear "two hallelujah females speak and sing for Jesus." Eliza Shirley kept William Booth informed of their activities and sent him newspaper accounts of their meetings.

While the General was trying to reach a decision about America, Railton, his right-hand man, asked to be allowed to go. Every man was needed on the home front, but Railton offered to take "sisters" (since there were more of them in the ranks) for his invasion force. William Booth capitulated and in February 1880 appointed seven "lassies" to accompany Railton to the United States.

Eva fretted because she was not old enough to be chosen. But she was delighted that Captain Emma Westbrook, their former cook and a favorite friend of her childhood, was one of the group. At their farewell meeting in Whitechapel, Eva told her, "If only I could go too."[11] She had no idea then that she would one day be appointed to the United States and would spend almost half of her life in America.

Mrs. Booth gave Railton two flags, one for the corps already established in Philadelphia, the other for the corps he was to open in New York,[12] and when the *Australia* docked at Castle Garden in New York on March 10, 1880, the people waiting on shore were amazed to see eight uniformed persons—a stocky, black-bearded man and seven young women—come marching down the gangplank, lustily singing hymns. On the bands of their black, derbylike hats were the words THE SALVATION ARMY printed in gold letters. The curious spectators crowded close to see what this uninhibited group would do next.

The strong March wind whipped their red-yellow-and-blue silk banner close to the faces of bystanders, who wondered about the small American flag in one corner of the strangers' flag and showed interest in the meaning of the words *Blood and Fire* which were inscribed on the yellow sun in the center.

As soon as thirty-year-old Commissioner Railton finished speaking on the text John 3:16, he told the newspaper reporters who pushed through the crowd to interview him that America was the first country outside the British Isles to be invaded. The Salvationists' frequent shouts of "hallelujah" caused the press to refer to them often thereafter as the "Hallelujah Army."[13]

Amos Shirley met the pioneer party at the ship in New York, and Railton commissioned him, his wife, and Eliza as captains. The Shirleys returned to Philadelphia with two of the lieutenants. Captain Westbrook and the other four lieutenants stayed with Railton in New York.

Railton shuttled back and forth from New York to Philadelphia, then to St. Louis, Missouri. While in St. Louis, working under great hardship, he published the first American issue of *The War Cry* on January 15, 1881.[14]

Approximately a year from the time he went to the United States, Railton was recalled to London. The Salvation Army was rapidly becoming an international force, and his help was desperately needed at home. While anxious about his American post and reluctant to leave, Railton saluted his General and began to pack. He was confident that the Army's work in America would survive its growing pains and continue to prosper under national leadership.

In London, Eva Booth also suffered growing pains. She wanted to be active in her father's Army. She knew the General used *The War Cry* as a gospel tool to tell nonchurchgoers about the Lord. One day she went to him and said, "Papa, the cadets are selling *War Crys* in the streets. Why can't I sell them too?"

"You're too young. You might get lost in the crowds."

"No, I won't. Please, Papa, just let me try one day and you'll see how many I can sell."

Receiving permission, she put on her uniform and chose to stand at the busy Liverpool Street station, where she proved herself to be a super salesperson. Before leaving home, she had read the current *War Cry* through and memorized the names of every town and country mentioned. Few could resist her calling out the name of their hometown and urging them to "read all about" what had happened there.[15]

But selling *War Crys* was not not enough for Eva. "I want to preach, Papa. I'm seventeen now. Send me out to preach." William Booth thought about it. Although she was eager to try her wings, was Eva ready yet to fly? This cherished child suffered, like her mother, from curvature of the spine. Was she strong enough to face the physical abuse she might encounter on the field? Finally, he called her to him and said, "Tomorrow you will go out with Elijah Cadman."[16]

Although disappointed not to be on her own, Eva decided to do her best with Cadman. They were a striking pair—Eva tall, pale, slender, with beautiful auburn hair and flashing brown eyes; Cadman a short, squat little man, broad in the beam, his bearded face shining with love for sinners. But his attacks upon sin shattered Eva as she watched him kneel on the doorstep of city fathers' homes and pray, "Lord, take him—take him away."

While Eva dared anything herself, Cadman's bizarre methods proved more than she could bear. After two days, she went to her father and said, "Papa, I can't go out another day with Elijah. He may be guided by God, but God isn't guiding me the same way."[17]

A few days later, the General sent her to assist Emma at the training home for women.[18] Eva was delighted and before long was Emma's most zealous helper. At a night-long prayer session, the staff and the cadets sought divine guidance as to how they could best help the London slum dwellers. The next morning Emma asked the staff, "Why not take a room in one of the worst districts and send a few cadets to live there? Let them dress as the people do (only be clean), visit, sympathize, and put before them the example of a good life."[19]

To this proposal, Eva gave enthusiastic support. She had felt for some time that they must do more than *tell* the poor around them about Jesus and His love for them. "We were ever calling them up without providing the ladder and going down to *show* them how to climb," she said.[20] Emma's suggestion would give them the opportunity to do this.

Emma rented a room in Drury Lane (Seven Dials) for Captain Hudson and four cadets who would live there and work under the supervision of Eva Booth and Staff Captain Blanche B. Cox. They became known as the Cellar, Gutter, and Garret Brigade.[21]

Along with the other girls, Eva donned a patched brown dress and long white apron and worked all day in a slum area where whole families—often more than one family—crowded into one room in great lodging houses. Going from room to room, they washed babies, straightened pallets on the floor—few had beds to sleep in—swept and scrubbed floors, nursed the sick, and listened sympathetically as weary, despairing mothers poured out heartbreaking tales to them.

At first the other dwellers in the Drury Lane area viewed the slum sisters with suspicion. "Wot're they doin' 'ere with their religion and white aprons?" they wondered. The girls had to dodge wet rags thrown into their faces by some tenants as they came through the doors,[22] and sixty-nine families once banded together to throw boiling water on them, but gradually they won entree into the homes and lives of the people.[23]

The people in the neighborhood soon learned that the lassies of the Cellar, Gutter, and Garret brigade had little time for preaching, although they did a lot of on-the-job counseling. When given an opportunity, they urged tenants to give Jesus a chance to help them.

Young toughs sometimes defended them at night when the crowds pushed and hustled them on the streets as they went to public houses or waited outside theaters to hand out tracts and try to talk to people about their souls. One young fellow roared, "Let 'em alone, well yer? I know 'em. They've been visitin' my lodging house and 'ave done me a power of good, they 'ave."[24] For Eva, these months prepared her for her next appointment—to the Great Western Hall, Marylebone.

6
Angel of the Slums

In 1885 Eva was given temporary charge of the women cadets at the training home while Emma was ill. At this time, the Army was engaged in a Purity Crusade to arouse the public about child prostitution, or what has since become known as the white slave traffic. Eva used every opportunity to speak in public meetings against this cancer in society. She led the cadets and training officers in raids on the city streets and public houses, selling *War Crys* that gave the latest news about the Crusade.[1]

When Emma was well enough to return to the training home, William Booth ordered Eva to take a short rest. Then he sent her from the training home to the Great Western Hall, just north of Westminster in what is now the borough of Marylebone. Middle-class people lived in Marylebone, just a stone's throw from the slums, not yet scheduled for clearance. The Great Western Hall, the largest building owned by The Salvation Army at that time, had become the Army's great white elephant, standing empty of people most of the time.[2] The General reasoned that if anyone could bring this corps to life, it was Eva.

When she arrived at the Great Western Hall, Eva

sized up the place—a mammoth auditorium capable of holding tremendous crowds. How could she get people to come there and listen to the gospel? "I wanted to find them, to go to them. I wanted to tell them as quickly and as simply as I could the greatest fact of all the ages—the never-dying love of God," she said.[3] To know them best, she would live among them.

She found living quarters—a room near the Great Western Hall. The room was furnished with a bed, a wooden table, two straight chairs, and an open grate to cook on. An iron kettle, frying pan, and saucepan completed the furnishings. But she thought it "dazzlingly attractive" after everything was painted white, including the walls. Only a crimson placard on the wall—"He loved us and gave Himself for us"—broke the stark whiteness.[4]

She soon became familiar with that world of the slums: its dimly lighted lodging houses, its damp polluted cellars, its fever-smitten courtyards, its blind alleys, its filthy stable yards. Under the dark recesses of a great bridge, she saw young teenagers and old men stagger out of sight.[5]

Eva carried old women's bundles and tried to comfort them as she climbed the rickety stairs of the Seven Dials lodging houses. But what hurt her most as she walked through the streets were the scruffy, half-starved little urchins who stood around in ragged clothes. She felt so helpless. She could not hope to feed and clothe them all, but she must do something. She thought of her own childhood—the fun with her brothers and sisters. But these children had nothing to do, no toys to play with. She had no money to buy toys, but what about trying to make some, or repair broken ones for them?

She went to a toy factory. Could she have the heads and limbs of imperfect dolls, discards that would be thrown away? Yes. Next to the carpenters for some sawdust. She found an energetic woman who agreed to get some of the mothers together to assemble the dolls and repair broken toys. After finding a cellar for them to work in, Eva posted a sign outside:

> *All broken toys mended here;*
> *Dolls manufactured.*[6]

All sorts of broken toys were brought to be fixed. One little boy brought some sick white mice. When he was given some healthy mice the next day, Captain Eva's fame spread. Wasn't this a miracle? Soon she was being called the "White Angel of the Slums."

Once the doll factory was established, Eva looked for a way to get closer to others in the neighborhood. She knew from working with the slum sisters that she could win the friendship of the poor more easily if she dressed like them. She took off her uniform, put on a tattered but clean dress, and threw a shawl over her head. With a little bunch of flowers in her hand, she joined other flower girls on the steps of the fountain in Piccadilly Circus.

They watched Eva and wondered about her. She was shabbily dressed, wore darned stockings and old boots, but her hands were smooth. They felt sorry for the "poor dearie" who had come down to this, but noted that she sold as many flowers as any of them.

Flowers were not the only thing Eva sold. When she was selling matches in Rotherhithe one day, a hot potato vendor told her, "Go home to your mother; you don't belong here." He gave her a potato to eat and "wouldn't charge her nothin' " for it.[7]

One night when a young Salvationist was pub-booming (taking *War Crys* into the public houses and talking to men about their souls), she saw a young woman with a hot potato cart. The Salvationist had drawn near to warm her half-frozen hands at the glowing coke fire when, to her amazement, she saw that the hot potato seller was her captain, Eva Booth, with a woolen shawl over her head and shoulders.

"Miss Eva, what are you doing out in the cold, and so late at night? You'll make yourself ill."

"I want to know what it feels like to be cold and poor and lonely. You can't really understand how poor people feel until you've had some experience yourself."[8]

One morning Eva awoke at six o'clock and felt a strong urgency to visit in the worst section of her parish. This was contrary to her plans for the day. After getting to bed at one that morning, she had decided to spend the day visiting her soldiers, but it was too early to start. Nevertheless, she felt impelled to go, and in her ragged clothes.

On the street some of the men and women hurrying to work recognized and greeted her. She returned their salutes and spoke to some here and there about their souls. Going up a narrow court, she told a big, brawny woman that she was going visiting in that area. "Oh," said the woman, "if you're lookin' for someone to visit, you had better go in there and see Bob. The sooner he's underground, the better."

"In there" was a lodging house where some of the most notorious characters in the neighborhood lived. Eva climbed the stairs and went into a musty little room.

Lying on the iron bars of an old bedstead, without mattress or bedding, with only a few old sacks under him and one covering his bony knees, was the rigid, shivering form of an old man. His face was pinched and drawn, and by his side was a cracked cup with a pool of dirty water at the bottom. Although it was a cold, bitter morning, no fire was in the grate. Sleet was blowing through a broken window. To Eva, it seemed that he must be perishing with cold and starvation.

"I've come to visit you, Bob."

"Oh, thank God! Thank God!" he gasped. Then, with a ravenous expression on his face, he said, "The crust, the crust over there. Get it me quick!"

Eva found a hard, dry crust which she could not break with her fingers. "You can't eat this, Bob. Let me get you some fresh and make you some nice hot tea."

"No, no, give it me; the crust, the crust!"

She gave it to him. He seized it from her and was about to devour it when he stopped. He laid the crust on his bony chest, put his transparent hands together, closed his eyes, and prayed, "Oh, Lord, for this food I am about to take, make me truly thankful." Tears rolled down Eva's face and she said in her own heart, Dear Lord, help me always to be "truly thankful" like Bob.

In a few minutes Bob had gnawed through that hard crust like a hungry wolf. Then Eva went out and bought some firewood and a sack of food for him. She made a fire and fixed Bob a cup of hot tea, with some fresh bread spread with butter and marmalade. After pasting some paper over the broken window, she found an old pail. "Bob, would you like me to scrub this floor for you?"

"Please, miss, I would."

After a long quest among neighbors for a scrub brush, Eva borrowed one. Never was a floor scrubbed so hard. In her enthusiasm to get it clean, she slushed the water on too generously. The door banged open. Looking up, Eva saw a woman who seemed to fill the doorway. She stood over Eva and said, "Stop this minute, or I'll take you by the back of the neck and throw you out the window. I'll have you arrested and put in jail."

"Whatever for?"

She pointed to the wet floor. "Because that water is coming through my ceiling and onto my floor."

"I'm sorry," said Eva. "Can I come down and help clean it up?"

"If you come down," she warned, "you'll never come up alive."

After the woman left, Eva continued to scrub, with perseverance but in moderation. When finished, she washed Bob's hands and face, then sat beside him and sang to him, playing her guitar.

Before she left, she asked, "Bob, will you put your hand on my head, while I kneel by your couch, and pray with me? Will you ask God that gratitude shall always be found in my heart, no matter what want or suffering or sorrow may come?" She always cherished his prayer.

A few weeks later, at three in the morning, she was wakened by the little shoeblack who slept in Bob's room.

"Come quick. Bob's callin' for you. I think he's dyin'."

Eva hurried into her rags. When she got to Bob's, she could see that the old saint was near death. "Sing it; sing it," he whispered. Trying to frame the words with his own thin lips, he sang with her the song Eva had sung to him the first day she visited him:

> I want to hear the flipping of the angel's wings,
>   When I die,
> And sing the song the angels sing, when I die.
>
> If you get there before I do,
>   When I die,
> Look out for me, I'm coming too, when I die.[9]

No matter where she went, Eva managed to mention the nightly meetings at the Great Western Hall and urge people to go to them. Some did and were surprised to find their shabbily dressed friend there in a Salvation Army uniform. Captain Eva's meetings were never dull but were filled with music and joyful singing. When she preached, her messages were fiery, dramatic, convincing. Sinners knelt at the penitent-form every night and prayed for forgiveness. Eva kept them busy the next day so they wouldn't go back to the public houses.

By this time, her congregation had increased from the fourteen who came to her first meeting to several hundred. The child who had preached to her dolls with such earnestness would soon be influencing thousands with her impassioned sermons at the Great Western Hall. She always remembered her father's advice: "Plunge in the sword, Eva. Plunge it in to the hilt. Reach the soul."[10] Spoken with emotion and sincerity, words to her were weapons.

Before each indoor meeting, she marched the converts to a street corner for an open-air meeting and asked them to witness to the change in their lives. In those days, the only mechanized vehicle on the roads was the steam roller, with a man holding a red flag walking in front of it, so the Salvationists had an open thoroughfare for their processions. They beat their drums, blew their brass instruments, banged their tambourines, and shouted their volleys of "hallelujah," "praise the Lord," "amen." Crowds gathered at the open-air service as Eva sang old hymns, accompanying herself on a guitar hung around her neck on a red ribbon.

Most nights after the meeting at the Great Western Hall, Eva took her guitar and a bundle of *War Crys* and went to the public houses to talk to men about their need of Christ. Like her parents, Eva thought of liquor as the Demon Drink and made no secret of her feelings about it. At first, the owners of public houses welcomed her singing, but they soon noticed that after she came through the swinging door, their business slowed down. As she strummed the guitar and sang, men stopped telling their coarse jokes and listened to her. Sometimes she knelt with a man and helped him pray for forgiveness of sin, beseeching God to keep him away from liquor.

The liquor trade did not look kindly upon anyone who took their customers away. Taking a drastic step, they organized a Skeleton Army, similar to others in England, whose members tried to break up Salvation Army marches and meetings. Instead of the Blood-and-Fire flag the Salvationists carried, the Skeleton Army bore a flag with the skull and crossbones of piracy on it.[11]

Members of the Skeleton Army attacked Salvationists with stones, brickbats, sticks, garbage, and anything else they could lay their hands on. When they tore the Army's red-yellow-and-blue banner from the flagpole, Eva would hoist the flagless pole high as though it were a victory symbol. They especially wanted to tear Eva's bonnet off her head or seriously injure her. One night she was struck by a stone and carried away, bleeding from a head wound. But it was difficult for her attackers to get at her, because by this time she had her own bodyguards around her, chosen from neighborhood gangs.

Eva recruited them skillfully. After discerning who the gang leaders were, when one of them came close to her, she would say, "Walk with me. I need you." Elated at the thought that this beautiful young woman wanted and needed him, the troublemaker would fall in step, now her ardent protector. His gang fell in line behind him and would-be rioters backed off. Sometimes she asked one of the "roughs," as they were called, to do her a favor—take her in his donkey cart to call upon someone. Seeing him driving Captain Eva around, the neighborhood soon got the message: anyone harassing her after that would have him to deal with.[12]

When the Skeleton Army attacked Salvationists on their marches, Eva's "roughs" often made the difference between life and death for some of her soldiers. Their tactics, as the name implies, were as aggressive as those of the Skeleton Army. After a bloody street fight, some of the Army's converts sat through a meeting nursing their battle scars.

Others besides the poor were now coming to the Great Western Hall in Marylebone. Before a meeting started, Captain Eva helped to settle people here and there, sorting out the more unmanageable. There were not only roughs in rags but roughs in top hats, known as the "walking-stick tribe."

On one occasion when William Booth was the speaker, a man wearing a top hat refused to take it off, sit down, or do anything Eva asked him to. Some of her roughs jumped up and, despite his resistance, hustled him out of the meeting, saying, "If you gentlemen don't know how to behave yourselves, we roughs will teach you."

But she let her roughs take out only the most unruly ones. That same night, two other men were causing a disturbance. William Booth said, "That couple of walking-sticks up there will have to walk off if they are unfriendly." The audience laughed and a contingent of the self-appointed orderlies started to put them out, but Captain Eva said, "Let them stay, boys." In a second, there was perfect order.[13]

Eva's expanding program required close attention to finance. When a visiting officer asked everyone to give a little in the offering, she interrupted, "Don't tell them that. I want five pounds. I tell them how much I want and they give it to me. Sometimes I hold up my gas bills and show them how much I need in money and tell them my troubles, and they help me." The crowd responded with a volley of "amens."[14]

Among the bandsmen at the Great Western Hall were two exceptionally talented musicians. One of them, George Fuller, many years later became the international staff bandmaster and held that post for eighteen years. The other, Bertram Mills, became known throughout Britain as he traveled and performed with the Bertram Mills Family Circus. Eva would meet him, too, years after she left Marylebone.

One man who often attended her meetings would stand out in any crowd: John Bright, England's great Quaker statesman and social reformer. She noticed him the first time he came—a strong, solid figure, distinguished-looking, with thick white hair and sideburns. After the meeting, he always checked to be sure she was dressed warmly before going out into the chill night air. "Take care of yourself, my child," he would urge. "Do not overtax your strength." And he wrote to William Booth, reminding him that Eva was only at the beginning of a life he felt would be valuable, and suggested, "Keep her in cottonwool."[15]

Lord Onslow, another eminent friend of Eva's father, had heard accounts of all she was doing at Marylebone. He discussed this daughter of William Booth with Earl Cairns, Disraeli's Lord Chancellor, and with the Earl of Shaftesbury, a great champion of labor before the day of trade unions. Onslow, Cairns, and Shaftesbury sent a messenger to Captain Eva asking her to come to the Houses of Parliament to tell them more about her work. There, in a red leather armchair, Eva talked freely to them.

When Lord Shaftesbury asked her what she would say to him if he were a drunkard, she told him she would tell him he should do something about his condition, ask God to help him.

"And if I was not quite convinced . . . ?"

"I should remind you of Christ on the Cross. He died to save. . . ."

The three statesmen looked at this slim young

woman and realized that all she did at Marylebone was centered around the gospel of the cross. Before she left, they took her down to the terrace by the Thames for afternoon tea. Evangeline never forgot the taste of those luscious Parliament strawberries and cream.[16]

Eva's pace at Marylebone never slackened. The days and often the nights were spent responding to needs of the people there. One Christmas night she went to bed at midnight, bone-tired but happy. A few minutes later, awakened by the crash of broken glass, she sprang out of bed and looked down into the street. Two men were fighting like beasts while a baffled policeman tried to separate them. When one of the fighters fell with a fearful thud, Eva knew she was needed. Without putting on her shoes, she threw a coat around her and ran barefoot into the snowy street, now red with blood.

The taller man was shaking the other like a rat. Jumping between them, she said, "Stop; I want to speak to you." When the bigger man released his grip; the smaller one scurried away.

The policeman brought out his handcuffs, but Eva said, "No, you mustn't lock him up on Christmas night. I'll take him to his home. Who is he?"

"He's Bones, and he's a terror."

The policeman waited while she dressed. When she returned, he walked with them to Bell's Court. Bones had hardly any flesh clinging to his massive skeletal frame. He lived in a cellar with not a stick of furniture, only a grating at the window. Eva bound his battered, bleeding head and put some water in a tin mug on the floor beside him.

The next morning, when she visited him, he asked, "Who done this?"—pointing to the bandage. "Thought I'd wake up in the lockup. Who fetched me here?"

When Eva said, "I did," Bones stared in amazement at her. She took bread and meat from a basket, and while she changed his bandage, he clawed ravenously at the food.

"It's drink that made you kick and beat on that man smaller than yourself," Eva told him.

"Drink! It's the only friend I've got. Wrong to kick a man? I was kicked into the streets when I was seven years old, and me father it was that did it. Me mother would come sneaking after me in the shed with a crust of bread. Reckon I don't owe no man nothin'."

She left him in the cellar and hurried home. She seemed to be running a high fever. Her lieutenant put her to bed and she was sick for several days. One morning she awakened to find Bones standing by her bed. She later found that he had knocked flat the man standing watch at her door because he was determined "see the little Captain."

When well enough, she went back to Bell's Court. Bones had added a soapbox to his cellar home. He drew from his ragged shirt three soiled leaves of paper, torn from a Bible—two from Matthew, the third from Isaiah.

"My mother give these 'ere leaves to me when she was dyin'. She said they'd be enough to take me to where I'd find her and where she'd be a-lookin' for me till I comed." The strong, hard-lined face quivered, and tears made white streaks down his unwashed cheeks.

Sitting there in the filthy cellar, with barely enough light, and with Bones, crouched beside her, Eva read to him the Beatitudes in Matthew and some verses from Isaiah: "He was wounded for our transgressions, He was bruised for our iniquities. . . ."

"Little captain, He didn't fight for Himself, did He?" It was the first of many visits and talks about Jesus. Finally, one day the champion fighter of Bell's Court, the terror of the police, and his own worst enemy opened his heart to God's love and found his mother's Savior.[17]

Dividing her days between the cadets attached to the Great Western Hall, the soldiers of the corps, and the poor of the surrounding neighborhood, Eva filled her days with an unceasing round of work for souls. When in trouble, the tough characters nearby sent her word. She often visited them in prison cells at Holloway, Pentonville, and Newgate where the more lawless were.

The corps and the people who lived near it were such burdens on Eva's heart that she was working far beyond the limits of her strength, trying to reach them for Christ.[18] William Booth realized that his daughter was at the breaking point, and although she did not want to leave, he wrote to her from Middlesbrough, Yorkshire, on March 4, 1887:

My darling Eva:

I am sure you are doing too much and I am, therefore, bound to make some arrangements to relieve you.

You must arrange to come out in a month from date.

You must sleep out *at once!* I cannot tell you how this is to be done but you must advise with the Chief and Herbert. I can see what a future is possible to you, and if you crack up as you must, living as you do, I shall be to blame.

Now, my darling child, you must take some little notice of my entreaties or you won't be alive in a month's time to come out. Let me know on my return how you are. Bless you; the Lord be with you. I made Bramwell promise that you will have some help. Your affectionate father,

W.B.

When Marylebone learned that Captain Eva was "ordered to farewell," as transfers were described, they petitioned the General to reconsider his decision. Could she not go away for a rest but come back to them? No, he had other plans for her.

But the General had to postpone those plans. Eva was so ill when she left Marylebone that for several months her life was despaired of. Stricken with a virulent form of scarlet fever during those months, Eva finally recovered, to find she had lost most of her beautiful, thick, curly auburn hair. One can imagine how this young woman, who all her life had been told how lovely she was and had come to take her appearance for granted, reacted when she looked in the mirror for the first time after losing her abundant hair and ran her fingers frantically through the thin patches that remained. When she asked, "Will it grow in again?" the doctor could make no promise that it would and suggested that she should get a wig.

Wigs were only whispered about in the nineteenth century. Today, women have accepted them as a convenience and time-saver, although if they were compelled to wear one because of baldness they would probably still be appalled. Certainly Eva was. Always high-strung, and now weakened by months of illness, she must have prayed desperately that God would restore her hair. But when she finally accepted the fact that it might never grow again, she began to wear a wig and did so the rest of her life. Actually, her wigs looked so natural that few people, aside from her family and some Salvationists, knew that she wore one. She was always embarrassed about her hair, but only those close to her knew this.[19] The way she shouldered this lifelong cross was a tribute to her courage and dynamic will to let nothing stop her from preaching the gospel.

7
Send Eva

The 1880s were turbulent years for The Salvation Army. Church leaders denounced from their pulpits the unorthodox tactics used by the Army to bring the gospel to the unchurched and bottommost masses. William Booth realized how foreign some of the Army's ways were to the conventional churches of his day. Refined and sensitive people shuddered when loud and sometimes discordant Army bands played on street corners, and they were amused when an uneducated but enthusiastic convert shouted out the date and hour when a "hell-deserving sinner . . . saw the light." Nevertheless, these nonconformist methods were proving successful among people whose lives had brought them nothing but suffering and defeat. They responded with hope to the Army's unstructured and joyous religion.

More serious than churchmen's disapproval, however, were the continuing attacks by street toughs, encouraged and often enlisted by the liquor industry, under the banner of the Skeleton Army. Salvationists had stones, mud, and refuse of all kinds thrown at them when on the march; they were pushed, beaten, and kicked by blood-thirsty mobs. But General Booth and his Army continued to march and sing and preach.

More serious still was the attitude of the authorities. In many places despite the Army's pleas for protection from mob violence, the police often refused to respond.[1] In 1882 alone, 669 Salvationists—251 of them women —were assaulted. The wife of the corps officer at Guildford was kicked into insensibility not ten yards from the police station, and a woman soldier was so injured that she died within a week.[2]

Skeleton Armies were appearing in many parts of England. When disturbances quieted down in one town, other towns erupted with violence. In some of these troubled spots, William Booth ordered, "Send Eva."

The town of Whitchurch was one to which she was sent. In Whitchurch, Mayor Melville Porter was himself opposed to The Salvation Army, but although Salvationists were abused and imprisoned, they continued their processions and street meetings, inviting people to the inside services.

Eva persuaded a butcher to give her a ride in his cart, then directed him to take her to the mayor's home. The butler reluctantly let her into the house but assured her that the master would not see her. Upon her insistence, he went to check this with the mayor, unaware that Captain Eva was tiptoeing behind him.

Once in the room with Mayor Porter, Eva talked to him about the Army and its desire to be a good influence to the people of Whitchurch. When she knelt to pray before leaving, the mayor knelt with her. He offered to send a guard with her back to the town, but she told him that would not be necessary.[3] This marked the beginning of the end of hostilities in Whitchurch.

Trouble of another kind broke out at Hanley where a gipsy boy, Captain Rodney Smith, was stationed. Gipsy Smith (as the captain was known) was drawing large crowds and selling 10,000 copies of *The War Cry* every week.[4]

Gipsy received farewell orders in August 1882. A group of citizens presented him with a gold watch in recognition of his services. To his wife and sister, they gave five pounds each. Gipsy knew that his soldiers had been thinking of making them a gift and he had stopped it, as General Booth had issued a regulation in October 1881 forbidding officers to accept gifts. But Gipsy did not think that the regulation applied to outside friends.

Two weeks later, however, he received a letter from headquarters telling him that the gifts must be returned. Unused to discipline, Gipsy ignored the letter. He next received a letter from Bramwell Booth, chief of the staff, telling him that since he had defied the General's wishes by accepting gifts, he and his wife could no longer work, and other officers were being appointed to Hanley.

Gipsy Smith, who became a world-renowned evangelist, harbored no ill feelings. He often thanked General Booth publicly for giving him his first opportunity as an evangelist.[5] But emotionally stirred friends resented losing Gipsy. The town committee rented a building seating 4,000 and asking him to stay on at Hanley, so he remained there for the next four years.[6]

When William Booth learned of the uproar in Hanley, he told Bramwell, "Send Eva." This was the biggest challenge his cherished daughter had faced. She found only a few stalwarts standing "true to the Flag"; the majority had followed the band to listen to Gipsy.

Someone asked Eva, "What are you going to do about it?"

She replied, "I shall preach the gospel as I always preach the gospel."

At first she spoke to empty pews. "Then," biographer P. Whitwell Wilson states, "the incredible happened. Of their own volition, the bands and the crowd marched back to their familiar hall."[7] Under Eva's leadership the corps had weathered the storm.

Another interesting battle during the 1880s was fought in the quiet seaside town of Torquay, in Devonshire. Torquay, with its medical baths and bathing beaches, seems a most unlikely place to find such bloodshed, persecution, and publicity that Parliament eventually would decide the issue, but there the town council passed a law in 1886 forbidding processions accompanied by music in the streets on Sunday.

Torquay had extremes of well-to-do and poor people. When the Army opened fire, some townspeople immediately rejected them, but many of the ordinary folk of the town became Salvationists. The officer had formed a little band from young men that held open-air services down by the harbor. The council's new law forbade music to be performed within a certain radius of the harbor, except for Her Majesty, the Queen's, band,[8] but Army members had been marching to music for years so they continued marching to it in Torquay.

One Sunday in January 1888 the police issued summonses against the corps officer, his bandmaster, and several of the bandsmen, charging them with infringing the regulation. On that same Sunday, the Friendly Societies of the town had hired a band to enliven their parade. After a court hearing, the Friendly Societies were fined ten shillings for each offender, but each Salvationist was fined five pounds for the same offense.

The Salvationists could not pay and were committed to prison at Exeter for one month. That night a local vicar could not sleep for thinking about these Christians imprisoned who had done no wrong, so he went to the police court the next day and paid their fines. The case, based on a Salvationist playing a concertina, was appealed to London. The high court found a technicality in the town's procedure and quashed the proceedings, and Army musicians, having stopped playing in Torquay pending the legal decision, again started blowing their trumpets and beating their drums.

On February 3, the local board served summonses on eleven more Salvationists, an action the *Torquay Times* deplored as savoring "somewhat of persecution."[9] The Salvationists were again fined, and from then on they were in and out of Exeter jail. When all the Torquay bandsmen were in prison at the same time, bandsmen were recruited from nearby towns. Hustling the prisoners to jail became a problem for the police because of the great crowds of spectators and sympathizers who turned out to give them a "hallelujah" sendoff to prison and welcome upon their return to Torquay.

In March, William Booth wrote to the local board and told them that he couldn't tell the Salvationists in Torquay to stop doing what was permitted in every other part of the British Empire and that "music is essential to the gathering into our barracks of those whom it is especially our duty to care for."[10]

Torquay was now split into opposing camps. One group continued to support the local board members, but many of the gentry, tradespeople, and ministers appealed to them "in the name of order and Christian charity to take off their hands from these, our fellow townsmen and fellow Christians, and in the name of God let them go free."[11]

However, the summonses and sentences continued. Families underwent privation while the husband was in jail. Welcoming prisoners home ceased to be a novelty and became a grim business. William Booth decided something had to be done and once more ordered, "Send Eva."[12]

Eva had regained her strength after her strenuous activities at the Great Western Hall in Marylebone and felt ready to tackle anything. As she took the train to

Exeter in April to accompany five Salvationists back to Torquay after their month's sentence, she wondered, What will happen to me in Torquay? Because, of course, nothing could stop her from marching to gospel music. Would she receive a summons, go before the magistrates, and be sent to prison?

By this time "Miss Eva" had become a symbol of Salvationism at its best to soldiers everywhere. They loved her and showered her with affection wherever she went. After a tumultuous welcome at the Torquay railroad station, Captain Eva and the released prisoners went to the Army's fort on Temperance Street for a welcome-home tea.

That night she paraded down the main streets of Torquay, with a strong brass band, to the Royal Public Hall. She played a banjo at the meeting and listened as one officer, a Captain Hopkins, related what had happened to him in jail. Because of an accident, he had only one arm, and while he was in jail his wooden arm was taken from him and never returned. Cries of "shame" greeted this, but he assured them, "They deprived me of my liberty but they could not deprive me of my Savior."

Although admission to the meeting had been by payment, Eva asked for a further offering on behalf of the families of imprisoned bandsmen. She then delivered a forcible address, often interrupted by shouts of "hallelujah" and "amen" from the audience.[13]

Eva returned to London and reported to her father on the condition of Army affairs in Torquay. He was deeply stirred and vowed, "We will go on, again and again." Bandsmen were volunteering from all parts of the West Country to replace those in prison. London's influential *Pall Mall Gazette* sent a reporter down to do a story on the Battle of Torquay. Eva returned to encourage the beleaguered Salvationists. Hotel proprietors shouted, "Ten pounds to the man who will quiet her."

The next Sunday night when she preached at the Royal Public Hall, fifteen hundred paid admission to hear her. She told them that she was staying in Torquay, and thunderous applause showed the crowd's approval. "Salvationists are not against keeping the laws," she said. "On the contrary, we uphold the law. . . . We do not want to be antagonistic to the local board, but we can't allow local boards, magistrates, or governments to prevent us from carrying out the work by which sinners are reclaimed."

She told about people who were converted at services to which they had been attracted by hearing the drum. "I am ready, if necessary, to beat the drum myself. God uses the drum to bring sinners to Himself. . . . We are fighting, not only for Torquay but for all the land. Thousands are praying for Torquay. When victory comes, as come it will, the bells of heaven will ring!"[14]

The next Sunday Eva encouraged the soldiers to adopt a new strategy. The town was expecting some casualties. Five hundred passengers, hopeful of seeing something exciting, came on the two o'clock train to Torquay. Thousands of spectators crowded around the open-air service. No one noticed that the Salvationists had two Army flags there instead of one. At the end of the service, lassies with their tambourines led the march to the Army's fort, the great crowd following. Eva Booth and the band stood at attention for several minutes, then marched, with Eva playing a concertina, in a different direction.

This raised two legal questions. Were tambourines at the head of a procession to be considered as music? Was a band permitted to march if there was no procession behind it? The magistrates decided that Eva's concertina was a musical instrument and that a band was itself a procession. When Eva heard that the clerk had said, "You don't propose, I presume, to summon Miss Booth," she sent word that Miss Booth "wishes to be summoned," and she received the familiar blue paper ordering her to face the court.

On the next Thursday when Eva faced the magistrates they did not press charges against her, but she made an eloquent plea on behalf of the bandsmen. "Gentlemen, you have seen some of these men. They have been brought before you in this court. You have imposed penalties on them for far worse offenses than playing a trumpet or beating a drum. You have fined and imprisoned them for being drunk and disorderly, for thieving, for other wrongdoings. What is to be said of you as magistrates when these men who are known to you as offenders against the law come back changed, sober, orderly, honest, and guilty of nothing but praising God with the instruments of music authorized by the Psalmist and blessed by the Savior of mankind?" Nevertheless, the prisoners were convicted as usual.[15]

The following Sunday, Eva again marched at the head of the procession and again received a summons, along with the other musicians. Wednesday night she told the congregation, "I led the band, and if anyone gets three weeks, I ought to have six. If anyone pays my fine, I will be very angry indeed."

The next day the courtroom was packed, with a large crowd milling around outside, eager to learn the verdict. Visiting jurists listened with those of Torquay as Miss Eva pleaded for the liberty of the bandsmen. She reminded everyone that some of the men being tried had been changed from drunkenness and debauchery to self-respect and good citizenship through the love of God. The silence was tense as her deep voice held them spellbound.

The magistrate said, "You have the voice of a crow but the face of an angel" and refused to commit her to prison, much to Eva's disappointment. She was anxious to share all the hardships of the fight.[16] As a result of the trial, however, the case was taken to the high court of London and came to the attention of the House of Commons. Henry H. Fowler, solicitor and member for Wolverhampton and also the most influential Methodist layman of his day, introduced a bill repealing the clause of the Torquay Harbour Bill forbidding processions on Sunday with music, and for the second time, Eva Booth was asked to come to the Palace of Westminster, this time as a witness.

The Army's lawyers instructed her to answer all questions with a simple "yes" or "no," and she followed their orders as she sat facing the members in a semicircle before her. Then the chairman, Sir Charles Russell, most dreaded by witnesses under cross-examination, said quietly to the slip of a girl in her blue uniform and big bonnet, "Now, my child, come up here and sit with me. Tell me all about it."

The crowded room grew silent as people listened to the rasping voice of the Queen's Counsel and the clear tones of Eva Booth speaking to him so freely. For the rest of her life, Eva cherished the opportunity she had that day for a one-to-one talk with Sir Charles Russell.[17]

The bill was passed and the Battle of Torquay was won. Captain Eva Booth was recalled to London, promoted to the rank of Commissioner, and appointed to be Field Commissioner of Army activities in and near London.[18]

8
Double Duty

Salvationists greeted their new Field Commissioner with enthusiasm. Her reckless daring and courage had made her a symbol of warfare to the soldiers and had won their admiration and affection. They loved her flamboyant way of speaking and showed it by the uproarious welcome they gave her wherever she went. She in turn truly loved people, which they seemed to sense.

William Booth was glad to have Eva back home again. It was an especial comfort to have her in London during her mother's serious illness. For in February 1888, Sir James Paget, a leading London physician, had told Catherine that a small tumor on her breast was cancerous and advised immediate surgery. When she asked how long she might expect to live without an operation, he replied, "Eighteen months to two years."[1]

After prayerful consideration, Catherine decided not to have the operation and went on with her work as usual, moving Emma's wedding to Frederick St. George de Lautour Tucker (known thereafter as Booth-Tucker) up to April 10 so that she could be present.

On June 21, Catherine Booth spoke publicly for the last time at the City Temple in Holborn. For almost a quarter of a century she had been stirring great crowds with her addresses. On this last occasion, she spoke for an hour, forgetful of all save her theme and opportunity. When she finished, she was so exhausted that it was almost an hour before she could be moved from the platform.[2]

Eva, along with her father and Bramwell, who lived close by, felt helpless as they watched her suffer and grow weaker every day. Nevertheless, Catherine Booth insisted that her husband continue his whirlwind campaigns in other countries, and upon his return she would rejoice with him from her sickbed as he told her of the meetings conducted and converts won for the Lord.

More than once Eva saw her father stumble from Catherine's room, after watching her agonized suffering, and go to his desk, where he wrote and rewrote throughout the rest of the night. One dreadful night while holding Catherine's hand, William felt her easing her wedding ring off her finger to slip onto his own.[3] Years later, Eva told Colonel Frank Guldenschuh, in America, "My mother wore this ring when I was born. Then my father, the Founder, wore this ring for eighteen lonely years. When he was dying, he kissed it and asked Bramwell to send it to me. It means so much to me; it has travelled around the world with me."[4]

When death drew near, the absent family members were called home. As they stood around her bed, Catherine Booth murmured, "Love one another; oh, love one another." Drawing Eva down to her, she whispered, "My Christmas box! Don't fret; you'll follow me. I'll watch for you.[5] And, Eva, don't forget that criminal you spoke to with the handcuffs on. Find him. Go to Lancaster jail . . . tell him that your mother, when she was dying, prayed for him . . . and hard as the ten years of imprisonment may be, it will be easier with Christ than it would be without Him."[6]

Through the long night, the family, household members, and her nurse, Major Hannah Carr, sang Catherine's favorite songs and knelt around her bed. The next afternoon, October 4, 1890, with William's arms around her, she was, in Salvation Army terminology, promoted to glory.

The Army's mother lay in state in the Clapton Congress Hall, where 50,000 persons filed past her coffin. On the lower half of the lid were laid her Bible, her bonnet, and the Army flag.

On October 13, twelve thousand attended the great service at the Olympia, in the West End. The funeral march the next day was restricted to 3,000 officers. Formed into fifteen sections, with flags and banners waving, the procession, with the help of the police, slowly forced its way through the dense throng of mourners. An honor guard of officers marched beside the coffin, which was draped in the Army colors and carried on a catafalque. The General followed, standing alone in an open carriage during the four miles to Abney Park cemetery. Eva rode in a closed carriage with her frail sister, Marian.[7]

At the cemetery when the General rose to speak, his long white beard, flashing eyes, and uplifted arm reminded the mourners of the patriarch Moses. *The Daily Telegraph* reported, "It was a most touching sight when the tall, upright General came forward in the gathering darkness to tell his comrades of the loss he, their General, had sustained. . . . He spoke as a soldier should who had disciplined his emotion, without effort and straight from the heart."[8]

It was not long after the funeral that Commissioner Eva, though saddened by her mother's death, was actively preaching to great throngs. One weekend at Rotherhithe, during the prayer meeting, a little girl about ten years old sat crying as if her heart would break. Eva, along with others, tried to comfort her but all she would say, amid her sobs, was, "My daddy won't let me get saved; he beats me every time I go to the penitent-form." The next morning Cadet Edward Joy was on duty at the front gate at Clapton. To his surprise he saw this same child making her way up Linscott Road. She had walked all the way from Rotherhithe, in London's West End.

"I want to see Commissioner Eva," she said; nobody else would do. When taken to Eva's office, the girl rushed forward and threw herself down by Eva's chair. "Oh, Commissioner, I can get saved now; my daddy died during the night." The cadet stayed long enough to see the Commissioner gather the tired little girl into her arms and kiss away the tears from the grimy, grief-stricken face.[9]

Eva loved children and looked after a group of homeless waifs at Clapton Congress Hall, which was now her headquarters. Some of the London officers lived near her office. Major Herbert Lord, on Eva's staff, lived with his family near Congress Hall. Often Eva would invite the four Lord children to play their favorite game with her.

"I remember marching around her table, singing Army songs at the top of our voices," said Mrs. Commissioner Owen Culshaw (née Lord). "We were small and she was young enough to enjoy playing Army with us. She made it so real. . . . One day I said to my brother, 'Bert, put my cape on me, please.' Of course, I had no cape but was pretending to have one like Commissioner Eva."[10]

By 1890 much of the rioting against the Army had died down. But at Eastbourne a mayor took office who publicly stated that he would put down "this Salvation

Army business"; that, if necessary, the town council would call on the Skeleton Army to help them.[11] The prolonged Eastbourne fight was one of the last ones the Army had to wage. Again, Eva provided galvanizing leadership.[12]

In 1892 William Booth needed a principal for the International Training Home, as it was then called, at Clapton Congress Hall. Ever since its opening, a Booth had been in charge of the cadets' training: Ballington, Emma, Herbert, and Lucy had all had a turn. Now Ballington was commander of Army forces in the United States; Emma was in India with her husband, Booth-Tucker; Herbert was going to Canada as territorial commander; and Lucy, recovering from an unhappy disappointment in love, had asked the General to send her to India. Bramwell, Booth's chief of the staff, could not be changed, and Marian's ill health kept her from leadership positions.

What about Eva? Booth wondered if he would be overtaxing her physical strength if he added training home principal to her already heavy responsibilities as Field Commissioner. Eva thought not and eagerly accepted this challenge for double duty.

Eva's lifelong love for cadets had begun years earlier when she had assisted Emma for a short time at the training home and was then partly responsible for the cadets in the Cellar, Gutter, and Garret Brigade. And while at the Great Western Hall, in Marylebone, she had had a brigade of cadets attached to the corps for field training. She assumed her new duties as training home principal with great ardor, and the cadets responded to her leadership with enthusiasm.

Sometimes they tested her sense of humor. She told the men cadets they must stop wearing starched high collars and cuffs, and the next time she was scheduled for a lecture, all the men in the front row were wearing high paper collars and cuffs.

"What is this?" she asked.

They stood and said, "This is farewell to the starched collar and cuff brigade," and she laughed with them.[13]

They vied with each other, however, to protect her from overtaxing her strength. The cadets often conducted meetings at the Regent Hall corps, almost eight miles from Clapton Congress Hall. So that she would not become overtired, the men cadets pushed her in a bath chair (a wicker chair with a small wheel in front and two larger wheels in back) from the training home to Regent Hall, in Oxford Street. The cadets always marched to the meetings, as there was no Sunday public transportation in those days, but they would not permit Miss Eva to walk.[14]

Years later in Chicago an officer asked Evangeline, then Commander of Army forces in the United States, "Do you remember the battles we waged? How hard, how fast, how fierce the conflict—often seven meetings a Sunday—the mass gatherings on Highgate Hill—the outpourings at Regent Hall—the crowded penitent-forms at Camberwell, nearly a hundred penitents kneeling in the mud, crying for mercy—the long marches, after midnight, back home, with three or four hundred cadets singing of His love all the way? You know, Commander, I got my greatest blessings at the end of a Sunday, wheeling you home in a bath chair on a moonlit night!"[15]

None of the cadets went to sleep when Eva lectured them. She warned them about being "weathercocks who changed with every wind" and told them, "There will always be winds—when on your knees, in lectures or meetings, while visiting people—to take your mind off what you are doing, but don't go with the wind. People become weak by never going against anything."[16]

In a lecture titled "Don't Walk on Velvet Carpets with Hobnailed Boots," she pointed out:

> The whole world is a velvet carpet. You are going out to tread on it. Don't use hobnailed boots; tread with *kindness*.
>
> Kindness is precious because there is so little of it. There is less kindly thought, kindly action, than anything else in the world. I don't mean *love*. You often find people who love intensely and yet are not kind.
>
> Kindness has nothing to do with the mind; it goes straight to the heart, and we want men's hearts.
>
> Kindness spreads because it is human. If you are too divine to be human, your place is up above, not down here.
>
> If you have kindness running out of your life, looks, and actions, He will bless it with His own blessing. Barbarians sometimes showed kindness. God's people should show great kindness.[17]

Eva always tried to put cadets at ease in her presence. After speaking to them one day, she had such a severe headache that she lay down for a rest before the public meeting that night at which she would be the speaker. A cadet was assigned to look after her. The chief officer for women told the cadet, "Nobody is to come in; nothing must disturb Miss Eva."

The cadet, awed by her great responsibility, tiptoed around the room. The fire burned low, so she went to the fireplace to poke at the coals. In her nervousness, she dropped the poker. It made a tremendous clatter in the silent room. Eva woke up, and the embarrassed cadet tried to stammer an apology.

Eva smiled at her and said, "Now, my dear, come over here. Tell me, what is your name?"

The cadet finally got it out: "Smiles."

Eva played on that word as only she could. "What a wonderful name. Just think, you're going out into the world to bring smiles to the downhearted, smiles to the poor, smiles to the sick, smiles to the discouraged, smiles to the troubled, smiles to those who haven't any hope, smiles to the elderly, smiles to the children, smiles to those in prison, smiles to the bereaved. . . ."

Cadet Alma Smiles (later Mrs. Brigadier Robert Young) never forgot how Miss Eva comforted her and calmed her down. She often retold the incident to her children.[18]

One of the cadets, Mary Welch, formerly lived in the Booth home. With her curly black hair and snapping, mischievous eyes, she reminded Eva of a gypsy, and after commissioning, Lieutenant Welch, affectionately called "Gypsy," became one of Eva's permanent staff members, remaining with her until the General's death.

All her life Evangeline used every opportunity to associate with cadets. As national commander of Army forces first in Canada and then in the United States, and later as General, with worldwide responsibilities, she could spend only a limited time with cadets. Nevertheless, she made the most of "spiritual days" at the Training College, praying earnestly and searching the Scriptures in preparation for them. Cadets anticipated these days with great enthusiasm and some trepidation. After all, they knew she could be a stern disciplinarian.

Colonel Emil Nelson recalled, "We prepared for a day with her as though she were a President or a King. She was our Commander. When she rose to speak to us, we were always 'My dear cadets.' Somehow she made us feel that this was not just an expression but what she really felt in her heart."[19]

Many women cadets tried to imitate Evangeline—

her voice, her gestures, even the way she threw her cape over her shoulder. As a young, impressionable cadet, Mrs. Commissioner Robert Hoggard thought the Commander glamorous. "We always attended her meetings at the New York Temple corps. She was so erect, her hair beautifully coiffed, her uniform perfectly fitted. She preached with such compassion and intensity. During the prayer meeting, although she must have been weary, she didn't sit down until after she had knelt to help those who were seeking salvation at the penitent-form."[20]

Eric Ball, distinguished Salvation Army composer, had heard all his life about "Miss Eva" from his mother, who had been one of Eva's cadets in the 1890s. In 1927, on one of Commander Evangeline's rare visits to Britain, he too "came under the spell of her presence." He wrote, "Three or four hundred cadets (perhaps more) at the International Training College would, if they had been asked, have followed her to the ends of the earth, hypnotized as they were by her stories, her humor, her rolling phrases, her authority, her humanity."[21]

After she became the General, Evangeline told another session of cadets in London, "Develop what God has given you." She held up her hand with a strip of bandage on two fingers. "They told me I shouldn't be lighting the fire, but you should have seen my fire. It was worth a couple of blisters. Work at yourself; it's worth the blisters! But don't forget that there is no work in the world so hard as that which you do with your brain."[22] Her guidance and advice to cadets then is still pertinent today.

The commissioning ceremony (similar to ordination) affects all cadets in much the same way. Their eyes glow with excitement; their hearts thump as they stand in line with their brigades, waiting to receive their promotions to officership and an appointment. The thousands commissioned by Evangeline Booth never forgot the special thrill of receiving their commission from her.

Lieutenant Colonel Lyell Rader expressed what many cadets felt at their commissioning—amazement that Evangeline could remember the "small fry" and give a personal word of counsel to each one.

When she commissioned the "Dauntless Evangelists" (a session or class of cadets), in Toronto, Canada, she remembered that she had heard Ernest Parr play as guest cornetist at the Metropolitan Opera House in New York and told him, "Parr, I wish I had half a dozen of you."[23] Kenneth Rawlins was reminded of his family heritage and told to live up to it.[24] She charged all the cadets, "Be worthy. Don't be afraid. Let no man make you afraid."

An officer on the staff of the New York School for Officers' Training for many years said, "Evangeline never resorted to puerile remarks to cadets, such as 'Do the best you can.' No; instead, she told them, 'Be an enemy—a fighting enemy of the world, the flesh, and the devil. Be an aggressor; carry the war into the enemy's camp. Be a fighter, a soldier, a man or woman who has the fire of war against sin in blood and bone'."[25]

9

Love Story

The Grecian Theater, later called the Old Grecian corps, played an important part in Eva Booth's life. After William Booth purchased the seventeen-year lease on the Grecian Theater and Eagle Tavern—part of a group of buildings notorious for the vice and immorality practiced there—he immediately set about to outsmart the Devil on his own grounds.

He closed up the Eagle, ordered some quick alternations in the buildings, and planned an early opening at the Grecian Theater. After alterations, this group of buildings was expected to accommodate 10,000 people.[1] This would provide ample room for an all-out offensive against sin.

When word got around that the Eagle was closed, the liquor interests wasted no time. They incited former customers, along with hundreds of toughs who enjoyed a fight, to protest the shutdown of the tavern. The day the Army took possession of the property, Commissioner Railton and the cadets' band headed up a march to the Eagle by way of City Road. A bad-tempered mob tried to stop them, and this developed into a riot. As the *Daily Chronicle* reported, "There were upwards of 400 constables on the scene by night."[2]

But William Booth refused to be intimidated. He was taken to court for not complying with a clause in the lease stating that the lessor should keep in operation "an inn, tavern, or public house." After much litigation, the court ordered him to either reopen the Eagle himself or rent it to someone who would.[3]

This placed the General in a terrible dilemma. All London waited to see what he would do. At last, rather than forfeit his lease, he rented out the small Eagle Tavern "for the sale of beer or spirituous liquor."[4] When his name appeared over the door as the licensee, he smiled. The Devil had won this skirmish, but with the fierce battle Salvationists would wage at the nearby Grecian, Booth knew that business would be scarce at the Eagle.

He placed brilliant young Major Thomas McKie in charge of the "Old Grecian," as it became known in the Army. McKie, tall, erect, and handsome—an attention-getter on any platform—packed in the people. So powerful was his preaching, old-timers maintain, that big men, with tears of remorse running down their cheeks, would climb down from the boxes directly onto the stage, rather than take time to come down the stairs to pray.

When Eva became Field Commissioner, she often was the featured speaker at the Old Grecian. By now, "Miss Eva" was well loved by everyone. Some of the roughest fellows around town had become her self-appointed bodyguards. When Miss Eva was announced as the preacher, an overflow crowd was on hand. McKie, along with others, fell under the spell of her impassioned preaching and magnetic personality.

At first, McKie dared not think of Eva except as the General's daughter. She treated him like any other of her father's officers. All the Booth children were given responsibility while very young and were adept at giving orders and expecting them to be obeyed. Eva carried this further than the others perhaps because, knowing that she was Booth's favorite, no one ever crossed her.

When she told McKie "Do this" or "Tell So-and-So I want to see him," he jumped to it like everybody else. But when the General promoted him to colonel, one can surmise that McKie told himself, "A colonel may some-day be able to talk about love to the General's daughter."

Until her late twenties, Eva did not seriously consider marriage. She always drew more than passing attention from men. No one knows how many proposals of marriage she received. When questioned about it, she would say with a twinkle in her eye, "I always sent the proposals to my mother."[5]

She had seen all her brothers and sisters married except Marian, whose health was poor. Eva had enjoyed the excitement that goes with a wedding and expected that someday she too would marry and have a family. But the man she married would have to possess many of the traits so evident in her father, who was her ideal. In the meantime, Eva's life was so full of new challenges, experiences, and heart-stirring happenings that she had little time for anything else.

By the time she was holding meetings for McKie at the Old Grecian corps, she had known him for several years. When she was in charge of the Great Western Hall, in Marylebone, Eva and McKie were participants in what *The War Cry* described as a "great council of war." Herbert, Emma, and Eva Booth, along with Majors McKie and William Elwin Oliphant, 200 cadets, and 50 officers, conducted a night of prayer and four days of meetings at Northampton. They inaugurated a new system of training cadets as well as an "attack upon the villages of Northamptonshire."[6] Anyone as observant as Eva Booth would have learned much during that time about the dashing, popular young McKie, five years her senior.

While Eva was at the Great Western Hall, she and McKie would have had many mutual problems to discuss. No doubt they often saw each other, too, at united Salvation Army meetings and councils.

After she became Field Commissioner, Eva had even more opportunity for association with McKie. The more she saw him in action, the more she realized that here was a man whose dynamic personality closely resembled her father's. Eva must have been aware, too, that she and McKie had much in common—physical attractiveness, military bearing, great platform ability. Both knew how to handle unruly crowds.

For his part, McKie admired Eva's quick thinking under stress and her repartee to hecklers. In fact, McKie liked everything about Eva Booth and in many ways let her know this. One day he could restrain his feelings no longer. When alone with her, he said, "Eva, I must tell you; I love you."[7] Although her reply is not on record, she surely said something like, "About time you told me, McKie."

Since Eva never did anything halfway, she probably started planning her wedding that day. She took it for granted that they could be married soon. Her father had never refused her permission to do anything she wanted to do; surely he would raise no objection to something as important to her as her wedding. After all, he had often told her, "McKie is one of my best officers." And she knew that the General had been happy to see Emma, Kate, and Lucy marry. One can imagine Eva trying out the sound of Evangeline Cory Booth-McKie, for every man who married into their family had to agree to the Booth prefix to his name.

McKie went to the Army's international head-quarters at 101 Queen Victoria Street to get the General's permission to be engaged and marry Eva. Then, as well as today, a Salvation Army officer must secure official approval from his superior officer before announcing his engagement or contemplated marriage. After a few preliminaries, McKie asked, "General, may I have your permission to marry Eva?"

The General's piercing eyes searched McKie's face. He could not help but know that Eva and McKie were interested in each other. But, like many fathers, he may have hoped that their attraction to each other would decrease with time if he was patient and did not interfere. Now McKie was asking permission to marry his darling Eva.

"I must think and pray about this," said Booth. "Wait here."

Half an hour later he returned and said, "As her father, I would like to grant permission for this marriage. It is difficult for me to refuse Eva anything. But as General, I must say no. You and Eva are both too important to The Salvation Army as individual leaders to be tied up together. The answer, McKie, is no."

McKie saluted his General and left his office, heavy-hearted. When he reported the results of his interview to Eva, she was astounded and angry. That night, although her father tried to explain to her his reasons for withholding his approval of the marriage, she refused to be placated.[8] Sometime later he wrote her a twenty-seven-page letter which Eva never destroyed. The following is a brief summary of it:

> I don't want you to marry for many reasons, and I want you to consider the matter carefully. You are each exceptionally good speakers, brilliant in many ways, strong-willed and used to being the leader rather than a follower.
>
> I am not sure that if you married you would be given every opportunity to use your many talents for the Lord. Your sister Emma and Fritz [Booth-Tucker]

have worked side by side in perfect harmony. I am afraid this would not be so with you because of your strong personalities. You are used to having your own way, my darling. Could you stand to be frustrated time after time?

If you really love this man and are determined to marry him I will not forbid it but leave it to your own heart. But I think I should bare my own heart to you and since you asked me, I must strongly advise you, No! No!"[9]

Railton and those who were close to the General sympathized with Eva and tried to persuade him to change his mind. The General was adamant and finally told them, "No more discussion. I have other plans for Eva."[10]

Soon after his interview with the General, McKie was promoted to Commissioner and sent as territorial commander of Germany. He eventually married a German officer.

Through the years, Eva's name was linked with such important and influential men as Dr. Herbert Bruce, in Canada, and John Wanamaker, General John J. Pershing, and others in the United States. Although her romance with McKie seems to have been the most serious, there are two other men that she evidently considered marrying. Reference is made about one of these in Wilson's biography of Evangeline. The suitor, Prince Galitzin, belonged to one of Europe's historic families.

Eva discussed with her father the possibility of marrying the prince, and William Booth reminded her of the time in her childhood when she stood before Doré's painting, *The Vale of Tears,* and decided that her life should be lived for the poor, the wicked, and the helpless. As they talked, sitting under an old tree, she looked into the scarlet of the setting sun and saw again Doré's painting. The next day she wrote to Galitzin, "I am not coming."

Two of the Prince's notes were preserved. The following one was written from Paris in 1894:

> My dear Dearest:
> I am still here trying to do my best to forget you a little, and to be able to go more bravely then to Russia. But it is not easy to forget you. I am working here very hard and seriously—in a private way. I have been much blessed, specially with the cadettes in lecturing. To-morrow I have to go to a little water-place near Havre on the seashore for about two days and afterwards Paris—Berlin—Petersbourg. . . . It is hard, very hard because it means Goodbye to you, my dear Dearest. I was thinking to go to London to see Mrs. Tucker and perhaps somebody else, but the *first* thing, I fear to meet somebody of the Army in London, and the *second* thing, it is too hard to say to you *Goodbye.* My heart knows that experience. . . . God bless you! Yours in Jesus, Galitzin[11]

Another suitor was J. Wilbur Chapman, the noted evangelist, but that romance never developed into marriage either.

Rumors of other love affairs pursued Evangeline for years. Without any effort, she attracted men with the charisma of her personality. In her later years, she told her secretary, "I would have been a wonderful wife and mother."[12]

Those who knew her best are not too sure that she could have adjusted to the role of wife, even on a fifty-fifty basis, but mother—yes! She loved children, adopted and reared four, and tried to gather the children of the world in her arms.

10
Crisis in the U.S.A.

Eva Booth often referred to the years she served as Field Commissioner and Training College principal in Britain as exciting and jubilant ones. The 1890s were years of great progress for The Salvation Army too. After the Eastbourne riots and persecution, there was little or no resistance to the Army's aggressive evangelism. Hundreds were seeking salvation at Army penitent-forms.

William Booth had much to rejoice about. His *In Darkest England* program was getting worldwide attention and making an impact on social reform in other countries as well as in England. His Army was opening fire each year in new territories. His own children were pushing the war on many battlefronts. Until 1896 there was no break in the close Booth family ties.

In January that year, while William Booth was on the last stage of a world tour, Bramwell Booth, acting for the General, sent "farewell orders," or transfers, to twenty-two leading officers.[1] All the Commissioners accepted their orders with the exception of the General's second son, Ballington, commander of forces in the United States.

Ballington and his wife, Maud, wrote Bramwell on January 31 protesting that orders came to them "without a word from the General himself," that they came at a time when they could not feel that the General had planned this with foresight, or that he made the move in the interest of America.

Ballington and Maud explained that they had lost confidence in the General and his autocratic system of government (in addition to several lesser complaints), and they felt they had no course open to them but to hand over their command in the United States and then step out of the Army as quickly and quietly as possible.[2]

As soon as Bramwell received their letter, he sent Colonel Alex M. Nicol to the United States to try to persuade the Booths to reconsider. He also wrote Ballington, refuting the statement that the General had not been involved in this change of appointment and reminding Ballington that the General had discussed the farewell with him both in England and in America over a two-year period.[3]

The stunning news of Ballington's decision to leave the Army came to William Booth when he was in India. Was there any way to persuade him to stay? The General thought of Eva, who had handled so many difficult situations for him, and cabled to Bramwell: SEND EVA.[4]

Meanwhile, back in the United States, when the *New York Sun* announced that Commander Ballington Booth and his wife had been "ordered to farewell," shocked American Salvationists and bewildered New Yorkers hurried to the national headquarters building for confirmation.[5]

Official notice of the farewell did not appear in *The War Cry* until two weeks later. In the meantime, friends of the Booths organized a mass protest meeting at Carnegie Hall, presided over by Chauncey M. Depew, prominent New York lawyer and public figure. William L. Strong, the mayor of New York, canceled a meeting in Albany to attend and voice his protest.[6]

The press played up the story of the farewell. Reporters applauded Ballington's decision to stay in America and charged that General Booth was attempting to "Anglicize" the American branch of the Army.

Ballington's farewell orders came at a time when diplomatic relations between the United States and England were strained over anti-English feeling engendered by a dispute between Venezuela and British Guiana over the Venezuelan boundary line.[7] The tension was so strong that one Saturday afternoon a howling mob assembled outside Salvation Army headquarters in New York and shouted, "Down with the English Army!"[8]

The American officers loved Ballington and appealed to London for the cancellation of his farewell orders. But when told that the controversy had gone too far, they realized that if the General insisted upon the farewell of twenty commissioners who were not Booths and then permitted his son to remain in charge of the United States, he would be accused of nepotism.

To further complicate matters, shortly after Nicol's arrival in the States, Herbert Booth arrived from Canada. The press reported that Herbert wanted Ballington's position, a charge that Herbert later denied to Eva.[9]

In his role as mediator, Colonel Nicol succeeded in getting Ballington to agree to go to London and talk with Bramwell before making a final decision to leave the Army. Then came the cable informing Nicol that Eva Booth was on her way to America.

Ballington, eight years older than Eva, was much like her in many ways. He too was a great orator and a talented musician, with a good sense of humor. Salvationists tended to idolize him, and he was well received by the public. His wife, Maud, the attractive daughter of a well-to-do Anglican clergyman, was also well liked. When Ballington and Maud came to the United States in 1887, like each of the national commanders who preceded them they took out American citizenship papers in order to handle Army property. After completing residents' requirements, they became naturalized American citizens. They were accepted and supported by all levels of American society, and during their regime the Army made great strides in all phases of its ministry.[10]

Ballington considered the coming of his younger sister an insult. When Eva arrived, he said, "So they've sent the pet of the family to convince me." But Eva, who had always been a favorite, was confident that she could heal the breach.[11]

On February 20, Ballington, Maud, Herbert, Eva, and Nicol met for a critical conference. After a heated discussion, Ballington and Maud spent the night cleaning their personal belongings out of their office at headquarters. They then placed their keys on their desks and left the building.

Ballington returned to headquarters only two more times. He went for a short meeting with staff members when he learned that the General had appointed Emma and Frederick St. George de Latour Booth-Tucker to succeed him and that, until their arrival, Eva Booth would be in command. The following day he went again to headquarters for a meeting with ninety officers who had intimated that they would follow him if he would declare the Army in America independent of international headquarters.[12]

Eva Booth had gone to her room to rest after several strenuous emotion-packed encounters with members of the staff. When Nicol leaned of Ballington's meeting, he hurried to Eva and urged her to go to it. Although Eva's attendant said Eva was too ill to attend, she left immediately with Nicol,[13] took the elevator to the fourth floor of the headquarters building, and demanded ad-

mission to the room where the officers were meeting.
When they refused to admit her, she went downstairs,
hurried around the block to the fire escape in the back of
the building, and climbed to the fourth floor. One can
imagine the effect upon the ready-to-secede officers
when Eva Booth made her dramatic entrance through
the window.[14] They were waiting for Ballington, now in
conference with his legal representative and staff officers
in an adjoining room, to come out and call upon them to
join a rival army. But here was Miss Eva asking for a
hearing, then making an impassioned plea for them to
remain faithful Salvationists.[15]

In his own account of this episode, Nicol states that
the seceders in the next room were informed of Eva
Booth's unexpected invasion. He believed that if Ballington had come forth with a counterblast manifesto,
"the eloquence of Miss Booth would have been as water
spilt on the ground." But Ballington hesitated and lost.
Eva showed a strong hand and won.[16] Ballington left
headquarters, never to return.[17]

Now the officers who had implicitly agreed to leave
the Army were chagrined. Under the Army's code of
discipline, mutiny deserved punishment. They turned to
Miss Eva. What would happen to them? She wisely promised that since the rebels were "largely influenced by a
brilliant leader, they would receive indemnity, on condition that they would personally express regret for not
having entered a protest when rebellion was suggested."
Nearly all were delighted to remain with The Salvation
Army, and the danger of a major split in Army forces was
past.[18]

However, Eva Booth and The Salvation Army still
faced many problems. A hostile press and rich and influential friends continued to urge Ballington to start a rival
army. On February 26 the *New York Daily Tribune* stated

that Commander Ballington Booth would either "turn over the property of The Salvation Army to his successor or make a stand, which they hoped meant that he would start an American Army." On February 28 the *New York Recorder* announced, "Ballington decides to surrender property because 'the cause of saving souls is too solemn and too momentous for us to enter into any schism or controversy.' " And the next day the press reported Ballington's decision to organize an American army under the name of God's American Volunteers, which was changed on March 21 to The Volunteers of America.

Eva Booth held her first public meeting in the United States on Sunday, March 1. Despite rain, four thousand people jammed Cooper Union, with two thousand left on the sidewalk in a cold drizzle. They all wanted to see the woman described by newspapers as the "minion of British despotism," and when Eva stepped to the front of the platform to speak, she was greeted with boos and hisses. The hisses, according to one newspaper, were like "escaping steam from a dozen locomotive engines."[19] But Commissioner Eva had faced more violent opposition than this. With a quick look around the platform, she seized a small American flag and waved it above her head. "Hiss that if you dare!" she told them. Startled into silence, the audience listened and then cheered her daring. Then she spoke for twenty minutes on the eternal joy derived from giving one's heart to Christ. The *World* reported:

> She wore a tremendous poke bonnet. It was out of all proportion with her slight figure, clad in a tight-fitting dark blue uniform. She commenced at once a religious exhortation. The volley of words rolled out in strong, almost rasping tones. She hardly paused to take a breath. Periods, there were none. She rose to a fervor of excited eloquence. Every minute she would

shoot an arm up its full length. Again she clenched her
fists and swung both arms horizontally about until she
whirled half around. It was the same vigor that her
father, the General, has so often exhibited in his ear-
nest exhorting.[20]

As she traveled through the United States conducting meetings, in addition to speaking, Eva sang her way
into people's hearts. She accompanied herself on a concertina and in her high soprano voice sang Salvation
Army words set to American melodies. She visited New-
ark, Philadelphia, Chicago, and other large metropolitan
centers, where she found little defection of officers. By
the middle of March, she could tell the *Morning Advertiser*, "Our American troops, with a few exceptions, in this
day of test are found at their post."

Eva also used the weeks in the United States to reas-
sure friends in the strong Auxiliary League formed by
Ballington and Maud that The Salvation Army would
continue its evangelistic and social ministry with as much
zeal as ever. Among these Auxiliary friends was Emma
Van Norden, daughter of Warner Van Norden, president of the National Bank of North America. About five
years before this, after carefully studying the Army and
its work, Miss Van Norden had become a recruit, donned
the Salvation Army uniform, and been an active worker.
She later decided to go to London and enter the Army's
International Training College.

It is surprising that the Army not only survived the
controversy in this tragic chapter of its history but
emerged stronger, rather than weaker. Although the loss
of Ballington must have been a personal tragedy to William Booth, he rejoined that "My American Army has
been true and loyal."[21] As for Eva, when she returned to
London, she was given a tremendous ovation at Clapton
Congress Hall. The General wired, TEN THOUSAND WELCOMES

HOME FROM YOUR FATHER. YOU HAVE DONE BRAVELY AND SELF-
SACRIFICINGLY FOR GOD, THE ARMY, AND THE GENERAL, and *The
War Cry,* terming it an historic welcome, noted that the
applause was so prolonged and enthusiastic that the
Commissioner mounted a chair and over and over threw
kisses to her delighted troops.

Eva spoke movingly of the loyal American Salvationists. "Truly I realized that I was the least of my
Father's house when the wire came, ordering me to jump
to the bridge. To me was granted the privilege of
strengthening hearts passing through the sorest test of a
lifetime and of being a little help in their midnight of
blackest despair."[22]

Looking back after more than three quarters of a
century, one can see that the primary issue behind Ballington's secession from The Salvation Army was William
Booth's system of government. As Ballington told Nicol,
"The one subject that separates me in spirit from my
father, as General, is the system that he persists in developing to the detriment of the work in America. I have
no quarrel against Mr. Bramwell Booth. . . . He is a thor-
ough system-worker. But mark this: it is not the system-
worker I object to, it is the system, and the author and
upholder of that system is my father. My quarrel is with
him."[23]

William Booth, Founder of the Army, was strong
enough to make his autocratic system work. However,
this matter of polity plagued the Army for years. It was
not settled until the 1929 High Council in London—a
Council that Evangeline Booth participated in.

11
Mustered to Canada

The year 1896 was a turning point in Evangeline Booth's life. Until then her entire life and Salvation Army career had been spent in Britain. She had never been strong physically. After the years at the Great Western Hall in Marylebone, she had been ill for months. And since then, Sir James Paget, who had diagnosed her mother's cancer, had told William Booth, "If you want to keep Eva, there is just one thing you can do. Put her on the back of a horse for an hour or two every day and get her out into the open air as much as possible. This will help the weakness of her spine and correct a tendency towards consumption."[1]

Where could I find more open air than in Canada? her father asked himself. He hated to think of sending Eva so far away from him. She had been a great comfort since her mother died, but for her own good as well as for the Army's, he ordered her to Canada. That great country would be another heavy responsibility for her, but he believed she would measure up to it.

When very young, all the Booths were given appointments with great responsibilities. Emma, "The Consul," was "training home mother" when she was twenty. At twenty-two Herbert, "The Commandant," was principal of the men cadets' training home at Clapton and later commanded Army forces throughout the British Isles. Kate, "The Marechale," was sent to open up Army work in France at twenty-two, and Lucy, at the same age, directed the International Training Garrison. Ballington, too, held high offices before he was sent to direct the work in the United States as a young man.[2]

When word got around that Eva was going to Canada, friends would stop each other on the street to ask, "How can the General send her so far away?" And everywhere she went, she was surrounded by groups of tearful supporters, new and old converts, who would ask, "What'll happen to us, Miss Eva?"

She assured them that the General would always have a good officer taking care of their needs. But in all parts of London, and in Whitchurch, Torquay, and other places she had been, Salvationists were telling each other, "Things'll never be the same without her."

Although she was saddened by leaving her father and the people she had worked with since her teens, Eva was excited at the thought of directing the great Canadian territory. The weeks she had spent earlier that year in the United States, after Ballington and his wife resigned, holding on to Army forces until the Booth-Tuckers arrived, had given her some idea of the opportunities she would have in the "New World" for service to God and to people.

Perhaps she was thinking, too, that in a new country it might be easier to forget Commissioner Thomas McKie. She still wasn't reconciled to the fact that while six of her brothers and sisters were married, her father had refused to grant her the same privilege. But busy days gave her no time for self-pity.

Herbert, who was farewelling from Canada and going to Australia, sent her a hundred-page brief, going into great detail about the country and the four years of his command there. Eva read it hurriedly and decided to wait until she was aboard ship to study it more carefully.

Shortly before her sailing date, the General called her into his office for a personal talk. He thought of the children Eva cared for as her own. He knew she was especially interested in a little boy, Jai; a tiny girl, Dot; and baby, Pearl. Surely she wouldn't think of taking them with her. But knowing how unpredictable she could be, he decided to prevent anything like that from happening by dealing with the matter beforehand. "Eva," he told her, "you won't have time, going into a country new to you, to look after these children you have had under your wing here in London. None of them are to go with you to Canada. That's an order; no children go with you. You understand?" Eva nodded her head. She understood, but for the first time in her life she decided not to obey.

At her farewell meeting in the great Exeter Hall, "the people laughed and cried, shouted and prayed." When Commissioner Eva rose to speak, there was a standing ovation for several minutes, with tears streaming down many faces. How could they part with this beloved leader who had played a personal part in so many of the lives?

"Please," she begged, "no more tears. I want to remember this as a happy evening, surrounded by friends who have fought with me for years in the battle against sin. Your love and prayers have upheld me. Now wish me godspeed as I leave you."

"We do, Miss Eva, we do!" they shouted.

The meeting finished with a "hallelujah" windup, Commissioner Eva marching back and forth on the platform, carrying the Salvation Army flag and leading the Salvationists in singing "I'll be true; I'll be true; true to its

colors [the flag], the yellow, red, and blue." They finished
with the Army doxology:

> Praise God, I'm saved [left arm lifted high],
> Praise God, I'm saved [right arm lifted high];
> All's well, all's well [both arms remain uplifted]
> He sets me free [lower arms slowly and clap loudly on
>   "free"].

Commissioner Eva was escorted to Liverpool Station
by hundreds of her devotees.[3] No children were in sight
when she boarded the train with her companions, Gypsy
(Major Mary Welch) and Adjutant Carrie Pease. She
arranged for someone to take three of the children ahead
to the boat train, where they would wait in another coach
for her. When her ship embarked for Canada, Dot, Jai,
and Pearl were with her.

We have no way of knowing why she defied her
father about this. She may have reasoned that since he
refused her a husband, he had no right to deny her the
company of three small children.

Commissioner Eva kept pretty much to her cabin all
the way. For one thing, she was seasick most of the time.
Then she wanted to unwind, study Herbert's brief, and
get ready for her new charge.

The long report was very informative. "You will
have to adapt to a different kind of people, for the most
part well educated and religious. But there is a real need
for born-again Christians." Eva thought about this. So
the people would be different from those in London
slums? But basically, people were people everywhere,
with the same internal needs, weren't they?[4]

Herbert discussed the financial depression Canada
had just gone through and told her that the Salvation
Army was on the verge of bankruptcy. It had overex-
panded with buildings to accommodate the huge crowds

that responded as revival fires swept across the Dominion.[5] Eva made a note: "No money." On the other hand, optimists were prophesying a great wheat crop in western Canada this year. Perhaps the worst of the depression was over.

Climate might be a problem for her—five climates, according to Herbert, varying from arctic severity to the mildness of an English winter.[6]

Distances would be great between the corps. In addition to the Canadian corps, she would be responsible for those in the states of Washington, North Dakota, and Montana in the United States, known as the Pacific province.[7] "Great distances," he said, which meant she would be often out of doors, just as the doctor wanted.

All during his tenure, Herbert had been plagued by personnel problems with his top leadership. In 1892 Brigadier Peter Philpott had led a minor revolt against the Army which many in Army circles still refer to as the "Great Split," described this way in the book *What Hath God Wrought?*, by Arnold Brown (later General):

> Many of those who left melted eventually into church or mission congregations. For a time some were known as Christian Workers. Others, like Brigadier Peter Philpott, around whom most of the controversy centered, continued their work of preaching the gospel, and as the years have shown, under the blessing of God, with good success.
>
> In retrospect, "The Split" appears to have been the product of misunderstanding between strong personalities. That misunderstanding has long since vanished, and though some of the seceders never returned to the Army, they are today, like Philpott, among its warmest friends.[8]

Dr. R. G. Moyles, author of *The Blood and Fire in Canada*, has discussed the condition of the Army when

Eva Booth went there. "The Salvation Army started out in Canada as a camp-meeting, revivalistic agency," he said in an interview. "When it went into social work, around the 1890s, some people felt it was becoming too institutionalized. Others objected to the number of English officers coming to Canada. The only Canadian officer at that time was . . . Peter Philpott. When Philpott resigned, about twenty officers and forty or fifty soldiers went with him. So it really wasn't a 'Great Split.'

"Herbert Booth bore the brunt of it. The newspapers in the Toronto area took sides. The *Globe* championed one side, the *Star* the other." So things had not been easy for Herbert Booth. Commissioner Eva's years in Canada have been called the "Golden Decade," because everything both in the Dominion and in The Salvation Army was on the upswing. While Commissioner Eva was asking God to help her in the tremendous task she faced, Salvationists from every province in Canada converged upon Toronto for the great welcome meeting to be held June 11, 1896, for their new territorial leader. On that evening the troops were told to "fall in line" and Adjutant Watson, mounted on a white charger, led the great march down Yonge Street to the Geddes wharf. Each province (composed of several districts, each comprising five to ten corps) carried banners and wore colors to distinguish it from the other provinces.[9]

The cruiser *William Booth*, bedecked from stem to stern in bunting and flags, met Commissioner Eva's ship on Lake Ontario. Waiting on the wharf, the enthusiastic Salvationists kept up a continuous volley of "amens," "hallelujahs," and "praise the Lords" from the minute they saw the Commissioner standing on the bow, waving her handkerchief.[10]

Colonel Clement Jacobs, the chief secretary, welcomed Eva as she stepped ashore. She was scheduled to ride to the meeting in a carriage pulled by white horses. As she climbed nimbly into the carriage, saluting and smiling, a reporter declared that the volleys were "almost loud enough to be heard across the lake by our Buffalo comrades."[10] But the Salvationists' fervor and approval of their new leader—tall, slim, erect, young, and beautiful—was growing stronger every minute, and some of the men shouted, "Let's pull her carriage ourselves!" Swiftly unhitching the horses, about twenty of the male staff seized the ropes, and "human steeds" pulled the carriage up Yonge and Carlton streets.[11] Street cars stopped to make way for the marchers, but it must have been a long, hard haul.

When the procession passed the *Toronto Globe* building, the printers and employees, in high windows, saluted the Commissioner, who remained standing nearly the whole length of the march, smiling and waving her handkerchief.[12]

They arrived at their meeting place—a conservatory type of building called the pavilion, seating about 2,500—to find the grounds swarming with people, and the building itself packed. Superlatives described the welcome demonstration to the Commissioner: "A gorged building—they even crowd the roof—enthusiasm leaps to its highest pitch. The General's daughter welcomed with a tornado of applause repeated again and again. Her address a Niagara of sanctified eloquence."[13]

When the fanfare died down and she rose to speak, Eva assured them, "All that is in me and all that I possess is upon God's altar. Together we may push our way with the story of Calvary into the darkest and saddest corners of this territory. I will be in the thick of the fight, but success depends upon three conditions: I must have your sympathies; I must have your prayers; I must have your cooperation."[14] Thus, after roars of applause, shouts, blasts of trumpets, flags waving, drums beating, hands clapping, and handkerchiefs waving, Canadian Salvationists pledged their support and took Commissioner Eva to their hearts.

Next came house hunting. Eva wanted a home in the country with ample grounds to accommodate a horse and, if possible, the dogs she always liked around her. She found a place on North Yonge Street, in what was then Glen Grove Park, now North Toronto, about five miles from headquarters. Because it had been empty a long time and was reputed to be haunted, the house could be rented for ten dollars a month. Not squeamish about ghosts, Eva signed a five-year lease.[15]

Mr. Alex MacMillan, one of the family (otherwise spelled McMillan) who were part of Salvation Army history in both Canada and the United States, was a young teenager when the Commissioner came to Canada, and he remembers Miss Eva very well. His father was provincial officer in Newfoundland, in Winnipeg, and then in London, Ontario. When the Commissioner came to their province, she almost always was billeted in their home. The youngsters soon learned that Commissioner Eva loved sports and was always ready to join them in outdoor activities.

On one visit to Ontario, Alex's younger brothers, Norman, Bill, and Don, asked her to go tobogganing with them. He recalled, "The ground had quite a steep slope, right down to the river. But she wasn't afraid; in fact, she loved it.

"She was good at all kinds of sports. I joined her personal staff when I was sixteen. Along with others, I used to go skating with her at a place near her home. That was all wide open spaces or farms in those days. She was a good skater, too. And, of course, great at riding a horse. She had to keep at that—doctor's orders. That's what kept her healthy and helped her to relax."[16]

Alex MacMillan also remembers seeing her ride her horse to headquarters. "That was something you didn't forget—the young, attractive woman in Salvation Army uniform, with red-lined blue cape billowing out behind her, riding down Yonge Street." But he thinks that she usually drove to the office in an old English gig, a two-wheeled conveyance in which the driver sat up high and the passengers down below. She did most of her horseback riding before or after office hours, often riding the two or three miles from her home to the Army's farm, off Yonge Street, along the Bedford Park Road.[17]

Commissioner Eva found Canadian Salvationists eager to help her strengthen the Army's image in Toronto and throughout the Dominion. They soon realized she could turn out more work in a day than most people and expected everyone else to work equally hard.

Previous territorial commanders had been colorful, but none had been as outgoing and innovative about getting the gospel message out to people as this one. Even in a day when horses, buggies, and gigs were a common means of conveyance, Commissioner Eva heading up an Army march on a white horse attracted special attention. Compared to her brother Herbert, whose enthusiasm had been dampened, perhaps, by so many internal problems, the flamboyant "Miss Booth" captured their imagination.

At this time, the massacre of thousands of Armenians by the Turks was arousing worldwide indignation. The Salvation Army at Marseilles met and cared for refugees, who, though they had escaped the Turkish sword, were starving, friendless, and despairing. After this temporary aid, the Armenians were brought by the Army to other countries for more permanent provision. SEND US TWENTY, Commissioner Eva cabled international headquarters, and introduced the twenty-one who came to St. John, Halifax, to their Canadian friends at an

overflow crowd at the opera house, where they told
ghastly stories of family massacres. From there she took
them to Montreal for another large meeting in St. James
Church. In both places, audiences responded liberally to
the appeal for financial help.[18]

Before leaving Toronto, Eva had engaged Massey
Hall—the largest auditorium in the country—for a third
meeting. Some less courageous souls questioned whether
she was not going too far to expect to fill a building
seating 5,000. Arnold Brown, who had served as territorial commander of Canada, said, "Old-timers have told
me that some of the corps officers objected, 'This will
spoil our Sunday night meeting.'

" 'Oh, no,' she said, 'I don't intend to close the corps
Sunday night. I am just speaking to the general public.' "[19]

Many Canadians admired her daring and turned
out en masse to learn what this interesting young woman
would do. The *Toronto Evening Star* reported a "very
large gathering in Massey Music Hall last night" and gave
it good coverage. "On the platform were the Armenians,
ministers, prominent citizens, staff officers, and the Salvation Army Territorial Staff Band in their bright red
tunics. Mayor Fleming, who presided, accompanied Miss
Booth to the platform with a little Armenian girl (the only
survivor of a family of ten) and Little Willie."[20] (A short
time before, Commissioner Eva had added Willie, a
Canadian boy, to Dot, Jai, and Pearl at home.)

The Commissioner's message climaxed the emotion-packed meeting. She told them, "The few months I
have spent in Canada among you have convinced me that
my spirit is not the only one which has been lacerated by
the terrible reports of inhuman butchery and cruelty
which has reached us from Armenia's land." Again,
when she made an appeal for financial aid for the Armenians, the response was good.[21]

This was the first of many meetings in Massey Hall. Miss Joy Miller who was a child when Commissioner Eva was in Canada, has said, "Evangeline Booth spoke so often at Massey Hall that some of us young people thought the Army owned the building."[22] And Mrs. Major Norman Boyle recalled, "My father, Captain Thomas Peacock, was a big, husky man, and very tall. Often when Miss Eva was speaking at Massey Hall, the crowd would be so big that she couldn't get to the door. Then my father would pick her up, lift her above the crowd, and carry her into the building."[23]

Throughout the eight years she was in Canada, Eva gave evangelistic meetings top priority. In February 1897 she launched a two-month campaign titled "The Siege," an all-out "declaration of War upon Beelzebub, the great deceiver," and issued weekly "Orders," stressing the need for prayer, faith, and work to assure victory over the Devil.[24] Each year, in addition to the corps' on-going spiritual program, "The Siege" was waged during February.

One such evangelistic group was an all-women's brass band, booked far in advance. Another revival brigade, The Red Knights of the Cross, was a strong soul-saving force. When Commissioner Eva traveled with them, she too wore a bright red uniform. She was becoming so well known in Canada that by 1903, when she and the Red Knights were at Ottawa, the Sunday afternoon service was held in the Russell Theater to accommodate the crowd. Cabinet ministers and members of Parliament were among those who listened to her impassioned plea for them to "Turn to Calvary, look to Jesus, see His face. Seek His love, learn of His pity, ask His compassion, plead His grace."[25]

In those days, Army evangelistic groups, as well as many officers, used bicycles for transportation. On one campaign, titled "Wheeling on to War," the Commissioner, Jai, and Dot rode with the bicycle brigade for ten days, and Eva preached at one-day stands in corps about twenty miles apart.[26] These meetings on wheels were forerunners of the great motorcades conducted later in the United States and Great Britain.

Some questioned the propriety of Salvationists riding bicycles while doing the Lord's work. When Commissioner Eva was interviewed about this, she said in her incisive way, "Well, the fact of your finding me in wheeling uniform and on the eve of a bicycle tour should prove to you that I have thoroughly decided the question."

"But your hands are already so full. Will not such a new endeavor take you out of the well-known paths of usefulness?"

"On the other hand, it helps us to run along those paths at a faster speed, and takes us into new ones."

"But do you approve of Sunday cycling?"

"Of course I do if you're on your Master's business. What is the difference between walking on your two feet to *one* meeting and propelling yourself on two wheels to *two* meetings? Thousands of Salvationists are riding for the glory of God, and with every revolution of the wheel rolls faster on the chariot of war.

"Prejudice sometimes tells us, 'You never saw Christ on a wheel.' But neither did you ever hear of Him speaking through a telephone. The opportunities of today are wide and God-given, and we should be blind indeed if we failed to recognize and seize the greater facilities they give our holy fight."[27]

She was just as enthusiastic conducting a wedding ceremony. When her companion, Adjutant Carrie Pease, decided to marry Adjutant Thomas Stanyon, the Commissioner made the event a never-to-be-forgotten one for many besides the bride and bridegroom. The pavilion was the setting; flags the decoration. First, from the wings, came Commissioner Eva, wearing over her red tunic the white cords which marked a special occasion. Next came the bridegroom and best man. Then, the center of attention, the white-sashed slender bride. She was followed by eight white-robed children, four of them part of the Commissioner's family, and three bridesmaids. During the ceremony, when Eva came to the word "obey," she said to the bridegroom in an audible undertone, "Mind you don't ever tell her anything that she doesn't want to do."[28]

Evangeline Booth always looked for opportunities to meet the needs of people. Alex MacMillan recalled the time, around 1900 or 1901, when several young officers on the headquarters staff—Walter Peacock, William Arnold, Etta Whittaker (later Mrs. Arnold), Arthur Morris, and himself—decided to do something special at Christmas for poor children in an area known as "The Ward," adjacent to the Temple corps.

To raise funds, they wrote letters to prominent people in Toronto, working evenings in the finance department on stools at high desks, the kind used by bookkeepers. "Miss Eva heard about this, and to our surprise and delight she became one of us in this task. The dinner for one hundred children took place in the old Jubilee Hall on the basement floor of the building. I believe this was the beginning of the winter relief and Christmas dinners which have now become part of the Army's program."[29]

But while Eva went out of her way to help those in need, she demanded twenty-four-hour service from her staff and those closest to her.

When a cable for her was delivered to headquarters on a Sunday, Alex MacMillan would take it to her at her home. Since no streetcars ran on Sunday, this meant a five-mile walk each way for him. But he was not upset that she didn't offer to have someone drive him home. "I was glad to walk ten miles for Miss Eva."

The Commissioner was surprised to find that in Canada, although Salvation Army prison-gate workers met released prisoners at the gate with their "Red Mariah," they were not allowed to visit inside the prisons. She felt that the Army had a special ministry to men and women in correctional institutions and in time secured permission for Salvationists to visit prisoners.[30]

Shortly after one of her visits to the Kingston penitentiary, she received a letter from some of the inmates. They expressed their gratitude for her interest in them and said, "The fact that there are those who care for us, and earnestly desire our spiritual and temporal good, will serve to enlighten many a weary hour, and stifle many a bitter thought."

In the Christmas *War Cry* that year, Commissioner Eva sent a message to prisoners, reminding them, "The light and love Christ brought can get right through the grating of a prison cell and right through the terrible blackness of a prisoner's past. . . . Sorrow for sin is the first step towards forgiveness, towards His light and love."[31]

Eva thanked God that souls were being saved, that throughout Canada people were responding to the Salvation Army's ministry. But there was a great sore festering along the Yukon and Klondike rivers. Men were dying of "exposure, exhaustion, starvation, scurvy, and not a few of alcoholic poisoning."[32] The Salvation Army must do something about this.

"*I* must do something," she decided.

12

The Gambler and the Lady

"Gold in the Klondike!" This startling statement spread with the speed of lightning around the world. By 1898 it had sparked the greatest rush in history. But it wasn't only gold that drew people to the Klondike. Satan was busy too.

In Toronto, Evangeline Booth read the newspaper reports. Eight dead bodies had been picked up on White Pass in one day. "Only God can counteract the Devil's forces," she wrote her father in London, asking permission to carry the gospel to the stampede. Her brother Bramwell, the Army's chief of the staff, opposed her plan. "Her health is too delicate," he said. But the General said, "Let her go."[1]

On April 14 Eva held a "salvation rally" at Massey Hall to launch the Klondike expedition. To dramatize the situation, six men and two women officers, dressed in fur, climbed single-file up steep orchestra steps (representing the Chilkoot Pass). A dog pulled a sleigh, piled high with bundles and three canoes. On the platform they set up a minute bivouac with tent, folding stove, and other paraphernalia. In this picturesque setting, Commissioner Eva dedicated the eight officers under a new Salvation Army flag. She then spoke of "the needs of

Dawson City and how the Salvation Army proposes to meet them," concluding, "We need four thousand dollars for traveling, provisions for one year, and outfitting, including large tents. This is, I am told, a very moderate figure indeed."[2]

A few days later, the Commissioner left by train with her Klondike party to take the steamer from Vancouver. Fellow passengers visited her car along the route, visits that often turned into prayer meetings. At prearranged stops along the way, the engineer held the train while the Klondike party appealed to townspeople for help. Colonel Chester Taylor relates that at Bellingham, Washington, "Evangeline Booth marched at the front of a two-block-long procession, playing her concertina and leading the singing of martial choruses."

At Vancouver, Salvationists and friends filled all available space on the wharf. Passengers already on the steamer, the *Tees*, lined its rails. After leading the vast crowd in Isaac Watts's hymn, "Were the Whole Realm of Nature Mine," the Klondike party knelt on the rough planks of the wharf as the Commissioner prayed for God's blessing on this new venture.[3]

Royal Northwest Mounties accompanied the Commissioner's party and the ship's captain put his vessel at her disposal. While it docked at cannery ports, she preached Jesus Christ to hundreds of Indians on the wharves and in the rain-soaked wooden barracks.

All the way to the Alaskan port of Skagway, Eva prayed that she would have a personal encounter with Soapy (Jefferson Randolph) Smith, a thirty-eight-year-old Colorado badman notorious for the way he ruled—or, more truthfully, misruled—Skagway from his saloon, Jeff's Place. This former phony soap salesman and confidence man from Denver, already with a record of outlawry, crime, and terrorism, had been among the first to disembark at Skagway, which became the outfitting point for cheechakos, or tenderfeet, heading over the White Pass trail. At his combination saloon and gambling hall, he gathered an army of thugs, tinhorn gamblers, sharpers, bunco artists, shell-game operators, cutthroats, and disreputable women to prey on new arrivals on their way to the Klondike placer claims.

Soon Soapy Smith had taken over the town. He pacified the citizenry at first by collecting purses for the widows of men killed in gun battles and by making contributions to churches, but when his gangsters grew more brazen and ruthless, a vigilance committee was organized, known as the Committee of 101, which ordered all "objectionable characters" out of the area. Smith retaliated by forming what he called a Law and Order Committee of 303 with himself as chairman. He organized his men into a drill team and even wired President McKinley in June that he was prepared to offer his troops in the war with Spain. When Soapy's marchers came down the dusty street, townspeople locked their windows and sourdoughs leaped out of the way.

Word reached Skagway that a lady preacher was on the way, and when the *Tees* docked at the Lynn Canal port at sundown, a large crowd had gathered on the dock to greet her. The Salvationists' small band struck up "Onward, Christian Soldiers" and marched uptown to a corner between the Pack Train Saloon and Jeff's Place. There they held a street meeting and proclaimed the gospel of redemption to thousands who blocked traffic to listen.

Evangeline Booth wrote later, "Sinners they were: the old and hardened, the young tenderfeet just from home and plunging into degradation, the once well-to-do but now debased, the once-poor but now rich, the intelligent, the sharp and the brutal—there they all were,

in Western clothes with big hats . . . men on horseback . . .
boys standing on their cayuses."

They cheered and clapped as she stepped forward,
to plead with them for an hour to forsake their sins and
accept salvation through the blood of Jesus Christ. Hundreds raised their hands and asked her to pray for them.
Penitent men knelt by the large bass drum. A cold night
wind blowing down the Chilkat range caused her to
shiver as she led them in singing "His Blood Can Make
the Vilest Clean." But where was Soapy Smith, the man
for whom she had prayed? Someone draped a blanket
over her shoulders and whispered, "Soapy said to put it
around you." She had not noticed the man with the wide
pushed-back sombrero who had ridden a big white stal-
lion to the edge of the crowd.

The meetings continued for several days. One night
Soapy tossed $5.00 in gold on the drum. Eva used the
money to buy food, for men were starving in Skagway.
Another night he sent over some slabs of moose meat.
God had nothing to do with this meat, read the note. *Compli-
ments of Jeff's Place*.

The Army had pitched its tents among some trees,
and one evening the Mounties assigned to guard Commissioner Eva told her, "Soapy Smith and five of his
bodyguards are coming."

"Leave him to me," said Eva, and walked out to invite
the men to have a cup of cocoa. As they stood around the
campfire, she took Soapy aside.

"Why don't you give up this kind of life?" she asked.

"I can't. If they didn't think I'd kill 'em, there's
plenty would kill me."

Commissioner Eva said, "There are worse things
than death. Stop taking life. God wants to give you life."

"You talk like my mother," Soapy told her. "She took
me to Army meetings when I was a boy. I liked it. They let

me clap my hands when we sang. But that seems so long ago."

Quietly, in the flickering shadows of the campfire, the Commissioner talked to Soapy Smith about Jesus Christ. For three hours they sat, until finally Soapy bowed his head as she prayed. Eva had "opened the life-gate" for Soapy Smith. Her testimony penetrated the weak spot in his armor. He listened, hesitated—but it was very late. Six weeks later Soapy Smith was killed in a gun battle.

Did Evangeline Booth succeed in doing what no one else had even thought of doing: convert the wickedest man in Alaska? Was Soapy Smith possibly touched by God? We will never know this side of heaven.

A widow whom the outlaw had helped went searching for his body, found it, and had it removed to the morgue. Funeral services were conducted in a church which Soapy had helped to build. The minister's text was Proverbs 13:15, "The way of transgressors is hard."[4]

After she returned to Toronto, Eva wrote to the converts in Alaska, "My dear children in the gospel, 'hold fast that which is good.' As yet you are young in the faith; the Devil will lay many snares to trap your feet, to destroy your trust, and to rob your peace. You will need to watch and pray. Keep your eye upon Jesus. Seek to follow His example. You must cast aside all things which would hinder your spiritual growth, and seek after holy living. Stand together. Stand by your officer! Stand by the flag! Take an active part in the fight."[5]

As a result of their many stops at ports en route to Alaska, Evangeline Booth started the Indian work in northern British Columbia. The Indians liked the Salvation Army—the uniforms and music, the free-and-easy meetings. When she returned to the area in 1899, Eva found that many Indians had given themselves titles like commissioner and colonel. She demoted them all, which caused some dissatisfaction, but they soon adjusted to the captains and lieutenants she sent in to their Indian villages. The Salvation Army operated farms, built schools, and to a great extent looked after the whole community.[6]

The impetus of another visit from Commissioner Eva, plus the return of Adjutant Tom McGill and Ensign Fred Bloss from Dawson City to Skagway, caused many natives there to turn "from their totem worship and fanatical potlatches to the radiant religion of Christ as expressed through the Army."[7] The work pushed on throughout Alaska and North British Columbia, with officers and support from the Canadian territory for over forty-six years. Then in June 1944 the Alaska work was transferred to the United States Western territory.

When Commissioner Glenn Ryan was in Alaska in 1961, he talked to a Salvationist who as a girl of nine had served as an interpreter to the Tlingit Indians for Commissioner Eva on one of her trips to Alaska. "Her stoic features became animated as she talked about Miss Eva. She told me: 'I can never forget how she pleaded with us, "Go back to your village. Tell your people about Jesus, that He will save them and keep them from sin." My brother went back home, helped start the Salvation Army, and became a captain. Everyone loved Miss Eva. She ate with us—seaweed, dried seal, and dried fish dipped in whale oil. We told her we were sorry not to have hooligan fish for her'."

No doubt Miss Eva was delighted not to have this delicacy. Before going to Alaska, Commissioner Ryan had read in Robert Ripley's *Believe It or Not* column, "Hooligan fish are so fat, the Alaskans put wicks in them and use them for candles." Although skeptical when he first read that, after being in Alaska he felt that Ripley spoke with authority.[8]

Commissioner Eva rejoiced that everything seemed to be on the upgrade for the Army in Canada. Many "seekers" were kneeling at their penitent-forms, and social programs were flourishing. Things were going well for The Salvation Army in other parts of the world, too. In England, shortly after Eva left for Canada, William Booth had visited W. E. Gladstone, four times prime minister under Queen Victoria.[9] (Although Eva and the rest of the Booth family did not realize it then, Booth's visit with Gladstone would ultimately have a far-reaching effect upon The Salvation Army.) Eva's most loved sister, Emma ("the Consul") Booth-Tucker, and her husband, Frederick, were making great strides in Army "warfare" in the United States; Herbert and his wife, Cornelie, were doing well in Australia; and Kate ("the Marechale") with her husband, Arthur Sydney Booth-Clibborn, had overcome fierce opposition and were now well accepted in France. General Booth's Army was "opening fire" in many other countries, and Booth himself was beginning to be an affectionately acclaimed worldwide figure.

But in 1902 Commissioner Eva received heartbreaking news about family members. In January, Kate and her husband resigned from The Salvation Army in order to preach a "larger gospel." Booth-Clibborn, interested in faith healing and the immediate coming of Christ in person, offered his services to an American evangelist, John Alexander Dowie, head of what he called "the Christian Catholic Church" in Zion, Illinois.[10] How can Katie, darling Katie, who at twenty-two pioneered Salvation Army work in France, forsake it now? Eva wondered. William Booth wondered the same thing, but Kate went with her husband. William wrote in his journal, "I shall not attempt to describe my feelings at this utterly bewildering blow."[11]

Just a month later, Herbert and his wife also seceded

from the Army. Herbert, chafing under a growing dis-satisfaction with Army structure, disregarded Eva's ad-vice to "be patient" and left his command of Australia to become a free-lance evangelist.[12]

Grieving over the Army's loss of Kate and Herbert, Eva found solace in working harder than ever. She left on a ten-week revival campaign in Western Canada with her Red Knights of the Cross. On this third trip to Alaska, she found that nearly a hundred of the Tlingit Indians were now Salvationists,[13] and when the General came to Canada that fall, Commissioner Eva could happily report that things were "looking up for the Army in Canada." She traveled with her father on a strenuous tour where the General spoke in meetings across the Dominion. The Canadian Pacific Railway provided a private car for the use of the aged founder and his party. Here, no doubt, Eva and her father spent many hours talking about the family and discussing future plans for the Army in Canada.

Between the West Ontario meetings and the To-ronto Congress, the commissioner arranged for the General to have a few days of quiet and rest in a cottage at Lorne Park, near Port Credit. The then Lieutenant Alex MacMillan, on Commissioner Eva's personal staff, drove her horse and gig to the cottage and met her and the General at Port Credit. The General took his secretary, Major Fred Cox, with him, and the Commissioner took Gypsy Welch with her to prepare meals.

Alex MacMillan still remembers those idyllic days, "the white-haired General, reminding one of Moses or another Bible patriarch, sitting in a great armchair by the fireside with Miss Eva on a footstool by his side, reading the Scripture to us. Then he would pray with us and for us. I'm afraid I didn't keep my eyes closed during prayers. His face was so transformed, it was a benediction.[14]

Commissioner Eva drove the General around the country, mostly fruit farms in those days. They took long walks in the forest, recalled incidents before Eva had left England, and talked about the Army. On one of these walks, while singing a little song to her father, she began humming another tune which stirred "the passions of his soul." This became her musical composition, "Why Don't You Come to Jesus?"[15]

During the years Evangeline Booth served as Field Commissioner in Canada, she instigated many "firsts" and consolidated some programs that were already started. The annual soul-saving "Sieges" begun by her in 1897 continued to make a great spiritual impact throughout the land.

The training of officers was centralized in 1903 when the new Territorial Training College in Toronto was opened.[16] The Commissioner looked back with real joy on the breakthrough in prison work, recalling, "We had a struggle to get into the prisons. There was a strong prejudice against Salvationists meddling with the victims of the law. But after we got in, the results were so beneficial that we were allowed greater privileges, the Minister of Justice himself giving us every assistance."[17]

At the turn of the century, Canada had no parole system for prisoners. Commissioner Eva recommended to the government a system of prisoner probation and, as the Salvation Army leader, campaigned with other Salvationists for prisoner parole. The Salvation Army is in a large measure responsible for the parole system used in Canada today.[18]

The Canadian government liked the idea so much that they asked if she would release Brigadier W. P.

Archibald from officership to become Canada's first parole officer. "We'd like him to take over our parole system. This means that the Army will always be involved in it." Anxious for the parole system to get off to a good start and to help in a practical way, she released Archibald. On May 1, 1905, he became Canada's first national parole officer.[19]

Commissioner Eva was responsible for the first Christmas kettle placed on the street and for setting up a summer fresh-air camp at Oakville where three hundred mothers and children could enjoy a vacation.[20]

When she laid the foundation for the Army's immigration program in 1903, she set in motion a plan whereby the Salvation Army eventually brought more than 250,000 immigrants from England to Canada as settlers. Commissioner Owen Culshaw, who was associated with the immigration department at the Army's international headquarters in London for forty-two years, stated:

> "As I know it, the movement to Canada was the result of the Founder's visit to Canada in 1902. Going through the country, he saw the trackless wastes and he coined the phrase, 'The landless man for the manless land.' He came back to this country and started the migration movement. The first people to leave England were trained for work at the Hadleigh Farm Colony. They left in 1905 on a chartered ship for Canada. They sailed with the Salvation Army flag at the top of the mast. Other ships were later chartered. The bar of these ships was turned into a labor bureau where the immigrants were assigned to the job that had been allotted to them in Canada."[21]

One can picture Commissioner Eva and her father discussing the subsequent immigration program on that tour across Canada.

What may be considered one of the Commissioner's greatest contributions to Canada was her support of the Army's social work. Men's industrial homes and farms prospered. Rescue homes developed into homes for unwed mothers. The incorporation of Grace Hospital in Winnipeg, in 1904, with its nurses' training classes, set the pattern for present-day Grace hospitals, with their excellent nurses' training courses throughout Canada.[22]

The Commissioner was making plans with her staff for the 1904 International Congress to be held in London when on October 28, 1903, she received devastating news. Her sister Emma had been killed in a train wreck at Dean Lake, near Marceline, Missouri, on her way to Chicago to meet her husband, Booth-Tucker.[23]

While death in the Salvation Army is viewed as a "promotion to glory," Eva was nevertheless prostrated with grief at the loss of Emma, to whom she had always gone for counsel in times of personal crisis. But knowing how stricken her brother-in-law would be, she pulled herself together and hurried to New York. There she approved for him the order of service for Emma's funeral at Carnegie Hall which had been arranged by his staff.[24]

The General, who was "withered" at Emma's tragic death, wrote to Eva:

> Your precious letter of the 4th is just to hand. A few minutes before that time Bramwell gave me the cable news that you were not so well again, and that the doctor had recommended your getting back to Toronto as soon as you were able to travel. I do not know what to say to it all. God shield and sustain you.
>
> I shall go on. Time will dull the anguish, if it does not altogether heal the wound.
>
> So, precious Eva, we will go on—we must go on—with our Mission.[25]

A few months later, Booth-Tucker was recalled to England, and Commissioner Eva received orders to "farewell" from Canada and go to the United States. Before her departure, she led the Canadian delegation to the International Congress. The colorful group of Northwest Indians in native costume, the Salvation Outriders from western Canada, and the Territorial Congress band in scarlet tunics with white trimmings and maple-leaf insignia received tremendous ovations at "memorable meetings held in the Strand Hall, the Crystal Palace, and the Royal Albert Hall."[26]

Upon her return, on a whirlwind farewell tour, the Commissioner spoke to audiences crowded into every nook and corner of the largest buildings in the land. In Winnipeg, one man said as he left the opera house, " 'Tain't only her words, it's the 'bloomination' of her face."[27]

At the final meeting in Massey Hall, Toronto, Commissioner Eva urged her troops, "Hold fast to the flag of the Salvation Army. Contend for it! Uphold it! Be faithful to it! Stand by each other! Remember all the regiments of hell cannot break through the line. 'Unity' forms the red line of Calvary love.

"For my successor I can but ask that you will love and follow him as you have loved and followed me."[28]

Field Commissioner Eva left Canada, as she had left England, on the crest of a wave of tremendous popularity. In the United States, she knew she would face new and great challenges, but she thrived on challenges. She would also face some criticism, but like her father, she usually ignored criticism and forged ahead. All the Booths had a tendency to feel that a Booth was always right. Of course, when they disagreed among themselves, this created a problem for them and sometimes affected the whole Army.

13
March On

When Eva Booth came to the United States in 1904 to command the Salvation Army forces, she had already become headline news in the world's press. Some reporters in New York and other American cities remembered this brash young woman William Booth had sent to the United States eight years before, when Ballington and Maud Booth seceded from the army. She had impressed them then with her preaching and sincerity, and some recalled that at that time most Salvationists remained in the Salvation Army rather than follow Ballington and Maud into their "volunteer" army.

According to the newspaper grapevine, Eva had established a reputation in Canada by her daring Klondike expeditions and by her sheer ability to command people and administer Army affairs. With her gift of oratory, she had packed crowds into Toronto's Massey Hall. But would she pack them into Carnegie Hall in New York?

In the early 1900s life was more leisurely. Men were experimenting with steam-driven and combustion-engine autos, but Henry Ford would not introduce his Model T until 1908. Gas lights were still in use. Men worked fourteen and sixteen hours a day for eight or ten dollars a week. The Russo-Japanese conflict was front-page news, Theodore Roosevelt swung his "big stick" as a negotiator, and a number of cults were busy setting dates for the Second Coming of Jesus Christ.[1]

Immigrants from abroad swelled the larger cities. Settlement houses, such as Lillian Wald's Henry Street Settlement in New York and Jane Addams's Hull House in Chicago, tried to cope with social problems created by overcrowding and appalling sanitary conditions.[2]

The gospel of Horatio Alger's books—with their poor but clean-cut young heroes always ready to grasp opportunities—was the faith of the day. Hadn't Andrew Carnegie been a bobbin boy? And what about John Jacob Astor, who arrived in America with $5 in his pocket? Young girls sweated it out in factories and dreamed of a rich marriage, and, indeed, the dream that riches would reward hard work came true for some. For others, it faded in the despair generated by the filth and disease of the slums.[3]

Eva Booth had been around poor people ever since she could remember. She knew them and loved them. But she had also rubbed shoulders with great people. She felt comfortable with rich or poor, saints or sinners. At times she was even accused of neglecting the saints for the sinners. But she had a better understanding of human nature than some leaders of that day, who lived more sheltered lives. Although born and bred in England, she came to America determined to learn all she could about the United States. She mixed with all kinds of people, studied them, absorbed their thinking, and was aware of their needs and aspirations.

At her welcome meeting on December 6, reporters found that indeed Commander Eva Booth, perfectly groomed as always, had packed in the crowds at Carnegie Hall. Amid shouts of welcome as she came on the platform, the Salvation Army National Staff Band played an improvised version of "The Maple Leaf Forever" and "Yankee Doodle" as a link between her Canadian command and the one in the United States.

According to a *War Cry* reporter, when Commander Eva addressed the crowd, she "leaped through the open door of the people's hearts at one bound." She praised her predecessors, Commander Booth-Tucker and his wife, her sister Emma, and told the enthusiastic listeners that although she came to them "single file," she came to them from God, who would give her the strength to measure up to the great responsibility of her appointment to America.

She presented her first enterprise—the establishment of a slum settlement in Manhattan's vicious Cherry Hill district. The Army already had some smaller homes in that area, but she wanted to obtain a large property that would include a laundry where poor women could come and do their washing, a sewing room where they could make themselves warm garments, and a nursery where babies could be "properly and lovingly cared for while their mothers are at work." She pledged herself and "all that God is going to give me, for your blessing and help."[4]

A month later, the *New York World* ran pictures of a five-story building she had purchased for the Cherry Street Slum Hall, along with pictures of the slum sisters at work. In 1906 the Commander dedicated the Slum Settlement and Nursery, with accommodation for 100 children.[5] The Army carried on a heavy program there for the next forty-one years until, in 1947, the building was demolished to make room for a housing project.[6]

From the day she came to the United States, Eva Booth loved the country and the people, and they fell in love with her. An audacious person herself, she went along with the independent spirit of Americans. At times she pleaded with her father, "Let us do it our way," and the wise old General usually gave permission. Eva never disappointed him with the results of a proposed activity or project.

At first, William Booth worried about the physical and mental strain upon Eva, fearing he had "laid more upon her" than she was able to bear. He soon dismissed these misgivings, however, and wrote her in a prophetic letter, "Your career has been a remarkable one, but destiny, unless I am mistaken, has something in store for you more wonderful still."[7]

Soon after arriving in the States, Eva met Frances Elizabeth Willard, founder of the world's Woman's Christian Temperance Union. Miss Willard advised her to begin using her full name, Evangeline Cory Booth, for the added dignity she thought so essential to a woman with public responsibility.[8] Some people criticized the Commander for following Miss Willard's suggestion, asserting that she gave herself the name of Evangeline. While it is true that her father recorded her birth as Eveline, in 1888 he wrote to her as "My dear Evangelyn." At any rate, she ignored the criticism and, except by the family and friends of her youth, was thereafter known as Evangeline.[9]

Since Evangeline was only one where there had been two in charge of Salvation Army forces in the United States, General Booth decided to make the Western half of the country a sort of sub-territory, with Commissioner George Kilbey in charge, under Commander Evangeline. The Department of the West, as it became known, with headquarters in Chicago, extended to Honolulu. In addition to her duties as national commander, she administered affairs directly in the Eastern states as well.

All her life, Evangeline chose exceptionally capable

people to work with her. We saw how, as a teenager, she used the gang leaders of that day to keep order in her meetings, with the result that some who had intended to lead the fight against her took over the self-appointed job of bodyguard. In Canada she soon had gained a strong, loyal territorial staff, with able officers in charge of provinces throughout the vast Dominion. When she left Canada, she took with her Captain Richard Griffith, her personal secretary and aide, and, of course, Gypsy (Major Welch), who had been with her since Gypsy's cadet days. Within a few years, other officers would become familiar names to Salvationists in the United States—McMillan, Pugmire, Arnold, Smeeton, Bale, Margetts, Stanyon. She arranged for their transfer when she felt she needed them.

In the United States, she found a more than competent staff. Her national chief secretary the first year, Colonel Edward J. Higgins, would one day become the Army's third General. When Higgins was transferred to international headquarters in 1905, the Commander replaced him with Colonel William Peart, who remained in that position for sixteen years. Brigadier Edward J. Parker assisted her with the Department of the East.

Others played an important role in Army history— Brengle, Miles, Marshall, Reinhardsen, Damon, Chandler, Barker, Bates, Estill, French, Cowan, Fynn, Jenkins, and many, many more. But four men—William A. McIntyre, Richard E. Holz, William Evans, and Adam Gifford—became known as the "Big Four." They were all idea men, and perhaps because of their proximity to New York, they had easier access to the Commander's ear. Whatever the reason, they were men of powerful initiative whose suggestions were often followed.

The Commander was always able to hold her own with men of stature. She recognized and welcomed idea people. Actually, she did not keep anyone around her very long who was devoid of ideas. She has often been accused of using people and dropping them, picking them up again when needed.[10] This probably happened, but was no doubt a contributing factor to the great progress made by The Salvation Army under her leadership. In this trait, too, Evangeline was much like her father. He often told officers, even when they were doing a good job, "That and better will do." Evangeline expected the best from her officers.

Younger officers watched the way she managed her top staff. One said she handled the Big Four just like an expert driver would handle a four-horse team. She made each man feel important. Her strategy was to tell each one a little but no one the whole story. She kept them divided but united, each one working through her.[11]

Someone has described her as "having a short fuse—impatient, expecting people to jump at her command."[12] Most people would agree with this but would add that this was what made her such a pace setter. She never required more of others than she did of herself. People did scramble to do the least little thing for her. If she dropped her handkerchief, as one person said, "men cracked heads to be the one to pick it up for her."[13]

In New York, Evangeline found as much poverty amid great wealth as she had encountered in London. For the 70,000 children going to school without breakfast, she started a meal program, along the lines of the "farthing breakfasts" in England.[14] She spent her first month in America in an all-out effort to raise the extra funds needed to provide Christmas cheer and winter relief for people. Long before "Heart to God and Hand to Man" was a slogan of The Salvation Army, Evangeline had helped William and Catherine Booth practice it. All the Booth children were imbued with this philosophy.

The day before Christmas, the Army had 5,000 baskets filled and ready to give to the hungry people who tramped to the Grand Central Palace, at Forty-third Street and Lexington Avenue. From bare tenements and crowded lodging houses they came; from park benches and bivouacs under bridges, from doorways and street corners—a long line of haggard, ragged, and hungry people. In the distribution of baskets, Evangeline worked alongside other Salvationists, whispering words of encouragement with her "God bless you." Another 5,000 sat down the next day to a hot Christmas dinner. As reports came in from other parts of the country, the Commander learned that 30,000 had enjoyed a traditional Christmas dinner.[15]

During the holidays, despite a blizzard which made traveling more difficult than usual, she visited the Spring Valley (New York) children's home. She and the three officers with her went by train and then two miles by buggy. For a few hours Evangeline forgot problems and stresses as she mingled with the children, played games, and enjoyed refreshments with them. On the two-mile drive back to the station, with snow blowing up their sleeves and down their necks, no one complained.[16]

The Commander set February 5 to March 14 for the Seige, a special revival campaign like those she started in Canada, and the *War Cry* cover featured a declaration of war against King Beelzebub. This hot war against sin and Satan was waged in freezing temperatures. On February 11 the worst blizzard since 1888 paralyzed traffic in the Northeast and Midwest. The Seige continued annually until 1919, when it was replaced by the Flaming Revival—another month-long effort.[17]

In the same year of 1905, George Bernard Shaw's play *Major Barbara* set off a chain of controversy in America as well as in other countries. The play considered the wisdom of a Christian organization's accepting tainted money. Shaw did not go along with the Army's policy of using money "even from the Devil himself," in order to help people and spread the gospel. (To William Booth, the ends justified the means. When he was criticized for accepting a donation from a professed agnostic, he replied, "We will wash it in the tears of the widows and orphans and lay it on the altar of humanity."[18]) Shaw himself enjoyed the way he astonished London when he made his heroine a major in The Salvation Army and substituted a Salvation Army barracks instead of a drawing room for the conversion scene. Years later, when some of his old plays were revived, he said, "*Major Barbara* proved to be the most alive of them all."[19]

Evangeline felt that the Army could stand unashamed under the spotlight of criticism; that the popularily of Shaw's play won friends for the Army rather than alienating people.

Just as she was beginning to feel at home, news of the San Francisco earthquake, America's greatest disaster since the Chicago Fire, reached the Commander on April 18, 1906. For one terrible moment, San Francisco shook and trembled. Buildings crumbled, water mains snapped like dry sticks, and a fire started that raged unchecked for two days, destroying four square miles of the city. Evangeline responded like a cavalry war-horse to the sound of a bugle.

A wire from Colonel George French assured her that the Army was setting up a refugee camp at Beulah Park, three miles from Oakland. Wagons and carts were being used for ambulances and conveyances to take people there. She learned later that in San Francisco the mayor announced the death penalty for looting and called in 1,500 U.S. soldiers. However, in Oakland, the Salvationists' blue uniforms maintained the law and order needed. For five days, no officer removed that uniform, even to sleep. Sixteen thousand shocked people found refuge at the Beulah Park camp, where China-town Salvationists cooked and served beef stew and chicken dinners and 6,000 almost naked people received clothing.[20]

In New York, the Commander held a short meeting, to pray for the stricken families in San Francisco, and then began organizing her Army for duty. Like her father, she was a practical Christian. She once said, "Some people pray all night over an emergency and are too tired next day to deal with it."[21] Within forty-eight hours she had spearheaded one of the most notable gatherings of its kind ever held in New York City. Presided over by the Honorable Joseph Choate, ex-ambassador to England, the two-hour meeting in Union Square opened with the singing of "Rock of Ages" led by the Salvation Army band. Men in frock coats and silk hats stood side by side with men in their working clothes. In her appeal for a relief fund, Evangeline told them, "You may not be able to pay for a carload of provisions, or nurses or doctors, but you can send a bandage, or a blanket, or bread, or a tent." Baskets were quickly filled with money and checks, totaling $12,000. A month later the fund totaled more than $15,000, including $1,000 from William Booth at international headquarters, and money collected through an unseasonal use of Christmas kettles. The Commander herself visited the devastated region, traveling 8,000 miles in twelve days.[22]

Along with heavier responsibilities, Evangeline was often asked to officiate at weddings, a task she thoroughly enjoyed. She started doing this, along with dedicating babies and commissioning cadets, when she was young and was still doing it more than sixty years later. Many of the people involved have treasured records of such occasions.

For instance, a minister's wife still has the newspaper account of her mother and father's wedding, held amid volleys of hallelujahs, at a Salvation Army camp meeting in the early 1900s. Evangeline used the occasion to do more than perform the wedding ceremony. With her flair for the dramatic, after the evening service in the camp auditorium, all the cottages were illuminated and she led a serpentine march through the grounds, everyone singing. At eleven o'clock, all lights went out with the last stanza of a song, and she declared the campground officially closed for the season.[23]

It is impossible to estimate accurately the number of babies Evangeline dedicated to the Lord in her lifetime. At one service, typical of uncounted others, in New York City's Hippodrome, the Commander took the daughter of Brigadier Edward J. Parker in her arms and said:

> "I take from the arms and heart of her parents this baby. By the express desire of the parents I consecrate her to Him who loved us first and gave Himself for us; Whose unerring wisdom can direct our paths; Whose outstretched wings can shield in danger, Whose infinite compassion remembers our frailties; Whose boundless grace can keep from evil; Whose everlasting arms enfold us in death, and bring us into the desired haven.
>
> "Calling this great gathering to witness, I dedicate to Thee, O Lord, Mildred Estelle Parker, believing Thou art able to keep the charge committed unto Thee until that great day."[24]

General William Booth stopped to see his favorite daughter for three days on his way to Japan that spring of 1907.[25] They no doubt talked about the family. Both still grieved that Emma had died so young, and neither could understand how Ballington, Kate, and Herbert could leave the ranks of The Salvation Army. Evangeline would have told her father that everything was not smooth sailing for her in the United States. People still confused members of the Volunteers of America, of which Ballington was now the General, with The Salvation Army. Evangeline did not like the idea of ex-Salvationists, whom she thought of as deserters from the fold, mistakenly assumed to be members in good standing of her beloved Army. She was also annoyed that Herbert, now a transatlantic free-lance evangelist, could pop in and out of the United States for meetings, often without her knowledge, but Herbert probably saw no reason why he should keep his sister informed of his schedule.[26]

In September 1908, General Booth visited the United States for the last time. Evangeline accompanied him as he conducted meetings in the principal cities of the east and midwest. In Chicago he was seriously ill with dysentery for nearly a week and some of his meetings had to be postponed, but he made all of them with the exception of Cleveland. In Washington, President and Mrs. Theodore Roosevelt had a luncheon for the General and Evangeline.[27] She sat at the President's right at one end of the table, while the General sat in a similar place by Mrs. Roosevelt at the opposite end. The President asked the General to tell them about his trip to Japan and of the Army's work with different nationalities.[28]

William Booth, now seventy-eight and broken down physically, was still a commanding figure, resembling the prophet Moses more than ever. In meetings, he seemed to be on edge at times, although when speaking he still electrified audiences as he denounced sin. His speeches were, as always, lighted with flashes of humor—such as one of his favorite stories of the man who confessed between sobs, "I'm a convert all right, General, but when

I came into this place, I'm damned if I had any idea of getting saved."

When he sailed for home in November, Evangeline accompanied him. As the band played "God Be with You Till We Meet Again," the old General knew that this might be his last visit to America.[29]

By 1909 Evangeline had shifted her staff around. Alex M. Damon came on to territorial headquarters as field secretary, and Samuel L. Brengle became the National Traveling Spiritual Special. The Big Four provincial commanders had moved, too. Holz was now in Philadelphia, McIntyre in New York, Gifford in Boston, and Evans in Cleveland.

One of the Army's staunchest friends and supporters was John Wanamaker, eminent retail merchant. He greatly admired Evangeline Booth, and she consulted him about many things. When she first took up her command in New York, he warned her against wasting her gifts on small and unimportant engagements. She would do much better to reserve her oratory for big occasions, he said, and people would soon realize what a privilege it was to hear her. Since there were so many calls upon her time, of necessity she was forced to space herself and had to refuse some invitations. When asked to meetings in Philadelphia, where John Wanamaker usually served as chairman, she always tried to go and looked forward to those occasions. But one weekend, everything seemed to go wrong.

The Commander was under great pressures and tried to leave her worries in New York, but she was not her usual ebullient, stimulating self. The staff tried to ease the tension for her, but many things—mostly trivial—upset her. She became irritable and made life miserable for everyone around her. Crowds were good, penitents knelt at the altar and prayed, but Evangeline knew she had made things difficult for the staff, who had done their best. Altogether, the two days had been an ordeal, both for her and for everyone close to her.

On Monday morning, Colonel Holz called the Atlantic Coast provincial staff in for a postmortem. He loved the Commander and was feeling gloomy because he knew she had not been satisfied or happy about the weekend. He fingered his mustache, gave it a twitch on one side, and with his strong German accent said, "The Commander has come"—twitched his mustache on the other side—"and t'ank God the Commander has gone."

The colonel's grandson said, "He was really saying, 'Well, boys, we had a bad one; let's forget about it.' Actually, my grandfather and Commissioner McIntyre (then Colonel) were her strongest supporters and would do anything for her. But that was one time when he felt it was good she had gone without his scalp."[30]

William Booth kept his eyes on what Evangeline was doing in the United States and liked what he saw. He often teased her about the way Americans seemingly had "money to burn" but accepted her explanation that sometimes it was necessary to spend money to secure the future.[31] She always knew she had her father's strong support.

One morning when the Commander started to the office, she was amazed to find one of the early model automobiles parked as a gift at her doorstep. She asked her brother Bramwell, the chief of staff, for permission to keep it but he said no. Not satisfied with his answer, Evangeline wrote her father. She told him she was tired of being a straphanger—could she keep the car? The General decided it was equipment for work and replied, "Accept it and don't break your neck."[32]

The Commander was never happier than when one

of the Big Four came up with a bright idea. In 1909 Colonel McIntyre proposed a Boozers' Convention for the regeneration of drunkards in New York City. Evangeline gave her enthusiastic approval and issued orders that McIntyre should have all the help he needed.

The first Boozers' Day was on Thanksgiving. For weeks previously, bold posters nailed on almost every telephone pole and billboard in neighborhoods frequented by alcoholics made sensational announcements about the upcoming program. The one that attracted most attention read FREE EATS ALL DAY.

On Thanksgiving Day, a fleet of borrowed Fifth Avenue coaches, each manned by three Salvation Army stalwarts and a driver, cruised around looking for drunkards. They stopped at the Bowery, public parks, Hell's Kitchen, and municipal lodging houses, scooping up human derelicts wherever they found them and taking them to the Army's Memorial Hall. Operators of flophouses and "joints" were delighted to get rid of their nonpaying clientele.[33]

A spectacular parade took place in the afternoon. All Salvation Army forces helped. Four or five bands kept up continuous martial music. Featured in the procession was a water wagon, loaned by the city's street cleaning department, drawn by four horses. On the wagon were drunkards of all descriptions. Uniformed Salvationists marched on either side, to catch them if they fell off. That night when Evangeline referred to the drunkards who had been "on the wagon," she coined a phrase. Today a man who is abstaining from alcoholic drink is often described as having "gone on the wagon."

In the parade, floats depicted the miseries of a drunkard's life. The Walking Whiskey Bottle, ten feet high, made of papier-mâché, bearing the label of some familiar brand, such as *Bourbon XX*, drew the most attention. Chained to the huge whiskey bottle was a man representing a drunk—ragged, bloated, and reeling. After him came a poorly dressed, thin woman, with ragged children trailing behind her, reminding spectators of the woes of a drunkard's wife. Newspapers featured cartoons of this.[34] As the parade marched along, they collected additional boozers for the audience.

The Commander felt right at home with this crowd; she had cut her eyeteeth speaking to similar ones in London. When she addressed them, she made just as great an impact upon them as she did when talking in parlor meetings with the elite of New York. Because she loved people, she knew how to talk their language. Her simple message, spoken with compassion, was effective. By the time the call for penitents was given, scores made their way to the altar in front. Strong coffee and solid food had sobered some of them sufficiently to know what they were doing.

While eternity alone will reveal the lasting effect of these annual Boozers' Conventions, word has come back to the Army from converts scattered all over the world. One of the most outstanding and well-known of these converts was Henry F. Milans, one-time managing editor of the *New York Daily Mercury*, who was dismissed because he had become a slave to drink[35] and finally became one of Skid Row's shuffling habitués. In a drunken stupor most of the time, Milans hated himself when sober enough to realize how low he had fallen.

One morning he woke up in the alcoholic ward of Bellevue Hospital to find a noted professor of the medical school of Cornell University, with members of his class, standing around his bed. He heard the professor tell the students, "This man can never be cured. He is an example of alcoholism at its worst. He must die as he has lived, a drunkard. You are looking, gentlemen, at *a hopeless incurable*."[36]

A Salvation Army girl persuaded him to attend the

1910 Boozer's Day meeting. Milans thought McIntyre
went too far when he claimed God would not only forgive
sin but that he would take away the very appetite for
liquor. He told himself, "The day of miracles is past. It's
too late; I'm done for."[37] Nevertheless, he returned to
the hall every night for a week.

On Thursday night, just a week after the Boozers'
meeting where he had first been urged to seek God's
help, Milans stumbled forward to the penitent-form. In
agony, he prayed for God's power to deliver him from
the desire for whiskey. At last, he thought he heard with
an inner ear a Voice which said, "Trust Me; I will keep
thee." Milans arose from his knees a changed man. The
appetite was gone.

Nineteen years later, he could still say, "From that
moment to the present I never have been tempted to take
a drink of anything with alcohol in it,"[38] and until his
death, Milans conducted a lively ministry by writing,
through correspondence, and, by giving his personal
witness in public meetings.[39]

Newspaper editors, jaded by routine news, jumped
upon Boozers' Day as a good story. After one of the
annual conventions, a clipping service announced that
over thirty-six yards of single-column space had been
given to the event by New York newspapers alone.[40]
These stories were picked up and reprinted by newspapers the world over, causing considerable agitation at the
Army's international headquarters. What was Evangeline up to now? Some of the officers wondered what
General Booth would do about it.

He cabled Evangeline to send him full details about
this crusade in New York's underworld which was causing more comment than any Army effort since his own
"Darkest England" scheme broke upon the world. Later,
the General told the worriers, "In America she's carrying

out wholesale what I've always demanded of officers: Go for souls, and go for the worst."[41]

Boozers' Day meetings continued as an annual event until the passage of the Eighteenth Amendment. Evangeline credited prohibition with drastically reducing the number of drunkards in New York. With the "supply" of drunkards relatively dried up, she felt the Army could best utilize its forces elsewhere and substituted for Boozers' Day a Festival for Children.[42]

14
At Home

Soon after coming to the United States, Evangeline realized that in order to keep her health she needed to get a house outside of New York City, so she could sleep outdoors as often as possible and also continue her daily horseback rides. She first rented a small farm with a Victorian house on it about a quarter of a mile south of Scarsdale's New York Central railroad station. A few years later, she bought a small estate in Hartsdale for a reasonable price because it was next door to a dog cemetery.

She had the wooden buildings on the Hartsdale place torn down and replaced with masonry buildings. The new house, similar to an English country home, was large enough to accommodate her personal staff. She named it "Acadia," after the French Canadians who left Nova Scotia to settle in the South—their story made famous in Longfellow's poem, "Evangeline."[1]

James E. Walker, the contractor who supervised work on Acadia, was the father-in-law of J. Leonard LeViness, Evangeline's neighbor. Three of Walker's men still worked on the stable and garage after the Commander moved into the house. One day Evangeline saw these men opening bottles of beer to drink with their lunch.

She brought them a pitcher of milk and three glasses. Snatching up the beer bottles, she said, "There'll be no beer drinking here; it's not permitted on these premises." According to Mr. LeViness, when Walker heard about it, he "laughed himself in stitches."[2]

Surrounded by flowers in summer, a miniature lake at the foot of the lawn at Acadia reflected the beauty of the grounds around it. Along with flowers, shade trees of different varieties dotted the lawn. Through the years, plants and trees were given to Evangeline. She named the trees for relatives or dear friends. The Founder's tree, best loved of all, carried her father's name. Two tall cedars became the theme of one of her greatest and most soul-lifting messages for officers' councils. She loved to take visitors around the grounds, identifying each tree and plant by name and relating something about its background.

In the beauty and quietness of Acadia, the Commander found refuge from the multitude of cares and problems always confronting her. Not that she could leave them behind in the office. She carried them home with her, but sometimes the solution came easier away from the hubbub of the city.

Naturally, people wondered about her home life. Who lived at Acadia besides her? What was it like there? Did she ever forget that she was the Commander? Not really. Even at home, the Lord's work, The Salvation Army, and its people were the Commander's primary concerns. She was never too tired to consider anything that would benefit those she always thought of as "my people." Much of her strict, Christian upbringing was reflected in her daily life.[3]

Gypsy, of course, lived at Acadia and had the oversight of the home. The secretary, Richard Griffith, who came with her from Canada, plus a cook and gardenerstableman, lived there too. During the years, others would live there from time to time to help with secretarial work, music, or special projects. Captain Muriel Creighton was one of these.

When first commissioned as an officer, Creighton lived at Acadia for two years. A good musician, she served as a transcriber of music when Evangeline was working on a musical composition. At other times, she assisted Griffith with his heavy secretarial work. Her health broke down under the pressure of working long and irregular hours, but she treasured the opportunity she had during that time for close association with the Commander. Although it was almost fifty years ago, she vividly recalled those days.

> "The Commander's whole life was absorbed by the Army. She was not a good sleeper. She kept her Bible, Salvation Army songbook, and a notepad on her bedside table. The Bible and songbook were her principal reading material. She rarely read other types of books unless they were relevant to her messages. She made notes during the night—a verse of poetry, a thought or two for councils, Scripture that would make a good text for a sermon."[4]

At an officers' council, Lt. Colonel Lyell Rader, then just a young lieutenant, listened to the Commander tell how she got inspirations during the night and how it always annoyed her when she had to get up, stumble around, find a light, and then realize that the inspiration had vanished. In about forty-eight hours, Rader had figured out a gadget—a pencil with a phosphorescent knob on top that furnished enough light to see while writing. The Commander was delighted with it.[5]

By six o'clock every morning, Evangeline was out riding Goldenheart, her spirited Arabian horse. Although the grounds of Acadia were not large, she had a small bridle path at the rear of the house. Her next-door neighbors, a wealthy family, offered her the use of the bridle paths on their huge estate, and Evangeline often cantered off into their woods for an exhilarating ride.[6]

Only an expert horsewoman could have ridden Golden. The Commander liked a challenge, and going for a ride on Golden often became one. Sometimes, with Evangeline on her back, the horse would prance around in the stable, refusing to go through the door. In the contest of wills, Evangeline always won. Golden, still defiant, would eventually back out of the stable, fighting to the very end.[7]

Evangeline loved all animals. Mazie, the German shepherd, was with her constantly, taking fences along with Golden when Evangeline was out riding. Mazie, trained to respond to a whisper, roused Gypsy one night in time to call the doctor when Evangeline was seriously ill and the nurse was out of the room. The doctor's signed statement that "Another fifteen minutes and there would have been no hope," earned a medal for Mazie.[8]

Helga, the boxer that Helen Keller gave Evangeline, was another favorite dog.[9] She also had birds of all kinds, some of them gifts from foreign lands. When young Ray Gabrielsen met her train in New York on the last lap of a trip he was surprised that she had brought fifty birds from Japan. "How did you get these into the country, past customs?" he asked. "No trouble," she answered. "They just said, 'All right, you can take them in.' "[10]

When people wondered at the affection and response the ducks, swans, and other animals at Acadia showed to her, she told them, "It is the voice."[11] She talked to them, and they seemed to be trying to talk back to her.

Evangeline usually arrived home from the office anywhere from seven to nine at night. Just before they left for the one-and-a-half-hour drive home, Griffith called Acadia to say they were starting, the signal to begin preparing dinner. If the day had been a difficult one, the Commander would have dinner in bed. Since she was always a light eater, a cup of tea with a piece of bread and jam would usually suffice. Then, by the time the hungry secretaries had finished dinner or even before, she had signed papers, planned the next day's work, and was ready to dictate letters to be mailed the next day.

This left little free time for people to relax. But Evangeline never tried to plan for free time. According to people who worked near her, she could not bear idleness in any shape or form. Between getting off telegrams and cables at night and having to take down the answers about six the next morning, Creighton had to take her daily bath in quick jumps in and out of the water.[12]

Some days Evangeline stayed home to work on sermons, messages for officers' councils, addresses for public meetings and congresses, articles for publication, and talks for all sorts of speaking engagements. She usually worked in the library near her room on the second floor. Here, in this chapel-like room, surrounded by her books, with a warm fire in the stone fireplace in the winter and a lovely view from the open windows in summer, she prayed for divine guidance as she wrote—and rewrote—trying to obtain the best possible results. She was always a perfectionist. This often taxed the patience and understanding of the secretaries who had to type and retype those messages, but none begrudged the labor expended when their Commander stood before an audience.

When working at home, Evangeline wore simple civilian dresses. She was not extravagant and wore her clothes for years. On her beautiful figure (a perfect 36 in those days), even the most inexpensive dresses looked costly. The Commander's uniforms were her dress-up clothes. Mrs. Vermulen, a Frenchwoman, made them.

They were always silk-lined throughout, perfectly fitted to allow her freedom for gestures when speaking, never so tight that they wrinkled.

The Commander was always loyal to her staff. She might dress them down but would defend them from anyone else. They, in turn, were often overly protective of her. She loved to have people around her, but her staff kept uninvited visitors away from Acadia. Invited guests were kept busy, at least part of their stay. When Major and Mrs. Fred O'Neil and Major and Mrs. Charles Bearchell were at Acadia one weekend, their job was to pull up the weeds in the ivy. All day Saturday, after pulling up the weeds, they put hairpins in the ivy and pinned it to the embankment to train it to grow that way.[13]

The summer of 1911 in New York was scorching hot. Evangeline wrote to a Canadian friend:

> Nothing can describe what the heat has been like in New York. In my sleeping camp at eleven o'clock at night it was over ninety; 107 in the shade on the pavement. Sixteen hundred horses fell dead in the streets of the city and hundreds of people were overcome by the heat. It was fearful. I battled against it for five days and then fell in a very bad faint. A series of faints followed and I became absolutely prostrated; in fact, I have been of very little use since.

That was probably the summer she went to Lake George, New York, to visit her friends, Adolph Ochs, publisher of the *New York Times,* and John Wanamaker, who had more than one home there. One day some of her friends said to her, "Commander, you should have a place up here. This is what you need. Look at that beautiful outlook all the way down to the lake. This would be a nice location for you."

She said, "There's just one problem and that's

money." Shortly after that, some of her friends bought the property, gave it to The Salvation Army for Evangeline's use, and stipulated that the Army could sell it when it was no longer needed.

A former Salvation Army property secretary said, "There was never a penny of Army funds used for the upkeep of her place at Lake George. Her friends took care of it for her."[14]

After that, Evangeline always spent July and August at Lake George. She used her middle name and was known as Miss Cory up there. However, her many friends, such as George Clinton Texter of the Marine Midland Trust Company, Frederick Kappel, of A.T.&T., and others like them knew who she was. Mr. Kappel would phone the Commander and invite her to dinner. "There may be a party of forty or fifty. You don't mind, do you? Tell us something about the Army." She was always glad to tell anyone what the Army was doing.[15]

Fifty years ago Lake George was a much more dignified summer resort than it is today. Residents could tell when someone had arrived by seeing a yacht at the dock. Officially known as Woodcliffe, the Commander's place, which she called Camp Cory, was located on a point and consisted of a guest-house—mainly for officers on vacation—and, nearby, a small cottage for Evangeline. Her secretary, Richard Griffith, now a colonel, also had a one-room office-bedroom that he called his doghouse.

There at Lake George, Evangeline could relax to some extent even though the months were more or less a working vacation. She had time for swimming, her favorite sport after horseback riding. She was an excellent swimmer and diver. After water skiing was introduced in the twenties, she became adept at that too.[16] She like to excel at any sport in which she participated. Once, she worked hard and faithfully to perfect a certain dive, even though she had a broken toe.[17] Despite her athletic prowess, however, she was never strong physically.

When Evangeline swam, she was dressed from head to toe. Long stockings, the exact length of her legs, were sewn to her swimming suit, which had long sleeves.[18] It must have been quite an exercise in agility to get into the suit, but it certainly did not hamper her mobility in the water. For years, Evangeline was the first one into the water at Camp Cory. Encouraged by cheering spectators, she would put on an exhibition of fancy diving from a high board. One summer, however, she dived into the lake and did not rise to the surface. A good swimmer dived in after her and found her caught in the coils of a wire fence that had been submerged. It was a near escape from death. After that, someone else tried out the water before the Commander dove in.[19]

Some have criticized Evangeline because she seemed to enjoy the limelight and applause. Since she was a very earthy person, she would probably remind her critics that there is no biblical reason for not responding with pleasure to *earned* applause. She required the best of herself, whether she was preaching the gospel or performing on the diving board. Sinners kneeling at an altar were the criteria by which she judged the worth of her sermons. But when playing a game or engaging in active sports, she did it for fun as well as for the strength it gave her body. She worked hard and played hard.

Replying to a letter from Bernarr Macfadden, widely known apostle of physical culture, she wrote:

> Yes, indeed, I do agree with you that physical fitness is not only a great asset but a matter of primary importance, for it is the foundation upon which the superstructure of our lives is built. . . . If physical culture is to bring to men and women the very best results, it must be regarded as a means to an end and never confused with the end itself. . . . The body should re-

ceive every care that can possibly increase its efficiency, but always with the view of the service to be rendered humanity, and as the medium through which is being worked out in the world the destiny of a soul.

People differ about whether Evangeline was a good loser. One officer who thought she was a poor loser said, "You couldn't blame her for that. From girlhood, she was always flattered and had her own way. She was so capable in this, that, and the other. When one is subjected to the limelight, to glamour and patronage all her life, it would be difficult to be a graceful loser."[20]

William J. Parkins, now a retired Salvation Army Commissioner, who was closely associated with Evangeline through the years, said, "No one beat her often because she was too skillful in sports and games. I remember one time when we were playing tennis. I think it was my advantage and I swung hard at the ball with a lot of overspin, and it went down hard. I yelled 'deuce' and she said, 'You won that game.' I argued, but she repeated, 'You won that game.' You didn't win often, but she didn't want a contrived victory."[21]

Young officers from headquarters were often invited up to Lake George for their vacation. Colonel William Arnold's daughter, now Mrs. Lieutenant Colonel John Busby, spent two vacations there. She and four other women slept in a tent. Everyone staying at Camp Cory ate together in a long tent those summers. Most of the time the Commander sat at the head of the table. One officer remembered that one of the best things about a Lake George vacation was the opportunity to hear Evangeline's comments. "They were always so interesting and uplifting. We appreciated every minute of it."[22] When there were smaller groups, guests ate on the porch of the guesthouse.

After supper some nights the Commander brought her harp into the dining area, where she and Colonel

Griffith, on the cello, played for the guests. Other evenings everyone played parlor games, with Monopoly and Rook the favorites.

Commissioner and Mrs. Holland French spent one vacation at Lake George. The Commissioner said, "The swimming and the evening fun times, with Evangeline the gracious hostess and the center of activities, were great. We played some quiet games, but she liked the active ones best."[23]

Not all was fun and games at Lake George, however. Some knotty problems were dealt with too. The Commander sometimes called officers up there for interviews that might decide their future in the Army. And once during each summer, she held a conference with her leading staff officers. The problem with that was she never decided until the last moment when the conference was going to be, which made it difficult for officers to plan their vacations.

One summer Mrs. Commissioner John McMillan said to her husband, "Now, we're going to have our vacation. We're not going to wait until the Commander makes up her mind about the conference; we're going now." So they packed up and departed in their car. The next day, the Commander decided to have the conference, sent State troopers after them, and they had to return.[24] Nevertheless, although she could be most demanding, she could also be compassionate.

Evangeline was especially considerate of officers who were in difficulty. One case should be cited without using the name of the man concerned. He had betrayed the Army's trust in him. His territorial commander felt that he should be dealt with severely and wrote to the Commander:

> How sorry I am to think you have to be troubled with such an awful problem when you are physically unfit. [She was often physically unfit and sometimes had to

cancel out on engagements, to everyone's dismay, including her own.] This wretched affair has been a horrible nightmare and should be acted upon. I understand that you want some expression from me so I think it should be dealt with hardly.

After praying about the matter and talking to the offending officer, the Commander decided some clemency should be shown to him. In reply to a note from Evangeline, he wrote to her:

How I thank you for your note this morning and the phone call. How they helped me, no one will ever know but oh, I am grateful. Before God, I have pledged myself anew to Him, no matter what the decision of the court martial may be. . . . I only want to live to work and do for you and the Army what I think I am capable of doing.

After taking a big demotion and being required to make restitution for his wrongdoing, this man finished up with years of honorable service to God in the Army. He always attributed this to the kind and compassionate heart of the Commander, who had been willing to give him a second chance.[25]

Evangeline deeply interested herself in the lives of young as well as more mature officers. One summer the then-captain Ernest Newton, the Commander's corps officer, asked if his family could pitch a tent on Acadia's grounds for the vacation period, while she was at Lake George. "She would not hear of it, but invited us to use her newly renovated home. For five summers we lived in her home, and our children enjoyed playing on the grounds."[26]

One of those summers, on her way to Lake George, Evangeline phoned Newton several times to inquire about her financial secretary, Colonel Gustav S.

Reinhardsen, who was seriously ill in a Mt. Vernon hospital. When she learned that the colonel was not responding to treatment, she had the driver turn around and they drove all night, arriving back at Acadia at seven the next morning. She visited the colonel, who died shortly afterward, and conducted his funeral before leaving again for Lake George.

Evangeline herself would soon face deep sorrow.

15

A New Era

During her first eight years in the United States, Evangeline knew that anything she wanted The Salvation Army to tackle would have the support of the General. Although William Booth had paid his last visit to the States in 1907, through correspondence and cable he kept in close contact with his daughter and encouraged her initiative in the rapid expansion of the Army's program.

Most of his letters to her were handwritten, and Evangeline could tell by his penmanship that his eyesight was failing. By 1908 the General knew that he had cataracts and that one of them was becoming very "troublesome." On December 16 he underwent successful surgery on one eye. He cabled Evangeline on Christmas Day, her birthday, LOVE UNCHANGING, INCREASING, ETERNAL.[1]

Within two months General Booth was traveling again—to Norway, Sweden, and other European countries. The white-haired patriarch was now a sought-after speaker throughout the world.

In July 1909 the indomitable eighty-year-old General started on his sixth annual motor tour in Britain. Because his sight was so weak, broad bands of white

ribbon were tied to the railings of platforms to denote
their edges. In August, Booth's eye became so painful
that the doctor ordered him to abandon the motor tour
and return to London for further surgery. When it was
over, the General learned that the sight in that eye was
gone. But he thanked God that he had one eye left, and
work that a half-blind man could do.[2]

He wrote Evangeline in 1911:

> Your letter has been read to me. My sight is much
> worse, or it appears to be, as you will see from this
> scribble. However, I cannot help feel that I must write
> you with my own hand as long as I can.
>
> The world is in a poor way and we must help it. Let
> us have faith in God—more faith than ever.

He told her he wanted to visit her again when "surely
we shall have time to talk our hearts out a little, if it is only
a little."[3] But the General's lessening strength prevented
him from making the long trip to America. In December
he wrote her again:

> This is the last day of the old year. All the years of
> my pilgrimage will soon be old years and be gone
> forever. You seem to have had a mighty Christmas so
> far as feeding the hungry is concerned. They are talk-
> ing about ten thousand dinners in London, and I sup-
> pose they have done something after the same kind all
> through the country, but everything is thrown into the
> shade by your performance across the Atlantic.[4]

Evangeline realized that time was running out for
her father, and during the spring of 1912 she visited him.
One day she stood with him at the window and tried to
help him to see the glorious sunset. He could not see it,
but she urged, "Try, darling, try to see the sunset." Finally he said, "Eva, I shall never see the sunset any more,
but I shall see the dawn."[5]

She was with him on May 9 when he told 7,000 people at the Albert Hall, "I am going into dry dock for repairs." His other eye was to undergo surgery. At this, his last public appearance, Booth made perhaps his greatest speech. Without the use of amplifiers his voice reached the highest balcony as he cried out:

> "While women weep as they do now, I'll fight; while little children go hungry as they do now, I'll fight; while men go to prison, in and out, in and out, I'll fight; while there yet remains one dark soul without the light of God, I'll fight—I'll fight to the very end."[6]

On May 18, William Booth wrote in his journal, "Eva left for the States. . . . The parting at Rookstone [his home] was very painful; it will never be forgotten. Lucy stayed behind to comfort me."[7]

Lucy Booth-Hellberg was with her father on May 23, the day the cataract was removed from his other eye. Although the doctors were optimistic at first, infection set in a few days later. The surgeon, Dr. Charles Higgens, who had performed the operations on both eyes, called in another consultant, Dr. Edward Treacher Collins. After examining the General's eye, they went downstairs to talk, and Bramwell Booth was informed that his father's sight was irrevocably gone.

Bramwell returned to the darkened room to break the news to his father as gently as possible. After hearing the verdict, Booth's hand crept down the bedspread to take hold of Bramwell's. "God must know best," he said, and, after a pause, "Bramwell, I have done what I could for God and for the people with my eyes. Now I shall do what I can for God and for the people without my eyes."[8]

In the following days he worried about his soldiers who had been praying for him. "My dear people, what shall we say to them? This is such a blow to their faith."

And he knew how the news of his blindness would grieve Eva. "Darling Eva," he told Lucy, "she will feel it very much."[9]

He dictated a letter to Eva on June 19 to comfort her, and on June 27 he wrote to her by hand:

> My very dear Eva:
> I am trying to write my first letter with my poor eye quite closed and I should like it to be addressed to your dear self. Well, I expect it will be a miserable performance, but the motive is all that your dear heavy heart could wish. I commenced this letter on Sunday. It is now Tuesday. . . .

He wrote again in July:

> I had your letter. Bless you a thousand times. You are a lovely correspondent. You don't write your letters with your pen, or with your tongue; you write them with your heart.

The aging General was close to death. Perhaps he knew it. His speech had begun to fail, and one day he said to Bramwell, "The promises—of God—are sure—if you will only believe."[10] A few days before his death he told Bramwell, "I want you to do more for the homeless of the world, the homeless men. Mind! I'm not thinking of this country only, but of all lands."

"Yes, General, I understand."

"And the homeless children. Bramwell, look after the homeless. Promise me." Bramwell promised.[11]

On August 20, during the night, the General died. The next morning, officers arriving at international headquarters were stunned to read this message in the window: *The General Has Laid Down His Sword.*[12]

The world mourned Booth's passing, and many people wondered if The Salvation Army would survive the death of its Founder, but Booth's Army marched forward without breaking ranks.

The day after the General's death, the Army's solicitors, Dr. Alfred Ranger and William Frost, met with the Chief of the Staff and Mrs. Bramwell Booth and ten Commissioners at international headquarters. After prayer by Commissioner McKie, the envelope sealed by William Booth twenty-two years earlier, in accordance with the Deed Poll of 1878 giving him the right to name his successor, was opened. As expected, William Booth had chosen his son Bramwell as the Army's second General.[13]

Evangeline returned to the United States saddened by the loss of her beloved father. In addition to her personal grief, she realized that from an official standpoint, it was the beginning of a new era for her. Things would never again be the same. Heretofore, she had always been able to count on her father's support for any Army activity she proposed to him. Now Bramwell would have the last word in official Army matters. This was as it should be; the General always had the last word. But always before, even when Bramwell as chief of the staff had differed with her—for instance, about going to the Klondike when she was in Canada—William Booth had intervened and given her the green light. However, she admired Bramwell's administrative ability. She could do only her best for God and the Army and pray that her strong will would not clash with Bramwell's authority.

As soon as she was home, Evangeline flung herself into hard work. Her love for children led her to respond with enthusiasm to General Bramwell's suggestion for expanded programs for youth. The names of newborn babies were inscribed on corps Cradle Rolls. Parents not affiliated with other churches were encouraged to bring their youngsters to the Army. Troops of Life Saving

Scouts and Guards, similar to Boy Scouts and Girl Scouts, were inaugurated. Sunday school attendance boomed. The Army conducted many character-building activities for youngsters after school and on Saturdays.

Meanwhile, evangelistic meetings in America also flourished, and hundreds were converted in Salvation Army meetings. Many of these converts did not become members of a Salvation Army corps but returned to their churches. People began to realize that the Army's primary concern was the salvation of sinners, not the proselytization to the Army. Non-church converts were, of course, encouraged to become Salvationists.

In November 1913, Evangeline opened the first Salvation Army building in the United States erected to the memory of William Booth—a rescue home (later known as a Home and Hospital for Unwed Mothers) in Grand Rapids, Michigan.[14]

Shortly after that Evangeline made a statement of her attitudes about suffrage when she told reporters, "No, I don't believe in militant women's suffrage. However, I am a suffragist—I made that known long ago. Men have not made such a good fist of it with the ballot that women would do any worse." She predicted a revival of religion because people were "craving for something better than ragtime in literature, ragtime in music, and ragtime in conduct."[15]

The International Congress of 1914 was the highlight of the year for Salvationists. The Commander arranged a great farewell meeting in New York City for the 700 delegates from the United States. Just before the meeting, she received word that the steamship *Empress of Ireland,* with 165 members of the Canadian delegation on board, had been cut in two on a foggy night by a freighter.

Young Annie Blurton (later Mrs. Commissioner

Glenn Ryan) was traveling with her father and a train-load of Salvationists to New York when word of the disaster reached them. They held prayer meetings the rest of the way for the survivors and relatives of those who had died. Upon reaching New York, they learned that 1,024 persons had drowned and only 20 Salvationists had been saved. Commissioner David Rees, the territorial commander, his wife, and most of the Canadian staff band members perished.

Mrs. Ryan said, "I remember Miss Eva standing in the center of the platform that evening, telling us how as the boat was sinking, the Salvationists sang, 'It Is Well with My Soul.' Then she sang it. I can still see her standing up there, filled with sorrow, but singing, "When peace like a river attendeth my way . . . It is well with my soul.' "[16]

The United States delegates sailed on the *Olympic,* with former President Theodore Roosevelt, a longtime friend of The Salvation Army, as a fellow passenger.[17] For two weeks in June 40,000 Salvationists, about half of them from Britain, the rest from all parts of the world, held meetings throughout London. When Evangeline conducted Sunday meetings at the Clapton Congress Hall, a line eight deep waited in Linscott Road to take the place of any who might leave the building.[18]

The next night, General Bramwell led "Four Hours with God." *The War Cry* reported, "Apart from the General's closing appeal for dedicated service from his soldiers, the only set address of the evening was given by Commander Eva Booth." The Commander based her message upon "The Promises of God" and reminded the great audience of the Founder's words: "The promises of God are sure—if you will only believe." She dwelt at some length on the promise, "And ye shall . . . find Me, when ye shall search for Me with all your heart," and emphasized, "The promises of God are unalterable, immovable, imperishable."[19]

The great wooden auditorium the Army had built in the Strand held only one fourth of the delegates. Therefore, on July 4, the Army went to the Crystal Palace building and grounds on the ridge of Sydenham Hill for a day of meetings and a grand parade, led by 5,000 bandsmen.[20] Evangeline Booth, riding a beautiful brown horse, led the American contingent. The London *Times* stated that she was the outstanding woman of the Congress and quoted English Salvationists, who said, "She's the Old General come to life."[21] As Evangeline rode by, old friends cried out, "Miss Eva! Miss Eva! Do you remember me?" Colonel William Ware, then a boy of fourteen, saw Evangeline for the first time that day and never forgot the sight of the erect, youthful figure on horseback, riding before the Americans, all swinging along in their red cowboy hats.[22]

But while Salvationists of all races and colors marched and rejoiced, storm clouds were gathering over Europe, and other troops were marching. The International Congress was still in progress when Archduke Francis Ferdinand, of Austria, was assassinated on June 28 in the little town of Sarejevo. Salvationists who remained in England or Europe a short time to visit relatives or friends before returning home saw the beginning of mobilization for the war which was declared on August 4, 1914.

16
Doughboys and Doughnuts

World War I had erupted by the time Evangeline Booth and her American Salvationists disembarked in New York Harbor from the steamship *Vaterland*. President Woodrow Wilson declared neutrality for the United States and urged Americans to be "impartial in thought as well as in action."

Along with other international religious organizations, The Salvation Army faced the dilemma of its members fighting in opposing armies. Evangeline Booth maintained a position of neutrality, and her heart went out to Salvationists of all countries. Many men who had been marching alongside American Salvationists at the recent International Congress in London were now marching in their nation's fighting forces.

The United States government, with its close ties to Britain and France, soon began shipping vast quantities of munitions to the Allies. Anxious to do something tangible for wounded soldiers and civilians, Evangeline appealed to the public through *The War Cry* and the newspapers to bring old linen to The Salvation Army. Enlisting volunteers to help, Salvationists stripped and rolled the linen into bandages, sterilized and packed them into bales, and shipped them overseas.

In New York City, the Commander herself supervised the "Old Linen Campaign." Every Salvationist in the metropolitan area went to the Old Memorial Hall to roll bandages. Eleven-year-old Alleyne Young and Myrtle Margetts came with their mothers. Alleyne recalled how the Commander, dressed in a white uniform, welcomed everyone and, by her encouragement, inspired the workers to turn out great quantities of bandages, even using staff bandsmen to play martial and patriotic music which set a swift pace for the workers.[1] By December 1914, thousands of pounds of bandages had been shipped overseas. Volunteers could not handle all the material pouring into collection depots, so the Army appealed for funds to hire the unemployed to help process the material. Evangeline urged, "Pity all you like, but for God's sake, give!"[2]

When President Wilson declared war against Germany on April 7, 1917, Americans, not having experienced the shock of a Pearl Harbor, were psychologically unprepared to participate in the "war to end wars." However, although she deplored all war except that waged against sin, Evangeline announced in a *War Cry* editorial, "The Salvationist stands ready, trained in all necessary qualifications in every phase of humanitarian work, and to the last man will stand by the President for the execution of his orders."[3]

With characteristic decisiveness she moved to meet the challenge for service to American soldiers, summoning a National War Council which resulted in the creation of a National War Board to direct Salvation Army war work. A supplementary War Board, under the leadership of Commissioner Thomas Estill, with headquarters in Chicago, was formed for dealing with matters arising in the Western States. She also appointed national, territorial, and provincial war secretaries so that the entire Salvation Army was placed upon a war-service basis.[4]

Soon the Salvation Army set up service centers,

known as huts or hostels, outside but adjacent to camps in the United States. These centers provided canteens, recreation, writing, reading, and meeting rooms, and libraries for servicemen. Religious services were held on Sundays. In addition to the huts and hostels, the Army provided facilities for servicemen in seventeen naval and military clubs, thirty-three rest and recreation rooms, and numerous railway station canteens.[5] But Evangeline wanted to do more than serve military men in the United States. "American boys are going to France," she said. "We must go with them."[6]

She decided that Lieutenant Colonel William S. Barker should go to France and find out how the Salvation Army could best serve the American troops. She knew that Barker was fearless and would be persistent if faced with difficulties. "If you want to see Barker at his best, you must put him face to face with a stone wall and tell him to get through it," Evangeline said. "No matter what the cost or toil, hated or loved, he'd get there."[7]

At one point in negotiations with General John J. Pershing, Evangeline told him, "I want to send my Army to France." He replied, "I have an army in France," and she came back with, "But not *my* Army."[8]

Lieutenant Colonel Barker and Adjutant Bertram Rodda sailed for Europe in June 1917. In London, Barker discussed Evangeline Booth's plans for American troops with General Bramwell Booth. In France, he presented a letter of introduction to the American Ambassador, the Honorable William G. Sharp, from Jospeh P. Tumulty, President Wilson's secretary. The Ambassador gave him a letter of introduction to General Pershing, whom Barker found cordial. The General put a sidecar at Barker's disposal and suggested he go out to the camps, look the field over, and report to him on his findings.[9]

Barker found that the advance guard of the American Expeditionary Forces (AEF) had landed in France, and other troops were arriving almost daily. They did not go to the front at once but were billeted in small French villages, where they learned more than they wanted to know about French rain and mud. More like Portland cement than anything else, the mud got into their hair, down their necks, into their shoes, and sometimes even into their hip boots. One soldier reasoned that soldiers wore wrapped leggings not to keep the water out but to strain the mud and keep their feet comparatively clean.

Soldiers who had expected to be participating in great battles found themselves drilling in mud from morning to night. An epidemic of homesickness spread through the troops. The officer commanding the First Division was willing to have The Salvation Army see what it could do to help alleviate the terrible homesickness.[10]

At Saint-Nazaire, used as a base for the reception of troops to France, men who had been cooped up on transports stayed in a rest camp for a few days. Besides being a target for camp followers, soldiers were drinking so much French wine that the commanding officer welcomed the idea of having Salvationists in Saint Nazaire to help cope with the problem.[11]

Back in the United States, Evangeline Booth had been praying that the Lord would open up the way for the Army to serve in France. As evidence of her faith that the prayer would be answered, she borrowed $25,000, to finance the beginning of the work, and later another $100,000, from international headquarters. When some of her staff worried about the debt incurred, she told them, "It is only a question of our getting to work in France, and the American public will see that we have all the money we want."[12]

General Pershing authorized The Salvation Army to

open its work with the AEF, and Barker cabled, SEND OVER SOME LASSIES.[13] Evangeline determined to send only the very best to France. "I felt it was better to fall short in quantity than to run the risk of falling short in quality," she stated. "Quality is its own multiplication table. Quality without quantity will spread, whereas quantity without quality will shrink."[14] Although the girls in France were surrounded by thousands of adoring men, no hint of scandal touched any of them.[15]

The first group of officers—a married couple, four single women, and five single men—sailed for France on the *Espagne* on August 12, 1917. At their farewell meeting, Evangeline said, "These officers are not going on any pleasure excursion; they are not going out of any sensational curiosity to see how things look, or test how it feels to be at the front. They go authorized by a specific commission, with their Commander's confidence that they are fitted to accomplish the specific work inscribed upon that commission. Anyone failing will be shot! It is quite enough for us to pay their expenses to be a success—we could not contemplate paying them to be a failure."[16]

Turning to the departing officers, she said, "You are going overseas to serve Christ. You must forget yourselves, be examples of His love, willing to endure hardship, to lay down your lives, if need be, for His sake. In your hands you hold the honor of The Salvation Army and the glory of Jesus Christ. I rely upon you for unsurpassed devotion to the brave men who are serving their country under the banner of Stars and Stripes. I also rely upon you for unsurpassed devotion to the banner of Calvary . . . by the standards of which, alone, men can be liberated from all their bondage."[17]

Evangeline personally gave a charge to every group that went to France. Colonel Florence Turkington recalls that she never forgot the challenge to her own group. "As she spoke, although I am very short, I felt myself getting taller and taller. She made us realize our great responsibility. She finally said, 'I promise you nothing. I don't know what you will go into; it may be life, it may be death; it may be sickness, it may be loss—I promise you nothing.' But it made us feel tall to know that such a great woman had faith in us. We determined we would never let her down no matter how much work or danger was involved. She could be warm and gentle on the one hand, but she could also be stern and demanding. She demanded the best from everyone."[18]

Evangeline cabled Barker that eleven officers were on the way to France and that funds, when needed, would be supplied to him. This group arrived at Bordeaux eight days later and went to Paris to be outfitted with the khaki military uniforms that General Pershing had decided they should wear. They then went to Demange to work with the First Division in a tent 25 by 100 feet until a larger "hutment" could be built.[19]

Soon other Army huts were operating in front-line camps. The word went around. "If you're hungry and broke, you can get something to eat at The Salvation Army." The doughboys noticed that Salvationists catered to their needs rather than hobnobbing with officers. As instructed by Evangeline, none went near an officers' mess. They trudged through the sticky mud to the chow line to get in line with their "boys."

Rain continued day after day and men crowded into the Army huts, bringing their problems to the girls along with their mending. At night the religious meetings drew overflow crowds. The morale of troops near Salvation Army huts grew better. As the military moved closer to the front, the Salvation Army moved with them, sharing their hardships. Thousands of soldiers sent money orders, issued on Evangeline Booth blanks to the Salvation

Army's New York headquarters to be dispersed to their families through 1,000 Army posts in America.[20]

It was the doughnut, however, that became the symbol of The Salvation Army to the doughboy. By October 1917 ensigns Helen Purviance and Margaret Sheldon had been appointed to the First Ammunition Train of the First Division, at Montiers-sur-Saulx. After thirty-six days of steady rain, a blanket of depression hung over the whole area. Purviance and Sheldon agreed that "we ought to be able to give them some real home cooking," but supplies had run out and were difficult to buy locally. Purviance went to the commissary and found that the only things they could purchase there were flour, sugar, lard, baking powder, cinnamon, and canned milk.

"What about pancakes?"

"No good cold, or without syrup."

"Doughnuts?"

They eyed each other. A good idea. "But doughnuts without eggs, Helen?"

Helen Purviance put on her tin helmet and went to the village in search of eggs.

She knew little French, but she knew how to say eggs: *des oeufs*. She saw a young doughboy talking to a Frenchwoman. The woman was laughing hysterically. The boy wanted a chicken but could not pronounce *poulet*. He finally blurted out, *"Oeufs, sa maman"*—not eggs, but the mama of the eggs. He left with his chicken and Helen Purviance with her two dozen eggs.[21]

The first doughnuts were patted out by hand, but soon a grape juice bottle substituted as rolling pin. Since they had no doughnut cutter, they used a knife to cut the dough in strips and then twist them into crullers.

While Margaret Sheldon prepared the dough, Helen Purviance coaxed the wood fire in the low, potbellied stove to keep it at an even heat for frying doughnuts. Because it was backbreaking to lean over the low fire, she spent most of the time kneeling in front of it. "I was literally on my knees," she said, "when I fried those first doughnuts, seven at a time, in a small frypan."[22]

The tempting fragrance of frying doughnuts drew the homesick soldiers to the hut, and they lined up in the rain, waiting for a taste. Private Braxton Zuber, from Auburn, Alabama, was the first man to eat one. He grinned as he bit into a big, fat, sugary doughnut and said, "If this is war, let it continue."

Despite their heavy military uniforms, the girls were always cold. At night they shivered themselves to sleep, dozing off from sheer exhaustion. One day they were delighted to receive a package from Evangeline—warm wool sweaters. Pinned to each sweater a note said: "This sweater is made from wool that was given to The Salvation Army by the President of the United States." As an economy measure during the war, President Wilson used sheep to keep the White House lawn clean and trim. In addition to the money they saved the government in mowing costs, the White House sheep were a boon to the Salvationists in France.[23]

The doughnut girls saw death frequently. During major engagements, they often worked in field hopsitals. Soldiers who had died during the previous twenty-four hours were buried each afternoon. Sometimes only a few people could be present. Always the girls sang at the graves and prayed. Off to one side, the Germans were buried. When the simple services for American soldiers were over, the girls would say, "Now, friends, let's go and say a prayer beside our enemy's graves."[24]

In the spring, Evangeline Booth sent American flags to France so that all graves of American soldiers could be decorated on Memorial Day. At many cemeteries, in silence broken only by the boom of battle nearby, the military commanding officer walked down the long rows of graves, took a flag from one of the two Army girls following him, slipped it in the staple back of the cross, stood at salute, and went on to the next grave. The girls added their offering, gathered the day before, of flaming poppies, creamy snowballs, and blue bachelor buttons.

Near Cambrai, the plane of Lieutenant Quentin Roosevelt, Teddy's son, had been shot down in action and fallen behind enemy lines. When the spot fell into the hands of the Allies, a new white cross replaced the rude one which marked the lieutenant's grave, and on Decoration Day, Colonel Barker placed flowers there for Evangeline Booth.[25]

As news correspondents began sending stories about the doughnut girls back to the States, there was talk of saboteurs in America becoming active against The Salvation Army. On February 21, 1918, a fire thought, but not proven to be the result of arson (a staircase smeared with oil) severely damaged the Army's New York Training College. Two men cadets died. As the others reached the street, clad only in their nightclothes, they were hurried across the street into the Ninth Regiment Coast Defense Armory. Soldiers loaned clothing to the men and brought blankets to wrap around the women.

Early the next morning Evangeline met with the survivors to encourage them, contributing much of her own wardrobe.[26] As they came in for the meeting, all cadets were given a suit of long underwear. After speaking to them, Evangeline said, "Let's all sing 'We'll Never Let the Old Flag Fall' and wave our handkerchiefs." Lacking handkerchiefs, the cadets waved their long johns.[27] And despite the fire, Evangeline commissioned 114 cadets as officers a week later and sent some of them to France.[28]

A few months after the United States declared war, the Judge Advocate General of the War Department ruled that The Salvation Army was a religious denomination.[29] This allowed Evangeline to send chaplains to France. Three sons of those chaplains—Richard and Ernest Holz and Norman S. Marshall—are Commissioners in The Salvation Army today.

As the Army's war work expanded, Evangeline realized the need for an all-out effort to raise funds to support it. Against the advice of a few on her staff, she announced, "We're going out for a million dollars, and the Lord will help us to get it." While many Salvationists were staggered at the thought of the Army's trying to raise a million dollars, at her insistence everyone tried to think of new ways to approach this task. One of the most original and successful efforts was initiated in Chicago by Major Fletcher Agnew, the special efforts secretary.

One morning he asked Estill, "Would you approve a plan, Commissioner, to get the two thousand letter carriers of Chicago to go over their delivery routes one evening in uniform to solicit their patrons for funds for Salvation Army war work?"

"That's a ridiculous proposal. But if you can get the postal authorities to agree to the plan and the letter carriers will do the soliciting, you have my permission."[30]

By Friday, November 23, 1917, the Postmaster General in Washington agreed to the proposal and the Chicago postmaster set December 7 as the evening the postal carriers would solicit funds. When finished, the carriers took their money boxes to the nearest police station. Two Brink's armored trucks picked up the money the next morning and took it to the First National Bank, where it was counted and placed to the credit of each letter carrier. That one night, they collected $49,267.25 for the Salvation Army's war work.

Evangelist Paul Rader of Chicago spent the next six weeks as a volunteer fund raiser, presenting the letter carrier plan in large Western cities. By March 1918 the Department of the West presented the Commander with $200,670.89, of which $124,503.27 was collected by letter carriers.[31]

In October Evangeline recalled three men and three women officers to the States for a short time to tell people what the Army was doing in France. The three women stayed in the New York home of bank president Warner Van Norden, Evangeline's friend since her first visit to America. The Van Norden servants took care of the cooking and housekeeping, leaving the women free to go with Evangeline to parlor meetings. There she told wealthy and influential people about the Army's war work, and the women were available to answer questions. All six overseas officers spoke almost nightly at public meetings.[32]

The women officers were still in New York on November 11 when the Armistice was signed. A few weeks later they heard the tooting of a ship one Sunday morning and knew that the first troop transport was pulling into New York Harbor. They dressed hurriedly to get down to the pier to meet the men as they came off the ship.

The Friday night before, one of the officers, Helen Purviance, had spoken at a church in Brooklyn. The million-dollar campaign was over but they gave her the $200 collection and said, "We want you to spend this for the soldiers." On the way to the ship that Sunday morning, as they passed a newsstand, she said, "We can't go empty-handed to the pier." They bought all the newspapers the man had, called a taxi, and went over to Hoboken. The soldiers were thrilled to get an American newspaper again.

The women officers saw men from Western Union at the pier with telegraph blanks and decided it would be good to send telegrams on behalf of the men to notify their families that they had arrived and would soon be home. After all the men had disembarked, the officers went to the headquarters building to type up those telegrams, sending them in the name of Evangeline Booth. The $200 took care of the newspapers and telegrams that day. Later, as the boats came in, the telegrams grew to such a volume that it took twenty-five stenographers to handle them. Chocolate bars replaced the newspapers.[33]

In France, after the Armistice, three ports were chosen as departure points for troops returning to the States: Brest, Saint-Nazaire, and Bordeaux. The military turned twenty 66-by-100-foot steel airplane hangars over to the Salvation Army. Two of the hangars, placed end to end, made an auditorium seating 3,000 men where religious services were held. Adjoining that, another building was used for a canteen and rest room. In addition to being at the embarkation points, Salvationists went with the Army of Occupation to Germany and stayed until September 1919.[34]

In October 1919 President Wilson awarded the Distinguished Service Medal to Evangeline Booth with the following citation:

> For exceptionally meritorious and distinguished service as Commander of The Salvation Army in the United States. She has been tireless in her devotion to her manifold duties. The contribution of The Salvation Army toward winning the war is conspicuous, and the results obtained were due in a marked degree to the great executive ability of its Commander.[35]

Evangeline accepted the honor, happy in the knowledge that this was America's way of showing its appreciation for the Army's war work. She knew, however, that the spirit of the Salvationists in France was the same spirit

they had shown for the past almost forty years throughout America. As she often told people, "The Salvation
Army has had no new success. We have only done an old
thing in an old way."[36]

There were never more than 500 Salvationists in
France with the AEF.[37] But for the first time, the American public was aware of The Salvation Army and eager to
let them know it.

William and Catherine Booth, founders of The Salvation Army, with their first five children in London about 1862. Children (left to right) are Catherine, Emma, Bramwell, infant Herbert, and Ballington.

Catherine Mumford, a strong feminist, was married to William Booth in 1855. As a woman preacher, she aroused controversy in Victorian England.

William Booth, onetime pawnbroker's apprentice who became the founder of The Salvation Army.

Eva, as she was called by her family, showed signs of leadership even in her teens.

Evangeline Booth liked to don costumes for her speaking engagements, often appearing as a shepherd with traditional crook, holding a tiny lamb.

Evangeline with two of her adopted children, Pearl and Willie.

Evangeline Booth was an accomplished horsewoman, often appearing on her steed at Salvation Army official functions and parades. She was also an able swimmer and diver.

Commander Evangeline stands at attention during a ceremony beneath the Arc de Triomphe.

In 1919 President Woodrow Wilson decorated Evangeline with the Distinguished Service Medal.

When Salvationists were jailed for disturbing the peace in several Devonshire towns, Evangeline won their release and their right to witness.

Evangeline Booth traveled extensively around the world to countries where her Army had gained a foothold. Here, aided by an interpreter, she speaks to a Japanese crowd.

Evangeline stands by a plaque commemorating her father and the Army's "invasion" of the United States.

Notable in her own right, Evangeline Booth appears here with Amelia Earhart, first woman to make a solo flight across the Atlantic.

Under Commander Evangeline's thirty years of leadership in the United States, The Salvation Army experienced phenomenal growth and national acceptance. Here she is shown with President Herbert Hoover.

General Evangeline is greeted by Alake Albeukuka, a West African chief, at a royal garden party at Buckingham Palace.

Always interested in the welfare of disadvantaged children, General Eva inaugurated a children's playground in England.

Fourth General of The Salvation Army, Evangeline was welcomed in New York by civic leaders, the Honorable Richard Patterson, Jr., and Mayor Fiorello H. LaGuardia.

Seated with General George Catlett Marshall on the platform of ceremony in Kansas City.

Astride her favorite steed, Goldenheart, Evangeline leads a procession.

Evangeline had her detractors as well as admirers, but none questioned her ability as leader of the compassionate Army she served for a lifetime.

17
Music Maker

All the Booth children were musical. As a child, Eva had made her father laugh by singing him popular ditties like "Waiting at the Church."[1] William and Catherine had watched and listened as their children played harmonicas, violins, guitars, banjos, and concertinas. Then one day they asked for a piano. William hesitated, not because he objected to their playing but because he was afraid his talented offspring might eventually be lured onto the concert stage. But Catherine reminded him that their children had been born with a musical instinct that demanded expression and that in the Bible music was the one art referred to, even in celestial regions. She allayed William's fears, and the piano was installed.[2]

Through the years, William Booth and seven of the Booth children contributed fifty-five songs to the Army songbook. Commissioner Paul Kaiser commented, "The Booth children were all very independent and all great poets. Our songbook is rich from their contributions. That's probably the only place where they lay quietly together."[3] William Booth's song "O Boundless Salvation," known as the "Founder's Song," is loved and used perhaps more than any other in the songbook.

When its author was criticized for using music-hall

165

melodies with sacred words, he replied, as Martin Luther had, "Why should the Devil have all the best tunes?"[4]

Catherine Booth, who concentrated on speaking rather than singing, nevertheless valued music as an effective soul-winning tool, and she too defended the Army's right to use secular songs. "I contend that the Devil has no right to a single note," she exclaimed, and pointed out that the Army used music to entice people from the public houses to their meetings.[5]

Although Evangeline agreed with her parents that any tune could be used for evangelistic purposes, she wrote the music as well as the words for her own compositions. These songs often came to her as the result of her encounters with people. One day she visited a man serving a long sentence in the great Holloway Jail, London. He told her that once he had been a minister of the gospel but, little by little, sin had begun to control and erode his life. He said, "I fell—I fell as a star from the heavens to a cinder in hell." Thinking of his despairing cry, she wrote "And Yet He Will Thy Sins Forgive,"[6] a song that has blessed thousands throughout the world.

In 1904 she received with mixed feelings "farewell orders" from Canada. Her new appointment to the United States indicated the confidence her father had in her ability to measure up to the heavy responsibility of commanding Army forces in another great country. She looked forward to the new challenge but as she thought of the past wonderful eight years in Canada, she realized how much she would miss the people who had so warmly taken her to their hearts.

After attending a farewell banquet in 1904, marking the end of her years in Canada, Evangeline rode horseback down a road between great fir trees, near a small town outside Toronto, and thought of the people she had just left. That night the song "I Never Knew" was born,[7] emphasizing Christ's tears, pain, love, and grace, for her and for all who need Him.

Those who knew Evangeline never thought of her as a placid, easygoing person. Rather, she was known as one whose dynamic personality kept people on tiptoe and things stirred up. Mrs. Colonel Hazel Stretton remembers that Evangeline lived in a state of extremes in her thinking and in her spiritual life, that "when she hit the high moments, she was simply superb, both in her music and in her talks."[8] Few would dispute that, but even in some of her low moments she produced beautiful music. One of her earliest and best songs was written when her heart was broken over those she ministered to in the London slums. She had returned home late one November evening, after battling with cold, sleet, and misery, and was trying to forget the day's terrible scenes. "One picture I could not banish," she said "was the beautiful face and golden head of the little fifteen-year-old mother . . . the fast and bitter tears falling on the human mite dead in her arms; the despair in the frightened blue eyes as she said, 'Look, there is no place for us in life, or in death; no place for the baby, or for me. Where can I hide the baby? Where can I hide myself?' At one o'clock the following morning I wrote the song: The wounds of Christ are open . . . There for refuge flee."[9]

After the death of her father, Evangeline found it difficult to overcome the "unutterable emptiness of life without him." One day when alone with the "poignant realization" of her loss, she tried to imagine "that magnificent spirit as it soared toward a better and brighter world. Suddenly there seemed to throb around me the music of celestial spheres in a tumult of welcome and reward. I fancied I could see my father at his finest and best, stepping forward to meet on the threshold of glory the One he had loved so long and served so faithfully, while through the gates I caught a glimpse of the throng, ten thousand times ten thousand, passing up the steeps of light—the redeemed who through my father's life of sacrifice and toil had gone before him. And in the confidence of that vision there sang this paean through my soul, 'Fling Wide the Gates!' "[10] Of this song, Commissioner Richard E. Holz has said, "It is perhaps her greatest song . . . played by evangelical radio stations all over the world. With the voices and the music adapted from the Erik Leidzen band arrangement, it is absolutely a thriller. The beautiful thing about Evangeline Booth's music is that it is not a temporary thing. These songs are living on. 'The Wounds of Christ' is often sung. I always use 'The World for God' in a soldiers' enrollment."[11]

"The World for God" is the song that Evangeline carried around the world with her, and she thought it was her greatest.[12] She wrote it at three o'clock in the morning "bowed under the immeasurable burden of the stupendous responsibilities of the call that had come to me on being elected General of the international Salvation Army."[13] When the General attended the Swedish Congress in 1935, Colonel Klaus Ostby led the Congress choir in her song. After the meeting, she told Ostby, "When I get to heaven, I will ask the Lord to let you conduct the heavenly choir in 'The World for God.' "[14]

A reporter once asked her, "What is the greatest honor you ever received?" Although she had received medals and honorary degrees, she replied, "The greatest honor was listening to the children from a leper settlement in India sing: 'The world for God; the world for God; I give my heart; I will do my part.' "[15]

Evangeline often composed on her big seven-pedal Lyon and Healy harp. When she was traveling or too busy to play the harp for some time, she would sear her fingers with a hot iron to speed the formation of calluses necessary to play the instrument.[16] She also used a small organ that she referred to as the "Sankey organ" because Moody and Sankey had carried it with them on their tours and Ira D. Sankey composed his hymn, "There were ninety and nine that safely lay in the shelter of the fold . . ." on it.[17]

Not just a hobby, music was for Evangeline an important part of her life. During the years Muriel Creighton lived at Acadia, the Commander and some of her staff often met in the library for a musical evening. Evangeline played her harp, Griffith his cello, and Creighton the organ. Evangeline had her favorites among the classics, but the old hymns of the church and folk songs to which sacred words had been adapted appealed to her most. Always included was Samuel Wesley's hymn "Behold the Saviour," to the secular melody "Drink to Me Only with Thine Eyes," and Isaac Watts's "When I Survey the Wondrous Cross," to the tune of "Boston."[18]

Any musician on her staff had to keep pencil and manuscript paper near the telephone. One morning she awakened Creighton before five o'clock and asked her to put on her robe and come down to the library to write down a new melody. "Three melodies were born that morning," Creighton said. "Over and over she sang the melody and I wrote down the notes until she was satisfied with the results. After she had worked out some harmonies, she phoned Griffith to bring his cello. We worked and played until ten o'clock when a long-suffering Gypsy, whose patience had run out, called us to breakfast.

"Later, the Commander combined the three little melodies and named the composition 'Birds Singing for Me.' However, when they finally appeared in their printed form, the title had been changed to 'Streams in the Desert.' But the three little melodies were there intact just as she had sung them that morning so long ago."[19]

Wilfred Kitching, a brigadier at the time, who later became the Army's seventh General, described "Streams in the Desert" in *The Musician* as a "tone poem." It was introduced at a great national musical festival in the Royal Albert Hall, London, in 1936, when the Salvationist Publishing and Supplies Band, under Adjutant Eric Ball, played the composition. Kitching wrote, "I wanted to shout 'hallelujah' as I listened to the captivating power of the haunting melody." And Bramwell Coles, then a brigadier and head of the music editorial department, told the enthusiastic audience, "This is the first composition for bands to come from a General and the first brass band piece composed by a woman, fresh evidence of the most priceless of musical gifts—melodic invention."[20]

Gosta Blomberg, now a retired Commissioner, and formerly Evangeline's private secretary, always took his concertina and music paper along when traveling with her. He said, "I often got a telephone call at three o'clock in the morning. General Evangeline would sing a new tune she had just composed while I, with sleepy eyes, wrote down the new melody as fast as she sang it. Then in the morning when I played it over to her, she would either smile, recognizing the tune, or frown upon it, disowning it, saying, 'That is not the song I composed. You must have dreamt it.' But she wrote perhaps twenty-five new songs during the years I was with her."[21]

While working on a composition, Evangeline consulted with Salvation Army musicians such as Erik Leidzen, William Broughton, Richard E. Holz, Eric Ball, and others to be sure a piece was musically correct. Sometimes she argued with them. She did not want all the "freckles and warts touched off it."[22] She always knew the kind of harmony she wanted, and no one was permitted to change it.

Brigadier William Broughton told Colonel Douglas Norris that Evangeline was a hard taskmaster. One day she asked Broughton to listen to one of her songs and later to make an arrangement of it. After she played it for him, he said, "But, Commander, I would like to suggest one or two little changes." She answered, "Not one note, Broughton, not one note! I want it the way I have written it."[23]

Russell Crowell, a former Chicago staff bandsman, never forgot Broughton's story about another time he was called to Acadia. In order to conserve time, Evangeline had a horse saddled for Broughton so he could accompany her and her horse, Goldenheart, on their early morning ride. Broughton, unaccustomed to riding, had to write down notations for the music she hummed or sang to him as he tried to keep upright on horseback. Only his devotion to the Commander enabled him to help her under such unorthodox working conditions.[24]

Evangeline always had great rapport with bandsmen and singers. During her thirty years in the United States, she considered the New York Staff Band as her very own. She called them "my boys" and knew each one by name. William Slater never knew when he would be called to stand beside the Commander and play "Tucker" on his euphonium. After preaching a little sermonette on the melody, she would say, "Play, Slater, play."[25] Stanley Sheppard or William Parkins, also members of the band, might be asked to play a cornet solo. Frank Fowler, a baritone-bass singer, or Walter Mabee, a tenor, often sang in her prayer meetings. Colonel Emil Nelson, at that time a member of the band, said, "She made us all feel that we were important—that we belonged to her."[26]

William Maltby, a Salvation Army musician and now a retired colonel, first met the Commander when she toured West Virginia by train in 1920 and took a pick-up band with her. The Commander said she wanted to be introduced to each band member, so they lined up. "Bearchell and I were chums. We were first in line, then ran outside and got back in line again and shook hands at the other end. Although there were thirty-five of us, she recognized us and said, 'You rascals, haven't you been here before?' She could always see the funny side of something."[27]

Evangeline enjoyed taking the salute of officers morning and evening as she walked to the elevator in the lobby of the headquarters building. At one time Brigadier Fred Ladlow worked in her office as secretary. When he first came to headquarters, he was standing in the lobby one evening when she got off the elevator. She said, "Hello," and he answered, "Hello." She then said, "Don't you salute your Commander?" He thought she said, "Do you play a flute?" and replied, "No, I only play an alto," hoping she would invite him to join her little ensemble. She enjoyed the joke along with everybody else.[28]

The Commander was a soldier at the White Plains (New York) corps. Because of her crowded schedule of engagements she could not attend regularly, but she kept a lively interest in the small corps, going to a dinner meeting each year to speak to the soldiers informally. One year she took Captain William Parkins with her to play one of his brilliant cornet solos. The corps officer, Captain Ernest Newton, surprised her with a newly organized small band that played two hymns. The Commander listened attentively as they struggled through their numbers and clapped enthusiastically. "Beautiful,

Captain," she told Newton. She knew all the hard work that had gone into enabling the bandsmen to play those simple tunes.[29]

A few weeks later the band came out to Hartsdale to serenade her before she left for a series of meetings. She wrote to thank Captain Newton and then added, "I noticed that the two younger boys were very poorly dressed. Can you get any kind of uniform, second-hand or otherwise, for them? I should think that two inexpensive tunics might be made, perhaps by a White Plains tailor, if you select the material. Anyway, I'll send you $50 to help with this."[30]

Her personal interest in the musicians endeared her to them and encouraged them to strive for excellence. Parkins was only fifteen when he played his first solo, "Columbia," before the Commander at a big youth council in Boston. He was surprised to get a note from her the next day. She wrote, "You played 'Columbia.' It was a gem."[31] From that day on he thought she too was a gem, and young Billy Parkins became one of the Army's outstanding cornetists.

On a visit to the New York Training College, someone told the Commander that Cadet Olof Lundgren, a young Swede, had great musical ability. She decided to see for herself what he could do. A sergeant for the class of 1931 remembered the occasion: "He did us proud. We sang some of the Commander's songs, then Olof was introduced. Bowing from the waist to the Commander, he sat down at the piano and took over. He played the piano with one hand, the cornet with the other. Then he sang beautifully, hitting all the high notes, and finished with an intricate cornet solo."[32]

During the depression years of the early 1930s, the new Centennial Memorial Temple in New York City, seating 1,600, was often unused. Commissioner John

McMillan suggested to Evangeline that a weekly meeting of music and song be held there, to be known as Friday Evening at the Temple. The Commander liked the idea and gave it her enthusiastic support. From the opening service, November 1932, FET was a great success.[33] Erik Leidzen, musician, composer, and conductor, was revolutionizing Army band music in America with his compositions and arrangements. Under his direction, Salvation Army singers and bandsmen united to thrill large audiences at the Temple every Friday evening.

The highlight of the first series of meetings was a festival concert in May 1933 at which Evangeline Booth presided, listened to premier performances of her latest compositions, and brought a message. Dr. Edwin Franco Goldman, leader of the renowned Goldman band, was the guest conductor.[34] Erik Leidzen wrote a special march for the New York staff band to play and presented a handwritten score to Dr. Goldman. The march, entitled "E.F.G." from Goldman's initials, was built around those notes. Obviously it pleased him.

Evangeline, who always liked to finish a meeting in high gear, told the audience, "Now we'll all stand and sing the Salvation Army doxology. Let's have the band."

Erik Leidzen stood by the band and said, "We do not have that music, Commander."

"But I want the band to play."

"This band does not play without music," he said. Playing with music was always a strong point with Leidzen. "It's against regulation," he added.

"I'm the regulation," she said.[35]

As William Parkins, now a retired Commissioner but at that time a young officer and solo cornetist in the band, recalled, "We bandsmen were stunned as we listened. Here were two very strong personalities. We all loved them both and couldn't have had two stronger persons competing for our loyalties right at that time.

"Erik Leidzen put down the baton and repeated, 'This band does not play.' The Commander looked at him. Then she turned to me and said, 'Billy, you play.' Well, this was all right. I was playing the theme. I wasn't getting into any harmony. So I played it and she led the great crowd in the Army doxology. The rest of the band didn't play.

"After they finished singing, Erik Leidzen walked over to her. Since I was in the first chair of the band, I was kind of between them. I don't recall the exact words but Leidzen said something like, 'If ever God was blasphemed in a festival, He was tonight.' She said, 'Leidzen, those are sharp words.' He replied, 'Well, now that I'm through, I think I can say them.' The Commander looked at him and walked away."[36]

As Commissioner Parkins remembered, it was more than a year before there was any reconciliation between Evangeline and Leidzen. "Here were two strong personalities clashing, and neither one was willing to give. But I think she was looking for a way to make amends with Erik Leidzen. One day she had Dick Griffith phone him and say that she was going to Sweden and taking Lieutenant Colonel Walter Mabee with her to sing. She wondered if Erik would be kind enough to write out the words phonetically so Mabee could sing her numbers in Swedish. Leidzen said he would be glad to do it.

"Then Griffith said, 'The Commander would like to have you and Mrs. Leidzen come to her home for dinner.' But Leidzen said, 'Why don't you and the Commander come here for dinner. We would be delighted to have you.' Evangeline and Griffith went to the Leidzens, and after that evening no more was said about their disagreement at the concert. Salvationists often wondered who really gave in. Actually, neither one did, yet she was the one who made the first overture."[37] And Leidzen worked hard prior to Evangeline's departure for

Sweden on arrangements of music for the tour as well as on the phonetic translation of Swedish songs for Colonel Mabee to sing.[38]

In January 1946, Richard E. Holz (a Commissioner at the time this book was written) returned to the States after serving as an Air Corps chaplain in World War II and was appointed music director for the United States Eastern territory. He began visiting Leidzen, his old friend and bandmaster, and soon Leidzen again became involved in producing music for Salvation Army bands. From 1946 until his promotion to glory in 1962, Leidzen made a tremendous contribution to Salvation Army music.[39]

Evangeline's presence at any musical occasion always delighted musicians and audience alike. It was enough that she, the Commander and later the General, with innumerable claims upon her time, came to add the dignity of her high office to the gathering. More than this, however, they knew that as a composer she had an unusual understanding of the quality and significance of the music played or sung. During her years as General, she was often referred to as the "Musician's General."

Musicians strove to give peak performances when they knew Evangeline would be present. For a Chicago congress meeting, a staff bandmaster asked Emil Soderstrom to make a band arrangement of the Founder's song, "O Boundless Salvation." This enabled the staff band to accompany the 150-voice chorus when they sang her father's song. The band started with a fiery introduction at a fast tempo. They had played only four measures when Evangeline stood up, turned around, and said, "Captain, that's got to be slower." They started again and took it at the tempo she wanted.[40]

Before she went to England as General, Evangeline

wrote a number of songs, even her own funeral march. She liked to try out a new piece of music on someone to get the person's reaction. Colonel Maltby listened as she played the funeral march. He said, "It was very good. After she got to England, she had Eric Ball write it out in funeral march form and it has been published."[41]

Evangeline spent time going over music for her meetings with the soloist who would sing. Lieutenant Colonel Walter Mabee had a beautiful tenor voice but did not read music too well. He sang often in her meetings, but she always made sure he had the notes right and would sing them the way she wanted.[42]

Shortly after becoming General, she sent a message to all bandsmen and songsters: "Sanctified musical talent is one of the most powerful means God has given man to help in bringing the world to His feet,"[43] and at her first bandmasters' councils, she urged, "I want bands! Go get me bands! Make me bands! But only if I can have them consecrated to God. The band that is not so will be in my way because it will be in God's way!"[44]

Her great empathy with band and song leaders is demonstrated by an incident recalled by Brigadier Bramwell Darbyshire. "At a meeting at Westminster Central Hall, London, the Assurance songsters, under the leadership of Colonel Railton Howard, were singing. After the second verse, General Evangeline turned around and said to the colonel, 'That's enough.' Immediately, he cut the songsters off. He was not upset. He realized that she felt it was the right moment to bring her message and he obeyed her command with no ill feeling. No one else would have asked him to bring a song to such an abrupt end."[45]

Through the years, people have asked, "What about Evangeline's songs? Were these her own work? What about the musicians who helped her?" Eric Ball said:

"I played her songs and we would discuss them, criticizing, amending. She would accept criticism readily, but she also knew what she wanted.

" 'You don't like that chord, do you, Ball?'

" 'No, General, I don't.'

"Smiling, her hand on my arm, she said, 'But I *want* you to like it.' "

Ball said further, "There was no doubt about her talent for music—but a person who is at once a public orator, administrator, Commander, and, at last, General has no time to perfect musical techniques. . . . I, or others who helped her, could not have written 'I Bring Thee All,' 'The Star in the East,' 'Bowed Beneath the Garden Shade,' and 'His Love Passeth Understanding.' Without her, these songs and many others . . . would never have been heard—and the Army would have been the poorer."[46]

Evangeline wrote songs with a gospel message and practiced what she preached to others: "Never make Army music an end in itself; always make it a means to an end. Remember always that the Founder's one aim in recruiting music to assist in the Army's great warfare was: *'Souls first, and last, and all the time.'* "[47]

18
The World's Greatest Romance

Evangeline's lectures drew vast audiences, first in Canada, then in the United States. In 1897 the *Toronto Daily Mail and Empire* reported that "Miss Booth in Rags" drew a "monster" crowd at Massey Hall.[1] An American newspaper in 1908 estimated that eleven million people had heard her speak during the previous year, a tremendous accomplishment in an era before radio or television.[2]

With her innate sense of timing, Evangeline used the preliminaries to set the mood for her entrance. Music from the staff band, singing from a white-robed children's choir which included her own adopted Dot, Willie, and Pearl, a picturesque march onto the platform of officers dressed in costumes representing nations where the Salvation Army labored, then dimmed lights—all this built up tense expectancy in the crowd.

Just as everyone started to wonder, Where is Evangeline Booth? a strain of music sounded. A shaft of light focused on a lonely figure clad in ragged skirt and torn apron, her shoes tied with string and a fringed shawl around her shoulders. Playing a concertina, she walked across the stage ready to present her famous address, "Miss Booth in Rags."

Holding her Bible in her hand, she spoke eloquently

about the keys of love, sympathy, sacrifice, and action that had opened doors of service to her in the London slums. She recalled her experiences, such as the night she stood outside the massive gates of a local police court and temporary prison and heard loud voices and heavy footfalls coming nearer. A woman with matted black hair, her face heavily bruised and scarred, her clothes stained with blood, was protesting shrilly as policemen propelled her toward the prison. As the gates swung open, the woman twisted furiously, trying to free herself from her guards.

Eva asked herself, "What can I do? Offer a prayer?" No time. "Sing?" Ridiculous. "Help?" There was no help.

"Whether it was an angel's suggestion or not, I never stopped to think, but impelled by a burning desire to do something, as she passed me I stepped forward and kissed her on the cheek.

"Perhaps the policemen were taken off guard by my action, but the woman wrenched herself free, looked wildly around, and cried, 'My God, who kissed me? Nobody has ever kissed me since my mother died.'"

The next day when Eva visited the woman in her cell (dressed in rags as a personal friend), the turnkey told her, "She's gone mad at last. All she asks is 'Who kissed me?'" Eva sat with the prisoner, listening to her tell how her dying mother had kissed her and prayed with her and then telling her, in turn, about the Savior who loved her and died that she might be redeemed from sin. This woman accepted Christ as her Redeemer and for years ministered to other women bound as she had been.[3]

A lecture always finished with an impassioned plea for sinners to seek salvation at the penitent-form. Although spent emotionally and physically after speaking, Evangeline prayed with many of those who responded.

Soon after she arrived in the United States, Evangeline told Edward J. Parker, then a young officer,

"Parker, I want to see you." One of the matters she discussed with him was the task of staging the visual part of her lectures: scenery, lighting, and, sometimes, lantern slides. She would conduct daily rehearsals of each lecture until she felt sure it was as near perfection as they could make it.[4]

One of the few times Parker argued with his Commander was over an invitation she received to speak at a special occasion in Pottsville, Pennsylvania. Evangeline thought she was already overbooked on speaking engagements, but Parker continued to urge her to go. She berated him and finally said, "All right, Parker, I'm firing you. I don't want you around any more."

He started out the door, then turned and said, "I'll go if that's the way you want it, Commander, but I'll tell you one thing: you're losing a good man."

She laughed and that was the end of it. He stayed, of course; she went to Pottsville and had a wonderful time. The city presented her with a beautiful clock made from a large lump of coal, highly polished, with her name carved into the base. Evangeline thanked them and, back in New York, gave the clock to Parker, her way of saying "Thanks for making me go to Pottsville."[5]

Evangeline carefully checked the preliminary portions of any program on which she appeared. She knew the importance of having an audience psychologically receptive to her message. Always sensitive to the reaction of listeners, she wanted them keyed up but not worn out before she began talking.[6]

As she spoke, Evangeline focused on people individually.[7] People never felt tempted to count the lights in the chandelier when she was speaking. She could electrify any audience; they were riveted on every word.[8] She never watered down her message of Christ's redeeming love.[9] People felt they were part of the scenes she described. When she talked about the disciples and Peter in the Upper Room, and walked back and forth on the platform, in imagination her listeners heard the footsteps of the disciples and walked with them.[10]

Evangeline's dramatic ability was often compared to that of Sarah Bernhardt. In the days before microphones, public-address systems, and amplification, she could stand, a solitary figure with the spotlight on her, on a stage such as the New York Metropolitan Opera House or the Royal Albert Hall in London, or in the biggest auditoriums throughout the world, and hold the attention of the person in the last row in the gallery. With judicious pauses, she could lower her voice to a whisper and everybody would follow along and hang on to every word. There seemed to be something magic about it. Today we would call it charisma.[11]

Small mishaps appeared never to upset her. One evening when she was lecturing on the "Stars and Stripes," a button somehow came off her skirt. She finished speaking, holding her hand at her waist, and no one knew anything untoward had happened.[12]

In stature she was a little taller than most women. Her interest in physical fitness—horseback riding, swimming, diving, skating, and other activities—kept her erect, a woman with a superb figure which always drew attention. Before walking onto a platform, she often threw her cape over one shoulder in a familiar gesture as if to say, I'm ready for business. She usually had three or four key notes on a piece of paper—all she needed for an hour's talk.[13]

Evangeline used makeup, which many Salvationists, both in America and in Europe, considered worldly, and they criticized the practice. She told some of her friends that she felt justified in using cosmetics to cover up marks on her face that had been inflicted during riots against the Army when she was a young woman—that she did not want her appearance to be offensive to the public.[14] However, for the most part she ignored the criticism. And all agreed that she looked beautiful, standing before the footlights, and was someone of whom her fellow Salvationists could be proud.

Props for some of the lectures created local problems. She asked the officers in Atlanta to have a white lamb on hand for her lecture "The Shepherd." Since lambs were scarce in Georgia at that time, they had a black one waiting for her.[15] Evangeline held the black sheep and stressed the Great Shepherd's love for *all* his flock.

When Evangeline arrived in Chicago for this lecture, they told her, "Commander, we're sorry but we couldn't get a lamb. We had to get a poodle and had it clipped to look like a lamb. Will you hold that instead?"

She looked at them and said, "Yes, but one bark from that lamb and you've had it."[16]

Following her lectures, prominent citizens came backstage to meet Evangeline, who was always completely exhausted. As they gathered around her chair, asking if they could do anything for her, she usually replied, "Watah! Watah! May I have a glass of watah?" Someone would bring her the water and as she took it she always asked, "There's nothing in this, is there? There's nothing in this?" It was one means of driving home her constant crusade against strong liquor.[17]

Every year she went down to Washington, D.C., and spoke in the city auditorium, seating 7,000. Featured on these occasions, in addition to the New York Staff Band, would be the U.S. Marine Band or some other great musical group such as the Westinghouse Male Chorus.

One night Evangeline, nervous as usual before a performance, walked back and forth, seemingly highly disturbed. Actually, she was getting herself under control before going onstage. The group of staff officers around her were trying to help her decide whether to wear long black gloves or long white ones. She wanted to wear the white gloves, but the "graybeards" were afraid they would be too conspicuous. She put on the white ones and they shook their heads "no." Off they came and on went the black ones. It was getting close to the time of her entrance.

Finally she turned for advice to Staff Captain Ernest Holz, the divisional secretary. He knew she would not be happy until someone suggested the white gloves, and he thought they looked dramatic against her dark uniform and would give her added visibility, so he said, "Commander, the white gloves will be ideal. The people will love them."

She said, "See there. A staff captain knows more than you commissioners, colonels, or anyone. Let's go." And off they went.[18]

Evangeline often conducted the final weekend of the Old Orchard camp meetings in Maine. Old-timers remember the tremendous "battle for souls" in her meetings, with seldom less than a hundred seekers at the penitent-form. After the meeting, she would get into her car and drive right out onto the beach, on boards previously placed there to make this possible. A crowd averaging from 8,000 to 10,000 would come from the pier and from all over the surrounding area. She often began this outdoor meeting with the Salvation Army doxology "Praise God, I'm saved!", preach a short sermon, then finish with what she called the "lily field salute" (white handkerchiefs lifted into the air) as the great crowd sang a familiar chorus, such as "Glory, glory, hallelujah! His truth is marching on."[19]

Another summer engagement Evangeline looked

forward to was the Sunday at Ocean Grove, New Jersey, where all the gates and entrances to the city were blocked by chains at midnight on Saturday. For the next twenty-four hours, no vehicles were allowed to enter or leave. Everyone walked to the auditorium. On the Sundays Evangeline spoke, she always found an immense crowd of people outside waiting for her as she left the building. She established such empathy with her listeners that they surrounded her and walked back with her to her hotel.[20]

Those who attended her officers' councils will never forget some of the themes she spoke on for several consecutive days. The "Cedars of Lebanon" was one of these. She adjured them to be "inright, upright, downright, and outright" in all their ministry. Today, every time they pass a cedar tree, many officers are still reminded of the blessings they received in those meetings.

Officers anticipated her councils for months ahead. One year in Philadelphia John Wanamaker slipped into a back seat at one of the sessions. Noting the officers' surprise that he was there (no doubt at her invitation), Evangeline said, "He won't hurt anything, and I'm sure if Mr. Wanamaker took time out for this occasion, he will have something to say to us."

Wanamaker told the officers about the time his friend, Graham Bell, celebrated the success of long distance telephoning by calling him. Bell asked him, "John, isn't this the most wonderful day of your life?"

Wanamaker answered, "I had to tell Graham the truth. This is a wonderful day, but I must tell you that the most wonderful day of my life was, and still is, the day I became a Christian. Right over my heart I have a little Testament with the Psalms, and my verse is 'This poor man cried and the Lord heard him and delivered him out of all his distresses' (Psalm 34:6). Now, Graham, that was the most wonderful day of my life."

Evangeline took the phrase "the most wonderful day of my life" and used it effectively in her message.[21]

Sometimes under the pressure of administrative duties and a heavy speaking schedule, she became ill. This happened once in Chicago. After a heavy weekend of meetings, she was too ill to come to the first day's officers' councils. The next morning the disappointed officers wondered whether she would be well enough to appear. Finally she came, walking slowly from the back of the building, leaning heavily on an officer's arm. When she got to the steps of the platform, someone reached down to help her. "No, no," she cried, then ran up the steps and strode across to the center of the building. Thrusting her arms high into the air, she greeted everyone with a big smile and exclaimed, "Hallelujah! I'm still alive," and threw kisses to the delighted officers.[22]

In one of Evangeline's best-known lectures, "The World's Greatest Romance," she told the story of the thrilling romance behind the Blood and Fire banner of The Salvation Army. She started giving this lecture in the United States in the twenties. The New York Staff Band, with the help of cue cards, furnished instrumental and vocal music at strategic points in the lecture. Later, Lyell Rader developed an ingenius board with buttons which Evangeline pressed to signify different musical meanings—play softly, stop, fortissimo, etc.—to the bandmaster.

Evangeline wanted this lecture as well as all others to be a means of turning people to the Lord. One night before she spoke at Springfield, Ohio, an opportunist walked onstage and made a plea for funds (the financial campaign of the Federated agencies was in progress). As she heard the man appeal for money, it upset the Commander so much that she said to Commissioner John McMillan, "Something has to be done to stop him." Turning to one of the bandsmen, she said, "Maltby, can't you do something? Knock over a chair." He did, and it made such a commotion that it distracted the man and he stopped speaking.[23]

One winter in Florida, Evangeline became ill and, at the doctor's insistence, rescheduled "The World's Greatest Romance." That night William Jennings Bryan introduced her. After the lecture, he said, "Commander, I have a speaking engagement tomorrow night not far from here. I'll forego that if you will give your same lecture there tomorrow night. I'll guarantee you another large crowd." She thanked him but could not accept his invitation since she was still under doctor's orders.[24]

Catherine Bramwell-Booth, now a retired commissioner, had little association with her Aunt Eva until Evangeline returned to England as General. Commissioner Catherine was then at international headquarters, in charge of women's social work in Great Britain and Ireland.

"Aunt Eva was brilliant. She had a gift with words. She was eloquent in her officers' meetings and, of course, she was always a wonderful speaker. I can remember her speaking at the Albert Hall—walking backwards and forwards while talking. It was very effective. She knew how to use her voice. In our day, with microphones just coming in, we had to learn not to be afraid of the sound of our own voices."[25]

After retirement, Evangeline once gave "The World's Greatest Romance" in Scranton, Pennsylvania, when she felt too ill to do it. As she looked out at the great crowd in the Masonic Temple and realized how much the local Salvationists depended upon her to represent them, she struggled to overcome the churning nausea in her stomach. Turning to William Parkins, her aide-de-camp that night, she said, "Ask the bandsmen to pray for me."

But after speaking a few minutes, she whispered in an aside to the divisional staff behind her, "I don't think I can go on."

"You're doing fine, General," they encouraged her.

Several times during the lecture, she walked to the side of the platform and fought to overcome the nausea. Because she was such a great showperson, the audience never realized how ill she was. As she fought for strength to continue, for the first time in her life she became unnerved and lost the sequence in her lecture. All the lights on her cue board lit up. "What does that mean?" one of the bandsmen asked Parkins. He said, "I don't know but I think she's in trouble." Sure enough, she started toward the side of the platform without talking. Suddenly, as though instantly healed, she walked back and continued speaking.

The script for the band was useless. They just listened to her and shuffled music fast when something out of sequence was needed. As several remembered, "She was a spellbinder that night, even with her affliction." The audience listened enthralled as she finished with a climactic:

"We preach the gospel for all men.

"We preach grace. . . .

"We preach the Bible. . . .

"We preach hell. . . .

"We preach heaven. . . .

"We preach it in song . . . the eternal gospel. The inestimable, fathomless, boundless, measureless ocean of God's love.

"I believe the rocks will turn gray with age. The forests will become unmoored in the hurricane. The sun will shut its fiery eyelid. The stars will drop like burned-out ashes. The hills will stagger and go over. The seas will heave their last expiring groan. The world will wrap itself in a sheet of flame.

"But God's love will never die. . . .

"This is the world's greatest romance: God's Love!"

Despite a standing ovation, Evangeline felt she had let the boys down. Although her staff wanted her to leave immediately for her hotel, she waited to apologize to the band for her shortcomings and thank them for responding so magnificently despite the difficulty of following her without adequate cues.[26]

19

Full Steam Ahead

At the end of World War I, Evangeline Booth assessed Salvation Army assets in the United States and found them alarmingly depleted. Properties had been heavily mortgaged—"a few millions." When asked, "What about your plans for expanding your work?" she admitted that would take a few more millions. "We'll see that you get what you need, Commander," friends assured her.[1]

Anxious to do away with the tambourine collections that took up so much of corps officers' time, Evangeline decided that this was the psychological time to put the Army on a sounder financial footing.[2] She announced in the *New York American,* "The Salvation Army is inaugurating a campaign which will revolutionize its financial system," and went on to explain that in May of that year the Army would go to the public in one great national effort, except for the Christmas kettle, to secure funds for its year-round work . . . a sum that would put into effective shape and condition all the machinery The Salvation Army had at its command for all the new equipment needed.[3]

In April 1919 she stated her belief that "America will see to it that our hands shall not be tied" because of lack of funds.[4] In May she launched the Home Service Fund

Campaign in Madison Square Garden, to raise $13 million with former Governor Charles S. Whitman as the national chairman.

To get off to a good start, a stove was set up on the steps of the Treasury near Wall Street and Evangeline cooked a doughnut which was sold by auction for $5,000 amid cheers and laughter. Then she and General Cornelius Vanderbilt, chairman of the New York committee, holding between them a clothes basket into which were thrown bills and checks, led a parade up Broadway—the only ticker tape parade allowed for a fund-raising occasion.[5]

Americans everywhere rallied to the Army's financial need. Not only the wealthy and well-known, but tradesmen, farmers, factory workers, and business and professional people worked on the campaign. Servicemen returning to the United States added their praise for Salvation Army work overseas, which resulted in a tremendous outflow of contributions.

In large cities, people stood at street corners, on automobiles, or in wagons to solicit funds. Cadets boarded buses, made a little speech, and worked down the aisles with their collection boxes. People in small towns covered the rural areas for the campaign. Throughout the nation a continuous stream of people came to Army headquarters buildings, often placing their bills or coins in a huge container on the platform of the corps.

Many of the donations were in small change: nickels, dimes, and pennies. In New York City by the end of the week, so great had been the response of the public to the Army's appeal that the banks had a shortage of coins. When bank officials found out the reason for this, they sent their counting machines to the Army so they could get the money back into circulation fast. Cadet Llewellyn

Cowan and several other cadets worked more than two days in one room, scooping up coins with coal shovels from piles five or six feet high on the floor and tossing them into the old-fashioned counting machines.[6] The Army raised almost $15 million in that organized national fund-raising campaign.[7]

Every year at the National Horse Show in Madison Square Garden, the directors themselves paid the expenses connected with it and turned over the gross receipts to an approved charitable organization. In 1919 the money went to The Salvation Army. The directors asked Evangeline to welcome their special visitor, Edward, Prince of Wales. At the entrance of the building, the Commander walked with the Prince between ranks of Salvation Army women in uniform. On reaching the royal box, Edward brought on thunderous cheers when he set a chair for Evangeline Booth, who remained with him during the performance.[8]

A few months later, King Albert and Prince Leopold of Belgium were entertained at a dinner at the Ritz-Carlton given by Rodman Wanamaker, chairman of the Mayor's Committee. Of the two hundred guests, Evangeline was the only woman present. When Wanamaker presented her to the King, he took her hand in both of his and said, "One of the happiest moments of my life was when I met your noble father," and thanked her for her leadership of Salvation Army forces during World War I.[9]

During these days when Evangeline's administrative ability was taxed to the limit by the Army's expanding program, a soldier returning to the United States from France made an impact upon her family life. Three of her four adopted children had married and no longer lived with her. But Pearl, now a young Salvation Army officer, still lived at Acadia and was close to the only mother she had ever known. Pearl made herself useful to

Evangeline in many ways and knew the Commander planned to take her along as traveling secretary on her next overseas trip. However, the day young Arthur Woodruff walked down the gangplank changed all that.

Pearl, in her khaki uniform, was at the dock to greet the soldiers. When she learned that Woodruff was also a Salvationist, they talked a long time. Then she and Woodruff began meeting at the cafeteria next to the Salvation Army headquarters building.

When Evangeline learned that Pearl was romantically interested in Woodruff, she called her into her office and said, "What's this I hear about you and young Woodruff? You know, Pearl, you thought you were in love with someone else not too long ago. I've heard all I want to about these young men. I don't want to hear any more."

Pearl listened, but she continued to see Woodruff and finally promised to marry him. When she told Evangeline her decision, perhaps the Commander remembered how she felt those years ago when she wanted to marry Thomas McKie and her father withheld his permission. For whatever reason, she made the interview an easy one for Pearl.

The next day Evangeline sent for Woodruff and discussed his future with him. He decided to become a Salvation Army officer and entered the training college that fall with permission to marry Pearl after being commissioned an officer. Although she agreed to the wedding, the Commander did not want to participate in it. She arranged to do meetings in the Western states and Hawaii and asked Pearl to be married during that time.[10] Through the years, Evangeline and Woodruff built up a mutual respect and affection for each other.

In 1920 General Bramwell Booth stopped in New York to confer with Evangeline on his way back to London from Australia. Following their conference, the Commander announced in August that the United States would be divided into three territories, each with its own territorial commander. She would remain the national commander, supervising all three of the territories but with no direct responsibility for any one of them.[11]

In October, Commissioner Thomas Estill moved from Chicago to New York to assume command of the new Eastern territory. Commissioner William Peart went to Chicago as territorial commander of the new Central territory. Lieutenant Commissioner Adam Gifford went to San Francisco as head of the new Western territory. Evangeline replaced Peart with Colonel Walter F. Jenkins as her national chief secretary, and sent Colonel William McIntyre to replace Gifford in the New England province.[12] She spent the next few months installing the three territorial commanders and conducting officers' councils to help get the new territories off to a good start.

With the ratification of the Eighteenth Amendment to the Constitution of the United States on January 16, 1920, Evangeline felt that Salvationists had won a great victory. Ever since she was a teenager, she had crusaded against the sale of liquor. She had stepped up her crusade during 1919 when the Volstead Act (the enabling legislation to implement the Eighteenth amendment) was being debated.

Shortly after the adoption of prohibition, opponents began to wage all-out war against it, urging repeal. The liquor interests charged that prohibition was put across surreptitiously when servicemen were overseas. Evangeline refuted this, reminding people that forty-six out of the forty-eight states had ratified the amendment, and hailed prohibition as the "world's greatest moral triumph."[13] When people referred to the speakeasies that sprang up across the nation as evidence that "prohibition does not prohibit," Evangeline answered, "It would be about as sensible to engage in an effort to expunge the Ten Commandments from the Bible because of their nonfulfillment in the lives of men as it is to advance the theory that the prohibition law should be repealed because it does not prohibit. Because the laws against arson, theft, and murder are being violated, shall we abandon these laws and their penalties? Certainly not."[14]

Some began agitating for the return of light wines and beer. "What are they but the thin edge of the wedge?" the commander protested. "Our stand with respect to prohibition is what it always has been—absolutely teetotal."[15]

She attacked all attempts to modify the law and declared that 90 percent of drunkenness before prohibition was caused by beer. "How ridiculous to say the saloon shall not come back, but let us have light wines and beer! Everyone knows that wherever light wines and beer are sold, even if it should be on the doorstep of a rabbit hutch, there will be the saloon."[16]

When Evangeline returned to New York in 1922 after a seventeen-thousand-mile tour of the states, throughout which she had noted the good effects of prohibition, newsmen confronted her with upsetting news. James Speyer, internationally known banker and chairman of the Salvation Army's annual financial drive, was also vice-president of an Association against Prohibition. "Is this true? Mr. Speyer is a wet?" she asked reporters. "Mr. Speyer is an old and esteemed friend of the Army but he will have to change his views if he is to continue as chairman of our drive."[17]

James Blaine, president of the Marine Midland Trust Company, had secured Speyer as chairman of the Army's drive and now tried to be the go-between for Speyer and Evangeline. Finally, he took Speyer up to talk to the Commander. Afterward, Blaine said, "I never had such an experience in my life. I couldn't get them together on prohibition, but they're still friends."[18]

The *New York Times* commented, "The incompatibility of belief evidently is irremediable, but it is not often that two people with opinions so unlike agree so amicably to disagree."[19]

Among the Army's friends were many like James Speyer who continued to support the Army 100 percent except on this one issue. Many of them became members of Salvation Army advisory boards.

In 1904 when Evangeline first came to America, she realized the importance of seeking advice from lay people. She cultivated and retained the confidence and friendship of leading citizens and sought their knowledge of law, business, medicine, politics, and labor to help The Salvation Army more effectively serve their communities. She invited men and women of experience and position, who believed in the Army's principles and programs but did not feel called to become Salvationists, to help with their advice.[20] Eventually official advisory boards were set up. Members interpreted the Army's program to the communities and the communities' needs to the Army.[21]

The Army's first advisory board, in Chicago, set the pattern for the rest of the nation. This board was the outgrowth of a camp board formed fifteen years earlier when The Salvation Army purchased the Glen Ellyn fresh air camp, twenty-two miles west of Chicago.[22]

When unusually pressed for time, rather than drive to Hartsdale and back every day, Evangeline stayed at the Algonquin Hotel in New York City, a favorite hotel for actors, writers, and newsmen. The hotel personnel loved Evangeline. "We have some of the top stars here at times, but none to outshine Commander Evangeline," the manager told an officer.[23]

No matter how busy she was with matters pertaining to finance, properties, or the problems that continually came up, Evangeline scheduled much of her time for evangelistic meetings. During a visit to the West Coast in 1924, she dedicated Evangeline Residences (homes for young businesswomen) in Los Angeles and San Francisco, but the primary purpose of the trip was to launch the "Red Crusade"—a four-month revival and evangelistic effort.[24] By the time she returned to New York, she was physically and emotionally spent.

Typical of her meetings was one in Harlem. The cadets' string band accompanied her. Evangeline spoke from Isaiah 59:1. "The Lord's hand is not shortened that it cannot save." The place was packed, with extra chairs down the aisle. As she talked about the wonders of the human hand, the human foot, people began squeezing their hands and shuffling their feet. Some had trouble breathing. Evangeline, sensitive to the reaction of her listeners, never let things get out of hand emotionally. While she wanted to speak to their hearts and stir them, she also wanted them able to think clearly when she invited them to seek forgiveness of sins at the penitent-form.[25]

When she needed to get away for an hour or two to relax, Evangeline visited her brother Herbert and his wife, who lived nearby in Yonkers, New York. During the years since he had resigned as a Salvation Army officer to become a free-lance evangelist, Evangeline had kept in touch with him. She had also tried to establish a happy relationship with another brother, Ballington, now General of the Volunteers of America, but found this harder to do. However, at Herbert Booth's funeral, September 25, 1926, Ballington sat on a platform with Evangeline for the first time since he left The Salvation Army.[26] At Mrs. Booth's request, Evangeline paid a moving tribute to Herbert, the staff band played, Brigadier Walter Mabee sang some of the hymns Herbert had composed, and Ballington also spoke.[27]

After Herbert's death, Ballington met Evangeline at Cornelie Booth's home from time to time, where Evangeline also enjoyed brief visits with the Booth-Clibborns and their seven children. At times she even featured her sister Kate as a speaker in Army meetings.[28]

By the autumn of 1926, the Commander was so pleased with the way the three territories created in 1920 were functioning that she decided to create a fourth, the southern territory, and these administrative divisions exist today. On January 1, 1927, sixty cadets, born in the south, were transferred from the Chicago and New York training colleges to the new southern college in Atlanta. William McIntyre was promoted to Lieutenant Commissioner and appointed to command the new territory— fifteen southern states formerly part of the eastern and central territories.

Under McIntyre's energetic leadership, the fledgling territory grew. When she returned to Atlanta the next year to dedicate the newly acquired Ellis Street headquarters building, Evangeline took the salute of 600 uniformed Salvationists who marched down world-renowned Peachtree Street to the strains of martial music from southern bands.[29]

In 1927 at a White House luncheon with President and Mrs. Calvin Coolidge, she found them especially interested in the Army's latest work, the Mariners' League, organized to extend to international seamen the religious, social, and educational services of the Salvation Army.[30] When Commander Richard E. Byrd left on his

Antarctic expedition in 1928, out of the fifteen hundred emblems offered to him he carried only his fraternity pin and two small portfolios containing small silk flags of the Salvation Army's national Military and Naval League and the international Mariners' League.

Evangeline initiated a Commissioners' conference in 1928 at which national and territorial leaders met for three days to coordinate the Army's work in the United States.[31] At that first conference, three of the Commissioners were from the "Big Four" of early days—Gifford, Holz, and McIntyre. Evans had retired and Lieutenant Commissioner John McMillan was now the fourth one of that influential group. Of later Commissioners' conferences, Commissioner Edward J. Parker wrote, "Sometimes, after hours spent discussing some national problem or project, we would ask the Commander to come in for a summary. Frequently she would suggest a solution that had not occurred to any of us.[32]

At times Evangeline sought escape from the pressures of her work by wearing civilian clothes to avoid recognition and by using her middle name, Cory. One summer at Lake George she had Colonel Griffith phone Lieutenant Colonel Edward Laity, then a young captain at Glens Falls, New York, to tell him to bring his car and take the Commander to a quarry to purchase some flagstones. Evangeline's first instructions to Laity were, "Don't call me Commander, but Miss Cory."

When they reached the quarry, Laity talked to the owner about size and price of the flagstones. Suddenly the man, an Englishman, stopped talking and said, "Isn't that Evangeline Booth, of The Salvation Army?" Laity said yes, but he wasn't supposed to tell him that, to which the man replied, "You couldn't fool me. I would know her anywhere by her nose. She has her father's nose."[33] Although she had failed to conceal her identity,

Evangeline was always delighted when someone found
her in any way like her father.

In November 1929, Evangeline went to Japan, taking with her the table where her father knelt as a youth
and prayed, "God shall have all there is of William
Booth." She used the table as a penitent-form in Japan
and around the world. (When she became General, she
took it back to the Army's international headquarters on
Victoria Street, where it was lost in the bombings of
World War II.)

Fifty years ago women occupied a much lesser place
in the world than they do today. Japanese women especially were not featured in public life. However, when she
visited Japan, government officials welcomed
Evangeline and escorted her to the halls where she spoke,
through streets lined with Christianity-seeking Japanese.

Emperor Hirohito broke precedent by inviting the
Commander to the palace for a private audience. The
Emperor also gave orders that she be allowed to wear her
uniform and bonnet instead of the usual court dress.[34]
Evangeline had practiced certain formal customs, like
bowing three times as she approached the Emperor and
another three as she backed away from him. Two of the
chamberlains greeted her at the palace with, "Don't be
nervous, Commander Evangeline. We, too, are Christians."[35]

Both the Emperor and the Commander spoke
through an interpreter. After the interview, the Commander was requested to attend the Emperor's garden
party. Guests stood along the garden paths on the route
the Emperor would walk. He walked alone and stiffly
erect behind his courtiers. All present bowed their faces
toward the ground. In the silence, the Emperor broke
precedent again. He paused, turned on his heel toward

Evangeline, and raised his arm—a gesture of salute. He then resumed his "unsmiling, almost mechanical, walk past his subjects."[36]

When Evangeline addressed Japanese university students, "she swept everyone before her," said Mrs. Commissioner Ernest I. Pugmire, stationed with her husband in Japan at that time. "It was marvelous that a woman could lecture there, but she had that gift. When she came out of the building, students who were Christians tossed their Bibles into her rickshaw for her to autograph, and she did it graciously."[37] Rickshaw transportation became a great favorite with Evangeline, especially after she learned that the rickshaw was the invention of a missionary who had an invalid wife.[38]

When the Salvationists went to the ship at Yokohama to say good-bye to her, they presented to her a huge Japanese flag of pure corded silk. Standing on a platform of freight boxes in the customs shed, she thanked them, charged them to "lift high the banner of Calvary," commended them to "the care of the Father of us all," and prayed that they would be "kept in His love." Then, with the crowd surging about her, cheering and singing, their banners waving, she made her way to the gangway and onto the ship.[39] She found an opportunity to say to Colonel Pugmire, "Somehow, Pugmire, I'm going to bring you to the United States"[40] (Evidently she prevailed upon General Bramwell to transfer Pugmire to Canada and then to Chicago as financial secretary; many years later, he became the national commander of The Salvation Army in the United States.) And as the vessel moved out of the harbor, Evangeline stood at the prow of the ship, waving the Japanese flag to and fro as the Salvationists sang to her, "God be with you till we meet again."

John L. McNab, chairman of the San Francisco advisory board, and L. M. Voorsanger and Warren McBride, board members, met her at quarantine. She conferred with them, and with members of the Army's territorial staff, before leaving for New York.[41] Her triumphant tour of Japan and the evidence of the love and esteem of the Japanese Salvationists toward her would bolster her courage in the difficult days ahead.

20
Stormy Weather

As the 1920s began, Evangeline Booth and her lively, progressive Army were happy. World War I had brought their work to the attention of the American public. Evangeline had been able to expand ongoing programs and develop new innovative ones to extend the Army's outreach.

Nevertheless, in a world growing ever more democratic in its outlook, she was becoming troubled about the Army's autocratic system of government. Territorial commanders from other countries wrote to her expressing their feelings about the need for reform.[1] Evangeline had already seen two of her brothers, Ballington and Herbert, withdraw from the organization because of their inability to accept the directives of either General.

William Booth had discussed the Army's system of government in December 1896 with former Prime Minister W. E. Gladstone during a visit at the latter's country seat, Hawarden. Asking the General how his successor would be appointed, Gladstone was surprised to learn that successors were appointed by placing the new General's name in a sealed envelope to be opened only at the old General's death.

"A most unusual arrangement," said Gladstone. Was

there any provision for removing an unworthy or inactive General? Booth admitted that he had been too busy to think about such a remote possibility. Gladstone then suggested that the Army might find it useful to have a group within its ranks similar to the Roman Catholic College of Cardinals.[2]

William Booth thought about this, and after consulting with three constitutional lawyers, he drafted a Supplementary Deed to the Salvation Army Foundation Deed of 1878. He carried this around with him for seven years and, during his worldwide travels, discussed it with Army leaders. Finally, the Deed Poll of 1904 was approved and signed by leading officers at the 1904 International Congress.[3]

In this Supplementary Deed, means were provided (by calling a High Council of commissioners and territorial commanders) "for removing from his position as General of The Salvation Army any General forfeiting confidence, and also for the selection of a General if, through failure to appoint, or from any other cause, there should at any time, in fact, be no General."[4] At the time, little attention was focused on the 1904 Deed Poll, which would eventually play such an important part in Army history.

When the sealed envelope was opened after William Booth's death in 1912, Bramwell was named, as everyone expected, to be the next General and was unanimously hailed by Salvationists everywhere as God's man to lead the Army.

By 1920, Evangeline had been in command of the United States for sixteen years, more than three times the five-year term of most territorial appointments. On a visit to America that year, General Bramwell warned her, "You cannot expect to remain at the head of the organization [in the United States] all the rest of your life."[5]

Evangeline protested being moved, but before the General left for England, they spent a day together at the Algonquin Hotel in New York—a day that her biographer, P. Whitwell Wilson, described as "Black Friday."[6]

The General evidently agreed that she could remain another two years. At any rate, Evangeline heard nothing further about being transferred until September 15, 1922, when someone phoned to tell her that the *New York World* had printed a cable from its London correspondent announcing a change of appointment for Commander Evangeline, without saying where she would be going. Upset at receiving farewell orders in such an indirect way, Evangeline cabled her brother and received confirmation that she would be having a change of appointment. Although obviously agitated, she told reporters, "I shall obey the order when the date is set for me to go."[7]

Immediately, influential American citizens protested Evangeline's transfer, warning the General of the disastrous effects her removal would have upon the people of America as well as upon The Salvation Army. Evangeline, however, in a proclamation to her officers, assured them that she was standing by the General and reminded them that no date had been set for her departure. "I am taking no part," she said, "in any statement or protest that may be sent to General Booth."[8] Nevertheless the General continued to be bombarded with cables and letters opposing Evangeline's transfer from the United States.

For nearly three months the newspapers reported the controversy, and Salvationists in the United States were kept in a state of uncertainty.[9] Finally, in December, the General retreated from his position with a cable to American newspapers. He noted that the statement in the *New York World* in September had been interpreted by some as "being an official intimation for my sister, Commander Evangeline Booth, to farewell from her present command. . . . Certainly such information . . . would not have been conveyed to her through the medium of the public press." He went on to say that he had no thought of an immediate farewell; "nothing definite has been decided nor will be until I return from my campaign in India, for which country I embark today."[10]

After the furore about her farewell subsided, Evangeline tried to put it behind her, forget it, and go about her work as usual. But there was one thing she could not forget: the overwhelming response of Americans wishing to keep her in the United States. She thought of the many opportunities given to her to preach the gospel and to serve people through the ministry of her Army. She decided after much prayer that she could do even more if she became an American citizen. On April 10, 1923 (her father's birthday), Colonels Jenkins and Reinhardsen stood with Evangeline as she became a citizen in the United States District Court, Southern District of New York. The judge, in his private chambers, said, "Commander, this is the greatest honor conferred upon me as judge to accept your petition for citizenship, and it is hereby granted."[11]

By 1925 an increasing number of leading officers were writing to her, urging her to use her influence as a sister as well as her prestige as Commander of a great country to persuade General Bramwell to initiate democratic reforms.[12] She had not as yet spelled out in writing to the General all she meant by "reforms," but he knew she wanted him to modify his own unlimited powers and thought he should do away with the "sealed envelope" as the method of choosing the next General. Despite the fact that Evangeline urged Bramwell to remember that the postwar world was different from the world in which

William Booth lived, he may have dismissed her importunities for reform as her personal rebellion against a brother's authority.

Both Evangeline and Bramwell believed they were defending their father's policies. Since the Army was the primary topic when any of the Booths met, the Founder had probably discussed the future of the Army with both of them, and each had an individual interpretation of these conversations. Evangeline wrote to the General suggesting that she go to London to discuss some of their differences. He replied that since he was coming to the United States to conduct meetings the following spring, he would prefer to wait and talk things over with her then. Evangeline was an impatient person. It is not difficult to imagine her reaction to Bramwell's message. A short while later she became seriously ill.[13]

Bramwell's meetings in America got off to a good start. Although still not well, Evangeline attended his first one and presented him to a large crowd, which welcomed him enthusiastically. Following the meeting, she collapsed and was brought back by train to New York, with a doctor and nurse in attendance. She recalled later, "I dragged through seven long months of the worst suffering of my life."[14]

Before he left New York in May, the General addressed 1,400 officers in council. Since none of them mentioned grievances to him, and since in his talks with Evangeline he had sensed her love and loyalty despite differences of opinion, the General returned home with more peace of mind than he had felt when he came to America.[15] He did not realize that officers who favored reform might not feel free to discuss such a controversial matter.

In 1927 the American Legion invited Evangeline to be the honored guest and speaker at their Paris convention, in commemoration of the tenth anniversary of the United States' entrance into World War I. The seven days in Paris were crowded with activities. More than a hundred Salvationist Legionnaires proudly marched behind their Commander down the Champs Élysées to the Tomb of the Unknown Soldier. In the silence, Evangeline shattered tradition by offering a prayer, but "the gendarmes just disappeared."[16] She addressed the great public gathering at the Trocadero, visited with George Clemenceau, spoke at a meeting of Salvationists from all over Europe, and was honored at a reception given by President Gaston Doumergue.

When she arrived at the Cathedral of Notre Dame on the final day for the thanksgiving meeting, officers took her to a side room. Marshal Ferdinand Foch and General John J. Pershing asked her to go between them down the center aisle to the altar. That march, in the war uniform designed by Pershing for Salvationists in France, was one of the happiest moments of Evangeline's life.[17]

Leaving France, Evangeline stopped in Denmark and spent a day with Colonel Mary Booth, Bramwell's daughter, before going on to England. Once in London, Evangeline spoke at Westminster Central Hall, where she received a tumultuous welcome.

She paid a quick visit to Torquay, where she had appeared before the magistrates in 1888 to defend the Army's right to hold musical religious processions. At the public civic reception given for her by the mayor, an elderly man pushed his way through the crowd. Taking her hand, he said, "Commander, you will not remember me. I'm the constable who arrested your bandsmen and put them in prison many years ago. I shall never forget you. How you won our hearts even before you had won your case."[18]

Before leaving Torquay, Evangeline went to the old Town Hall, up the winding steps to the courtroom, and once again stood in the dock where she had pleaded the Army's cause.

More important than any public gathering, however, was the conference the Commander had with General Bramwell. At its conclusion, they were still far apart in their views. She presented her brother with a memorandum of fifteen points, listing what she considered were needed reforms in the Army. The two basic points were stated in numbers six and seven:

6. It would be considered wise statesmanship for the General to abolish the present system of appointing his successor, and establishing a method for the election of his successor. . . .

7. To have the High Council, or some such body within the Army, select the succeeding Generals would provide a safeguard for the future which would be of great strength to the organization and do more to elicit and mantain the confidence of our own people than anything else, and this would not in any way prevent the Army from carrying out the purposes of the Founder.[19]

A few weeks later, the General sent Evangeline a seven-page reply, rejecting her proposals and stating his position:

As to the appointment of a succeeding General, your suggestion aims at cancelling the General's most urgent duty—his duty to discern and name his successor; and it aims at this for no useful purpose, for if the named sucessor be a person whom the Commissioners generally consider to be fit for the office, why interfere? If, on the other hand, after due consideration and trial he be found to be unfit by the Commissioners, they already have the power of deposing him and of electing a fit person in his place.[20]

The General discussed the Army's constitution and referred to both the Foundation Deed of 1878 and the
Deed Poll of 1904. Evangeline was alarmed when she
read:

> And indeed if I felt it desirable to exercise, with the
> consent of the Commissioners, the powers of altera-
> tion of the Supplementary Deed given to the General
> by that Deed, it would rather be with the aim of pro-
> tecting the essential features of the Foundation Deed
> than otherwise.[21]

She evidently considered this as a threat that the General
would ask commissioners to support him in altering the
Supplementary Deed—the deed that William Booth had
written "as a safeguard against unsuitabilities in a General."[22]

In February 1928, after writing Bramwell a twenty-
one-page answer, she sent copies of their correspondence to all commissioners and territorial leaders of the
Army.[23]

On March, 6, Bramwell Booth found on his office
table a letter signed by seven active and two retired London commissioners. They expressed sympathy with the
Commander's views and asked him to abandon any idea
of altering the Supplementary Deed of 1904.[24] The General was shocked to learn that nine men he had considered his supporters had discussed the subject with each
other, but not with him, and were in agreement with
Evangeline.[25] When he learned further on March 13 that
copies of the letter signed by the nine London commissioners, which he had regarded as confidential, had been
sent to the Army's leading staff officers throughout the
world, he was understandably upset. In her biography of
him, his daughter Catherine states, "From this time anxiety began to make serious inroads on sleep. Bramwell

Booth was burdened with forebodings of ill for the be-loved work, and felt himself devastatingly alone."[26]

Feeling that a crisis situation had now developed, the General sent first a letter or cable and then a memorandum of his views to all commissioners and territorial commanders.[27]

His last day at international headquarters was April 12. He conducted the weekend meetings in Sheffield; then illness kept him at home until May 8, when he spoke briefly at the twenty-first anniversary Home League celebrations at the Crystal Palace. On his last public appearance, May 10, he laid a cornerstone and spoke at Denmark Hill for the William Booth Memorial Training College. Between April 28 and December 15, 1928, the *War Cry* reported on his condition in sixteen bulletins, with two more on January 5 and 12, 1929.[28]

All Salvationists read the reports of their General's illness with increasing alarm. Few, however, except staff officers were aware of the crisis situation developing in the Army over differences of opinion on constitutional matters.

When Commissioner E. J. Higgins, the chief of the staff, visited the General on November 13, 1928, Bramwell was "sleeping under the influence of a narcotic."[29] Evidently he looked so ill that the commissioner may have thought he was dying.[30] The newspapers that night announced this possibility.

The next morning the chief of the staff received from seven London commissioners the official requisition, asking that a High Council be called, and sent summonses throughout the world to Army leaders who were entitled to attend. William Frost, one of the Army's solicitors, informed Mrs. Bramwell Booth verbally and gave her an explanatory letter. She received a copy of the actual requisition from the Chief the next day.[31]

General Bramwell was too ill to be told. He learned about the High Council from his daughter Catherine on New Year's Day, 1929. After discussing the matter, the General said to her, "If I die, Catherine, remember, there must be no bitterness. I forgive; you and the others must forgive, too. They want to change the General's [William Booth's] plan; they must know I shall never agree."[32]

During the next weeks, the doctors reported some improvement in the General's condition. Meanwhile, sixty-three members of the High Council met at Sunbury Court on January 8, 1929. Only one was absent, because of illness. None came with light hearts. All were concerned that the proceedings should strengthen rather than destroy the Army they had been helping to build most of their lives. They elected Commissioner James Hay as president, and Lieutenant-Commissioner William Haines as vice-president.

Part of a long letter to Colonel Walter Jenkins, national chief secretary in the United States, from Commissioner Samuel L. Brengle, for years a close friend of Bramwell Booth, gives some idea of the climate of the High Council:

> The High Council is almost of one mind that a change must come. A resolution was passed asking the General to retire, and a letter was drawn up by a committee, of which I was one, expressing the love and sympathy of the members of the High Council for him and our firm conviction that at his age, broken under the weight of years of vast labors extending over more than half a century of ceaseless anxieties for the worldwide flock he has shepherded, it was the only wise thing he could do both for himself and the Army. A delegation of seven of us was chosen to present the resolution and letter to him. . . .

He received us kindly, called us each by name in a slow, hesitating voice; asked for time to consider his decision, which was readily granted, and prayed slowly with and for us. . . .

My emotions were mixed—a mingling of pain and chastened joy. Pain at seeing him whom I have loved, lying helpless and pressed by such duties and demands and faced with such momentous decisions; joy at once more looking into his face and seeing with my own eyes whether or not he is fit for his great office with its daily grind of work on worldwide problems which involve both the spiritual and physical welfare of millions in more than eighty colonies and countries.

He is certainly unfit at his age and in his helpless condition for his job. If he does not retire and we have to adjudicate, I shall have to vote against him. There is no alternative.

In his letter, Commissioner Brengle was also concerned about who could follow Bramwell as General. He wondered if Commander Evangeline would be strong enough physically at sixty-three to undertake such a job with its worldwide problems. He felt she would find it infinitely harder than it had been for her to take hold of the United States at forty when "we were all young and eager to help her and the aroused and determined wills and tongues of men were still in leash. Yet, in many ways, she is the logical candidate."[33]

The High Council was disappointed at the General's reply to their request that he retire. He wrote that his doctors had advised him that "in a few months" he would be "fully recovered." Further, that the request to retire was "little less than a threat of expulsion should I fail to comply with it."[34] It was now clear to the councilors that the General would quit his office only if compelled to do so.[35]

They were asked but refused to allow Mr. (later Sir)

William Jowitt, K.C., to speak on behalf of the General. Members of the High Council felt that Salvation Army regulations precluded the participation of anyone connected with the law in an internal dispute. The next day Commissioner Catherine, in a moving speech, defended her father. But that night the High Council voted 55 to 8 to depose the General. The General's wife, his two daughters—Commissioner Catherine and Colonel Mary—and his sister Lucy, Mrs. Commissioner Booth-Hellberg, plus four other commissioners, comprised the minority vote. Evangeline voted with the majority.

The Council adjourned until Friday, when they would elect a new General. However, on Friday afternoon a telephone call informed them that Mr. Wilfred Green, K.C., representing the General, had secured a temporary injunction from the Chancery Division of the High Court of Justice to stop the proceedings of the High Council until the following Tuesday on two counts: (1) the Deed Poll of 1904 was invalid, and (2) the General had been judged without a hearing.

The General's appeal to the courts shocked the members of the High Council and alienated from him three of the commissioners who had supported him. His action also offended the soldiers, who felt that the General had abrogated an Army regulation he had helped to write and enforce: A Salvationist shall not take another Salvationist into court.

Since they could not proceed with the election, the Council adjourned. While doing so, the vice-president, Lieutenant-Commissioner Haines, collapsed and, less than an hour later, died, adding to the depression of the Council members. Evangeline spoke on behalf of the High Council at his funeral.

The High Council reassembled on February 13. The court had ruled that they had a right to assemble but should not have come to any decision about the General without giving him the opportunity of being present himself or being represented by others. Two doctors and two former officers now spoke on the General's behalf, and for two hours Mr. Jowitt pleaded eloquently for him. After further discussion, the Council decided by secret ballot, 52 votes to 5 (four members abstaining, two members absent because of illness), that the General was "unfit on the ground of ill-health" to continue in office.[36] Evangeline Booth again voted with the majority.

The election of the new General followed, requiring a two-thirds majority of Council members. The two candidates were Commander Evangeline Cory Booth and Commissioner Edward John Higgins.

In a letter to Colonel Jenkins ten days before this, Evangeline had written:

> What I feel about the Generalship is this: I am neither trying to get it nor to evade it. If I went by my own feelings, I should certainly most emphatically withdraw my nomination—it looms up before me as such a terrible ordeal. But upon all hands I am told that the Army is looking to me to bring it through flags afly. I myself realize that we are at a critical juncture. If the High Council—and we have been together for some weeks now—feels that I am the one, then I feel that it would not only be cowardly but wrong to shirk the responsibility. I must look to God to carry me through.
>
> But I can honestly say that I have no will of my own in the matter. God must make His will known and make it known by the election that is to take place. I will abide by that decision. Pray for me. And then pray some more. Pray that my health will hold out.[37]

When the vote was counted late the night of February 13, Commissioner Higgins became the third General of the Salvation Army by a vote of 42 to 17.

The next morning, with other High Council members, Evangeline met with General Higgins for a meeting of prayer and rededication of themselves to God and service in the Army. At the General's first public meeting, February 18 at Clapton Congress Hall, she pledged to him her support as well as that of The Salvation Army in the United States. The *London Daily Mirror* reported, "Commander Eva Booth roused the audience to thunderous cheers. Then she kissed Mrs. Higgins on the cheek and sat down." Mrs. General Higgins prefaced her remarks with a tribute to the Commander as "the greatest woman leader the Army has ever known."[38]

Salvationists throughout the world weathered with amazing serenity the troubled and sometimes stormy days preceding and during that first High Council. Often confused and perplexed because of conflicting reports, they nevertheless had implicit faith in the divine guidance of their Army.

21
The Great Depression

At the ground-breaking ceremony in October 1928 for the New York Evangeline Residence, Evangeline Booth said, "For ten years I dreamed of putting up a homelike, protected residence here for young businesswomen where they would be comfortable at a price within their reach, but we did not have the money to erect such a building.

"Then one day I went to see Mr. John Markle, the great anthracite industrialist, to thank him for a $10,000 gift to The Salvation Army. While talking, I told him of my dream. He asked, 'How much would such a residence cost?'

" 'A lot of money, Mr. Markle; a lot of money—$500,000.'

"Without a moment's hesitation, he said, 'I'll give you that.'

" 'Give me what?' I asked, with pounding heart.

" 'The $500,000 you want.'

"The possibility of a dream coming true so quickly left me speechless, for once.

"He understood and with a twinkle in his eye, he clapped his hand to his pocket and said, 'I've got it right here.' "

Now ready to break ground for the residence, she turned to her good friend and said, "Mr. Markle, you have invested in a stock that will never go down. It will continue to increase and will, as long as you live, be making its returns in human dividends."[1]

One year later other kinds of stock crashed on Wall Street, causing the American economy to fall apart, and the Great Depression became a reality for rich and poor alike. Next to the Civil War, the Depression changed the face of America more than any other event in the nation's history. But for a while, people refused to accept what was happening and viewed this economic disaster as just a temporary setback.[2]

Although usually an optimist, Evangeline Booth rightly assessed the seriousness of the situation and called an emergency meeting of Army leaders. "Gentlemen, we've got to do something—and fast," she told them. "Get busy."[3] Plans were roughed out to get maximum use of all Army resources and expand them to house, feed, and clothe even more people.

It soon became evident that additional facilities would be needed too. By November 1930, New York City officials were afraid of food riots. The *New York Times* reported that 450 tons of food were given to needy people at five police stations but that hundreds with tickets were turned away because the supply ran out.[4] Mayor Jimmy Walker asked Commander Booth what The Salvation Army could do to help in this situation. After a meeting with her staff, she promised that the Army would have six more feeding stations open the next morning.[5]

Buildings of all kinds were obtained, some needing repairs. People who were lined up for food volunteered to help with the work, but lack of funds was a constant worry. Although friends—the Vanderbilts, Rockefellers,

Goulds, Wanamakers, Armours, Tafts, and others who still had money—gave generously, the need was too great for any small group to underwrite. Evangeline tried to think of some way to raise a large amount of money.

One of the most popular annual sports events had been the Army-Navy football game. Rivalry between the two teams was so intense that two writers claimed "the Army band feels it can play 'Anchors Away' better than the Navy band can."[6] Relations became strained between the teams over a difference in rules, and they had refused to play their games in 1928 and 1929. The Commander talked to Mayor Walker to see what he thought about asking the Grays and Blues to play a benefit game for The Salvation Army. He urged her to go ahead and, when approached, they agreed to do it. Grover A. Whalen accepted the chairmanship of the game. Tickets sold from $5 to $50, and Junior League members offered to be ushers.[7]

Evangeline realized that some Salvationists might criticize her for attending the game, just as she knew that some criticized her for mingling with sophisticated and wealthy people who financially supported much of the Army's work. But she wanted to go and asked Commissioner Samuel Brengle, the Army's evangelist, to accompany her since "nobody would criticize Commissioner Brengle."[8]

On December 14, 1930, the *New York Times* headlined "70,000 Watch Army Beat Navy, 6 to 0; Gate over $600,000" and declared that the game took place "in a setting of glittering color and excitement such as football, at least in this city, has never seen." Together, celebrities and John Does watched the thrilling game in Yankee Stadium. Surrounded by her staff and with Major Jimmy Walker and Grover A. Whalen, along with Secretary of War Patrick J. Hurley, chief of staff of the army General Douglas MacArthur, and chief of naval operations Admiral W. B. Pratt, Evangeline Booth, in her blue uniform and bonnet, saw her first football game.

Following the Army-Navy game, Evangeline established a Confidential Bureau, under the direction of Major Ethel Renton and Mrs. Brigadier Edith Nice, for the thousands of business and professional people, unfamiliar with economic stringency, who were suffering in silence during the unemployment crisis. Pride made men shrink from telling even their friends about the physical problem of obtaining food and keeping a roof over their heads. Some wrote to the Army on expensive paper, confessing their need for help. Men with good references gladly accepted $20-a-week jobs the Army found for them. And still the breadlines grew longer.[9]

Across the nation, those who could tried to alleviate the sufferings of millions. Men like E. J. Hutton, who at that time was chairman of General Foods Corporation, supplied 100,000 families with food for a week and for three years supported free soup kitchens for the unemployed.[10] Newspapers supplied coal to the poor; electric companies gave tons of coke.

Salvation Army emergency shelters for the homeless included two extremely large ones. Chicago's chewing-gum king, William J. Wrigley, Jr., donated a building at 509 North Union Street which became known as the New Start Lodge, housing thousands.[11] The president of the Heckers Flour Company, in New York City, donated a tremendous building at 40 Corlears Street, which the Army named the Gold Dust Lodge (for a product of the company). This building, too, accommodated more than 2,000 nightly.[12]

In addition to helping the homeless thousands in cities, the Commander urged officers to do all they could to help sustain family life for the "new poor" in every community. Once-prosperous businessmen were now peddling apples on street corners for a nickel apiece.

The Army corps across the country, Home Leagues—large groups of Salvationist and non-Salvationist women—repaired and remade donations of cast-off clothing, planted gardens in unused lots, cooked meals, and canned food for families.[13]

With the increasingly heavy demands upon the Army, it was evident that another great effort was needed to secure funds. Again, Evangeline sought the help of friends. Mr. E. J. Hutton talked with Deke Aylesworth, president of the National Broadcasting Company, who agreed to sponsor a benefit for The Salvation Army at Madison Square Garden. When John F. Royal went to NBC as vice-president in charge of programming, late in 1930, Aylesworth told him, "I'm committed to do this benefit" and turned it over to him.[14]

Royal started assembling what he termed "one of the greatest star groupings that has ever been in any place in this country." At the same time, E. J. Hutton got in touch with friends who would contribute $1,000 to the gigantic program, titled Radio Land. A women's auxiliary, with teams headed by women such as Mrs. Hutton, Mrs. Samuel Adams Clark, Mrs. William Randolph Hearst, and Mrs. Franklin Delano Roosevelt, enlisted hundreds of women to sell tickets. Madison Square Garden was packed that spring evening in 1931 for the Radio Land program.[15]

The show opened with a five-hundred-piece orchestra, led by Erno Rapee. Five stages, three in the center and one at each end of the Garden, were set up with continuous programs going. Well-known radio personalities—Bing Crosby, Major Edward Bowes of the "Original Amateur Hour," and more than seventy-five others, contributed their talents. Ten of the greatest composers of the day, including Jerome Kern, Irving Berlin, George Gershwin, and Sigmund Romberg, played their hit tunes on one of the Steinway grands. Then all ten played one number together.[16] Mr. Hutton handed over to the Commander $500,000 from the Radio Land program.[17]

At the height of the Depression, William Randolph Hearst asked star reporter Adela Rogers St. Johns to do a series on unemployed women for Hearst newspapers. She set out as an unemployed woman wearing horn-rimmed glasses, an old dress, and a coat frayed at the elbows. In a recent letter, Mrs. St. Johns said, "I couldn't be more grateful for the chance to say how greatly I admired Evangeline Booth and The Salvation Army. When I did the series on unemployed women, I picked The Salvation Army as the only charity organization I could recommend 100 percent."[18] And in her autobiography, *The Honeycomb,* Mrs. St. Johns wrote,

> "I hang on the drab wall of this world the warm rich glow of the Salvation Army Home for women. Room of my own. Clean bed. Few things I have experienced in the way of physical pleasure like the hot bath with *soap,* towels, and privacy after weeks without them. I don't know how they could love me, but they did. Like God. And the lassies had breakfast with me and cheered me on my way.
>
> "The Army was in debt, but they knew our Lord would see about it."[19]

The Lord did see about it. People responded to the Army's appeal for funds. Then the Commander called upon her troops to go the extra mile, asking Salvation Army officers to help meet the financial crisis by taking a 10 percent cut in their already low salaries. She also closed the four officers' training colleges for one year.[20]

With the failure of more than 1,400 banks in 1932,[21] Americans were on the brink of despair. Franklin Delano Roosevelt took office as President in 1933 and hastily created federal New Deal programs which took over the burden that had been carried in the early years of the Depression by local governments and private agencies.

The Salvation Army continued to operate lodges in small as well as large cities for transients seeking employment. But now the breadlines, sometimes all night long, were for persons standing in line to register for jobs provided in connection with the Civilian Conservation Corps and the Works Progress Administration, government projects to provide employment during the Depression. Cooperating with federal agencies, The Salvation Army played an important role in holding families together and helping the breadwinners get back to full employment again.

When a violent earthquake in the Long Beach area of southern California destroyed lives and property in 1933, the Army quickly set up emergency relief stations in the devastated area and dispensed food and clothing.

Shortly after this, famed humorist Will Rogers decided to give the proceeds of seven radio broadcasts to The Salvation Army and the Red Cross. He telegraphed Evangeline, "Here is how this rough and tumble broadcastin' thing come about; the Gulf Oil Company kept wantin' me to litter up the microphone with some Oklahoma grammar. I did want to make a contribution to a couple of good causes that had done such fine work during our earthquake and I didn't have the dough to do it so Mrs. Rogers figgered it out. She says you got the wind to do it . . . with just talk. . . . The only one I can see lose is the Gulf Company."

Evangeline replied, "I only wish there were more

litterers with Oklahoma grammar who were always mustering their littered gems for the reinforcement of good
as you have done. . . . All the gratitude our hearts can
speak is small compared to what our hearts feel. . . . The
most practical way I can think of to demonstrate this is to
assure you that if ever you want for a bed or a meal, you
will find it in The Salvation Army."[22]

By the end of the thirties, Salvationists could look
back upon the decade of the Depression as years of
hardship and trial but years that their stamina and courage had enabled them to live and work through with
pride.

22
Out of the Cloud

Although Evangeline's time was necessarily taken up in the early 1930s with expanding the Army's welfare programs and setting up additional ways to feed and house the new poor as the Depression worsened, she did not neglect the spiritual emphasis of the Army's ministry. Wherever she went, she told her officers, "Preach Christ! Preach His Birth! Preach His ministry! Preach His love! Preach His suffering! Preach His power! Preach Him!"

She decided to go ahead with the 1930 Golden Jubilee Congress to commemorate the Salvation Army's fifty years in the United States. In January she launched Golden Jubilee crusade meetings which continued throughout the nation until the opening of the national congress in New York City in May. Many officers traveled to New York on railroad passes, and during congress week New Yorkers became accustomed to seeing Salvationists on park benches eating their lunch from paper bags. The congress began with a pilgrimage to Battery Park, the site where Commissioner Railton and the seven lassies landed in the United States. From there 4,000 Salvationists marched to the music of twenty bands up Broadway to City Hall for a civic welcome, with Evangeline the central figure.[1]

All the congress meetings were on a giant scale. The historical pageant at the 71st Regiment Armory on Saturday night lasted for hours. One unforgettable number was a march written for the congress at Evangeline's request by John Philip Sousa and played by a massed band of 300 under Sousa's baton.[2] Two acts—a snake charmer and Hawaiian dancers—drew criticism from many Salvationists. Although the Sunday meetings resulted in a large number kneeling at the penitent-form seeking forgiveness of sin, Evangeline was still upset by the criticism of the Saturday night pageant.

Monday morning when Colonel Albert Norris went to her office, he found several Commissioners there. She said, "Come in, Norris, and tell me—was the Saturday night program as long as some of these people say it was?" She needed assurance that people would forget those two acts when thinking of the trememdous impact of the whole.[3]

Mrs. Franklin Delano Roosevelt chaired the mass congress meeting for women in Carnegie Hall and presented the Commander, "a woman whose faith we all admire and respect . . . we love her because of her loving heart and never-failing sympathy." Evangeline's address, "Women Who Have Made History," was later published by Fleming H. Revell as a small book, titled *Woman*.[4]

When giving her lecture "The Shepherd" in the old Opera House at Times Square, Evangeline, with her flair for the dramatic, wore a robe of layer upon layer of pale green chiffon and carried a lantern and shepherd's crook. Women cadets, wearing bright orange robes and carrying staffs, formed the background.

During the Congress, Evangeline dedicated the Centennial Memorial Temple and the adjacent territorial and national headquarters building which had been in the finishing stages when the Depression hit America.

After two days of officers' councils, the officers left New York feeling that no job would be too difficult to tackle.

In June at the commissioning of the "Trail Blazers," the graduating class of cadets from the Army's training college, the Commander inaugurated the Order of the Silver Star to honor mothers who had given, and would give, their children to be officers. Before she pinned upon one of the fifty-seven mothers the small silver star pin she had designed, she told how the Order was born:

"One day a woman introduced herself to me with the remark, 'Oh, Commander, I'm so glad to meet you. I've given seven sons and a daughter to the Army as officers.' That night I couldn't sleep as I thought about her and about a fine, intelligent young officer who told me of the sacrifice of his widowed mother, with three little girls yet to bring up, who refused to withhold him from officership. As I thought of these women, I saw long lines of mothers who had given their children for God's service. It was during those sleepless hours that the Silver Star was born." The Silver Star has since become an international Order.[5]

Now that Edward J. Higgins had been elected General, Evangeline was serving for the first time under a General who was not a Booth. Evangeline and Bramwell had not always agreed. As sister and brother they had freely discussed their differences. By nature, Evangeline was not a person who automatically said yes to every order. But in spite of their differences, the Booths were a closely-knit family.

When Bramwell was promoted to glory on June 16, 1929, Evangeline mourned the loss of a beloved brother. At his death, the three people Bramwell had named to be his executors—his wife, his daughter Catherine, and his solicitor, Mr. Frederick Sneath—became trustees of all Salvation Army assets vested in his name. A few months later, the executors transferred to General Higgins, "for the purposes of the Army, all the property and funds vested in them by his predecessor."[6]

General Higgins had pledged to the High Council that he would carry out reforms in the Army which would assure the election of future Generals, fix an age limit for their retirement, and form a trustee company to hold the properties and capital assets of the Army in place of the sole trusteeship of the General.[7] In order to carry the approval of Army leaders, General Higgins called a Commissioners' Conference to meet in London on November 11, 1930, to "discuss reforms and other matters upon which he wanted the counsel and opinion of the leading officers of the Army." He wrote Evangeline and urged her to attend.[8]

Although not willing at first to be present at an international conference where her views might spark some controversy, she finally wrote the General that she would come.

That summer when Evangeline and her staff left for a few weeks at Lake George, a young man recently from Scotland, George Russell, was among the group. The Commander felt that Russell was officer material and that under Griffith's supervision he would learn much about the Army.

One day Griffith gave Russell a cable from General Higgins to decode. After decoding it, Russell took the cable back to Griffith, suggesting that he might want to give it to the Commander himself because the General was "dressing her down." Griffith read it and said, "Take it to her, George."

When Russell handed it to her, he wondered how the Commander would react. "She read it, read it again, and still a third time, then looked up with a twinkle in her eye and said, 'Well, Russell, you know if I can't take discipline, I can't discipline others. He's the General. I may not like this cable, but I've got to salute. Take a reply.' "

Her reply: "General, I received your cable. If that's the way you feel, I salute you. Sorry I didn't meet your requirements, do what was expected of me. I'll try to do better."

George Russell, now a retired Lieutenant Colonel, based his decision for officership upon that summer when "time after time the Commander won my respect and admiration as a leader who merited the loyalty she demanded from her troops."[9]

In November the Commander and American commissioners left for the international conference in London. Journalists there had not forgotten the tension generated in the 1929 High Council. The *New York Times* London correspondent noted that Commissioner Catherine Bramwell-Booth visited Commander Evangeline at her hotel the day she arrived and that they were on friendly terms throughout the conference.[10]

Commander Evangeline and Commissioner Catherine, although seeking different objectives, were both opposed to having reforms approved by the conference perpetuated by Parliamentary enactment. Evangeline felt the reforms did not go far enough and still left the General in autocratic control of the Army. Commissioner Catherine opposed reforms which would alter the autocratic system.[11]

However, the majority voted for Parliamentary sanction, and a Bill known as The Salvation Army Act, 1931, was passed by Parliament and received royal assent July 31, 1931. It provided

1. That the High Council should elect a new General whenever the office became vacant.

   2. That a Salvation Army Trustee Company should be
formed, whose duty it would be to hold, as custo-
dian trustee, all property of The Salvation Army
hitherto vested, or which might subsequently be
vested, in the General.

The age of retirement for a General was regarded by
Parliament as a matter for domestic legislation and has
since been fixed (by the Army) at seventy years of
age.[12]

For several years some Salvationists and journalists
had felt that certain countries in which the Army operated might want to become independent of the London
administration. Colonel Brindley Boon remembered
how Evangeline refuted this possibility for America
when speaking after the conference at a large public
meeting in London.

After quoting her father and her brother, who believed "every land is my Father's land," she turned to
Commissioner Samuel Brengle, then conducting spiritual campaigns in many lands, and said, "It was never my
father's wish, Commissioner Brengle, that there should
be a Salvation Army in America, another one in Britain,
and another one in Australia. You must keep the United
States of America Salvation Army an International
Army." Commissioner Brengle stood, saluted, and sat
down.[13]

Before Evangeline left England, she and General
Higgins spent four and a half hours with Mrs. General
Bramwell Booth and Commissioner Catherine at Hadley
Wood.[14] All of them talked frankly and sought mutual
understanding of differences that had culminated in the
1929 High Council.[15]

Upon her return to the States, rather than succumb-
ing to the pessimism which like a dark cloud blanketed
the land, Evangeline stepped up activity to meet people's

spiritual needs. Perhaps remembering her father's motor tours through Great Britain, she decided that motorcades would be the best way to reach people in wide geographic areas.

Her first motorcade started at Times Square in New York City. During the following twelve days, Evangeline spoke sixty times in towns and cities in New York, Ohio, and Pennsylvania. Every detail was planned. A small advance party traveled an hour ahead of the motorcade. By the time Evangeline and her staff and territorial and divisional leaders arrived, along with the bus carrying the New York Staff Band members, crowds waited to greet them. Today it would probably be impossible to get stores, factories, and schools to close down for a motorcade, but many towns turned out en masse in the thirties. Meetings were conducted outdoors during the day, inside at night.

As the band struck up a patriotic march, Evangeline walked on to the platform. She drew all eyes in her pale-gray tailored two-piece uniform and straw hat—a lovely shade of bright red. Those who traveled with her marveled at her stamina. She worked hard all day under a blistering sun and retired late at night utterly fatigued. But her recuperative powers astounded her fellows, who found the pace she set a challenge to them physically.

The response to that first motorcade prompted her to have a second one the next month, from Harlem through the Hudson Valley, finishing up at her cottage at Lake George.[16]

That autumn General Higgins asked Evangeline to go as his ambassador to six European countries.[17] She returned shortly before Christmas and wrote to her 6,000 officers:

> Make this Christmas Day an epoch in your spiritual experience. There is a danger of the officer becoming

too small for the large work God has asked him to do. To guard against this, I plead with you to study with increased diligence the life and character of Jesus Christ that your mind and soul may be broadened.[18]

During the summer of 1932 she did motorcades in the Central territory, using members of the Chicago Staff Band and officers from the Central states to accompany her.

Colonel Tom Gabrielsen rode with Evangeline in the tri-state motorcade. "She would nudge me and say, 'Gabrielsen, how long is it before I have to talk? I haven't got a thought.'

" 'Twenty minutes, Commander. Lots of time. Don't worry.'

"But she was always concerned. She captivated her listeners. She focused on people. She never talked more than fifteen minutes and never repeated an illustration."[19] At Hoopeston, Illinois, for example, one of the greatest corn-canning centers in the world, she spoke on "Canned Religion," the brand that "isn't fresh from the fields of glory."[20]

Evangeline opened the 1932 national convention of the Democratic Party with prayer—the first woman to have had that honor. The night before the convention began, she spoke at a mass meeting of "drys" at Orchestra Hall. The Chicago Tribune reported, "Women in tears as Miss Booth denounces rum."[21] Evangeline prayed the next morning that the delegates would have "wisdom that will unravel the tangled threads of national problems." Ironically, the convention nominated Franklin Delano Roosevelt, who was elected President on a "repeal prohibition" platform.

On August 21, Evangeline addressed a crowd of 25,000 in the Hollywood Bowl at a meeting which climaxed the religious gatherings at the International Olympic Games.[22]

She appointed Commissioner Edward J. Parker to set up the Army's exhibit at the 1933 Century of Progress World's Fair in Chicago. In June, on the occasion of the Army's jubilee in Sweden, Evangeline Booth was nominated by King Gustav to be Knight Commander of the Order of Vasa, and received the Vasa Gold Medal, "for your work and for the work of The Salvation Army." This was the highest honor the king could bestow on a person not a native of Sweden.[23]

That autumn, while making a tour through the country to observe firsthand how the Army could best help those in rural areas, Evangeline stopped for several days' meetings in Kansas and Missouri. A Sunday night meeting in Kansas City, Missouri, was chaired by Governor Guy B. Park. Evangeline related how she had stood before a judge at Torquay, England, who reprimanded her for disturbing the peace, then told her, "If you can give me one good reason why I should not sentence you, I will not."

"If you will give me until tomorrow, Your Honor, I'll have thirteen reasons."

The next morning she marched in leading thirteen bandsmen, playing their horns, and told the judge. "These are my thirteen reasons. They either were or would have been men of the street, but by the grace of God, they are now Christian bandsmen." She did not have to serve a sentence.

The governor turned to Captain J. Clyde Cox, Evangeline's aide-de-camp, and said, "I don't believe that. It's just a story she has made up."

After the meeting, as Captain Cox was clearing the way through the crowd for Evangeline to get backstage, a man cried out, "I have to see her."

Cox said, "No, you can't."

In her deep, gravelly voice, Evangeline said, "Yes, he can."

The man followed them, and when they got to her dressing room, he fell on his knees and started kissing her hand. "Stand up," she said. "Now what was that all about?"

The governor, influential citizens, and several reporters waited for his reply. "Well, Commander, I'm one of your thirteen reasons. I run a little grocery store in Colorado. When I read that you were coming, I closed the store and came to see you." When she heard his name, Evangeline put her arms around him and they stood there weeping.

Cox looked at the governor, who said, "Don't say a word."

When they were back at the hotel, Evangeline told Cox, "I must see the governor early tomorrow morning." She had been reading news reports and making inquiries about the kidnapping of Mary McElroy, daughter of city manager Henry F. McElroy. After the ransom was paid, Mary had been released unharmed to the family. A man named Walter McGee was arrested, tried, found guilty, and sentenced to death for the kidnapping.

"I don't believe McGee is guilty so he must not die," Evangeline said. "See if the governor will come for breakfast tomorrow with me."

Around midnight, Cox phoned Governor Park at Jefferson City to see if he would come back to Kansas City the next morning. "After what took place tonight, I would go anywhere, anytime," he answered.

Evangeline and the governor discussed McGee's case, and the governor promised to review it. Sometime later he commuted McGee's sentence to life imprisonment.

Cox sent the news clipping to Evangeline, who replied, "Captain, some things are worth getting a Governor up at midnight for."[24]

Plans for Evangeline to conduct meetings in Australia and New Zealand in 1934 had to be canceled when she became ill and her doctor ordered six weeks' rest for her. Then, shortly after she returned to her office, General Higgins announced that he would be retiring, and a High Council was summoned to choose his successor.

For weeks before she sailed for London on the *Leviathan* with the American commissioners, Salvationists and friends discussed openly Evangeline's chances of becoming the next General. Was she not the best-known Salvationist in the world? Did not her thirty-year record as Commander of American Salvation Army forces speak for itself? But reporters and cameramen could get only noncommittal replies from Evangeline.

When she arrived at Plymouth, General Higgins welcomed Evangeline and traveled with her to London. She conducted a great salvation meeting in historic Congress Hall on Sunday night. For four hours the vast crowd sat enthralled, now in tears, then in laughter, as their Field Commissioner of former days piloted the service.[25]

Meanwhile, back in the United States, half-nights of prayer were held in hundreds of cities. The Commander's troops were besieging God, as were Salvationists in all parts of the world, that divine guidance would be given to the High Council.

Christine McMillan, now a retired brigadier, tells of a meeting at Regent Hall, London, where a great crowd of old-timers remembered "our Eva" from long ago and where her younger sister, Lucy Booth-Hellberg, was in charge. "Now we're going down to pray that God will bless the High Council members," Commissioner Lucy announced. "I want to stress, my dear comrades, that you do not mention any name. The Holy Spirit is to be the guide and the Holy Spirit will lead them without any help from us. We will pray that God will bless them, guide them, and direct them so the right person will be chosen."

After several prayers, one elderly sergeant stood up. "Oh, Lord," he prayed, "Thou knowest who we mean when we ask Thee to make the High Council choose the right person—we who have stood by her side, we who have stood alone by her dear father, her who is the brightest star in her father's crown." A lot of "amens" responded.

Entering the hotel after the meeting, Christine found the Commander's staff in deep gloom. Evangeline was depressed, nervous, and unapproachable. At the urging of the staff, and particularly Colonel Griffith, who pushed her into the Commander's room, Christine told her the story of Commissioner Lucy and the sergeant. The gloom vanished. Evangeline laughed and laughed and said, "Oh, I can just hear Lucy." Then, "Where's Dick and the others? Let's have some tea and toast!"[26]

The result of the deliberations of the forty-seven High Council members had been predicted by many. Evangeline received a majority of votes on the first four ballots but lacked the necessary two thirds until the fifth. The final voting:

Commander Evangeline Booth	32
Commissioner Henry W. Mapp	9
Commissioner Catherine Bramwell-Booth	4
Commissioner Samuel Hurren	2
Commissioner David C. Lamb	0

On November 11, 1934, Evangeline Booth became the Army's fourth General—and the first woman to hold that office.

23

General Evangeline

When Evangeline Booth, followed by the Army's leaders, walked onto the platform adjoining the locked and guarded room where the High Council had met at the Clapton Congress Hall, she evoked a spontaneous burst of applause from waiting journalists. Few noticed how weary she looked from the strain of the long day's session. She quickly forgot her weariness when asked by newsmen for a message for the "rank and file."

"Tell them," she said, "that my heart is still the same, that my spirit is as enthusiastic as ever in the service of my Lord. I am a chip off the old block." Then she went on to say, "I love the poor; I love the working people. I was born on Christmas Day—never mind the year—and I think perhaps I came into the world with an extra measure of love in my heart on that account.

"Years ago I fought the gospel crusade in London streets. We shall fight again, and we shall fight in good company, for the armies of the Lord are mustering on either hand."[1]

London newspapers carried banner headlines emphasizing that the Army's new General was a woman. As the *Daily Herald* commented, "It means that the equality of sex so vital to the Army has easily survived its extension into the East, where the idea of equality penetrates only slowly. If Commander Booth can hold the Army's internationalism high above national rivalries, she will have served not just her organization but the whole world."[2]

Hugh Redwood, one of London's leading journalists, wrote in the *News Chronicle,* "As General, Evangeline is fulfilling the prophecy of her mother. . . . When Mrs. Booth lay dying of cancer, Evangeline, then a young field commissioner, burst into her bedroom one day flushed with happiness because of a meeting in the East End which had seen the ingathering of many 'trophies' [new converts].

"As Major Carr [the nurse] came into the room, Mrs. Booth said, 'Do you know what I have been telling Eva? I have been telling her that if she keeps on, and if she keeps single, she will one day be General of The Salvation Army.' "[3]

Back in the United States, the *New York Times* carried a character sketch of Evangeline. "The personality of the new General is as complex as the vast organization for which she is now responsible. We see in her a remarkable duality. On the one hand, the charm, humor, sympathy, enthusiasm, eloquence of a woman who, almost certainly, would have succeeded in achieving fame had she chosen the stage to be her career; on the other hand, the tenacious purpose, the unwavering faith, the decisive and persevering and disciplined statesmanship of an able executive."[4]

Indeed, Evangeline's personality was many-sided. Why, as one writer put it, was it that "everything she touched in the salvation war flourished"?[5] She never expected special treatment because she was a woman but because she was the leader of a great Army. As commander in chief, Evangeline often gave orders, demanded obedience, and enforced discipline, but despite her imperious ways she retained the affection and admiration of co-workers.

Because her father was closely associated with Evangeline as an administrator, Brigadier Christine McMillan, as an army reporter, had the opportunity to observe the General in all kinds of situations. Her assessment: "With all her egocentric proclivities, her maddening goings-on, and even her follies, she was not only a charming, witty, and even alluring personality, she was farseeing, of keen mind, astute and brilliant. She had the style of a prima donna, but she was consumed by strange fires, immensely insecure, childlike, simple, and almost naïve upon occasion. She could be ruthlessly selfish, yet tender, compassionate, and forgiving. I do not think she ever really harbored a grudge, nor was she vindictive. Looking back now, I see that she needed to be surrounded by affection and esteem just for herself alone. None of the honors or clamoring crowds or roses or applause quite met that need."[6]

Those who knew Evangeline best often saw evidences of her need to be assured of their love. The first time she talked at length with Lieutenant Commissioner William Parkins's wife, Eva, Evangeline asked her, "Do you love me?" Eva replied, "Yes, I think everybody loves you."[7]

But not everyone did. Like most public figures, she had detractors. However, most people loved Evangeline because they sensed her overwhelming love for God and for them. Although she was at home with the wealthy and her name often appeared in newspaper columns along with the names of prominent citizens, her greatest love was for the poor. Many have referred to this "lifelong obsession." From the time as a child when she took her dinner out to the hungry man peering through the window, she identified herself with the poor until the day she died. They recognized her as their friend, not their patron, and responded to her love.

Women officers admired her and were inspired by her leadership to prize their high calling and to give their best. Colonel Florence Turkington, with others, has expressed the feeling that underneath Evangeline's austerity lay a fine compassion and understanding, and they knew that "she could be warm and gentle as well as stern and demanding."

One day Evangeline told Catherine Baird, now a colonel and one of the Army's great poets, "I've always been afraid to take too much notice of women officers because I am a woman and people would think I was giving all the favored jobs to women."

Sincere evidence of someone's love always delighted Evangeline, such as the time she had finished a heavy two days of officers' councils. After the last meeting, Commissioner McIntyre told the officers, "You can't all shake hands with the Commander, but she knows she goes with our love and devotion." Evangeline was throwing kisses to everyone.

Captain Charles Overstake scampered over the seats and hurried to the back of the platform. When she walked by him, he said, "Commander, I had to shake your hand before you left." She extended her hand, palm down, in a pat, but he kissed it. Her eyes lighted up as she said, "Oh, thank you, Captain."

A few years later when Overstake was the chief side officer at the Chicago School for Officers' Training, Evangeline went there to speak. He was taking her up to the lecture hall and said to her, "General, do you remember when you farewelled from Chicago a few years ago and a young captain kissed your hand?"

"Was that you?"

"Yes."

"Do it again!" she said.[8]

One of Evangeline's most endearing traits was her sense of humor. Helen Purviance, now a lieutenant colonel, sat near the Commander in a restaurant and heard her tell the waiter, "I would like tea, but I want it weak." Soon after he set the tea before her, Evangeline's long finger beckoned him again. "I asked you for weak tea, but I didn't want it helpless," she said.

Newsmen enjoyed Evangeline's quick-witted repartee and often quoted her. One day when she was hurrying to catch a train, a breathless reporter pushed through the crowd and gasped, "Miss Booth—I want to ask you—is the world getting better?" Her instant reply: "I'm doing what I can to make it better. What are you doing?"[9]

Always curious about why she had never married, a Boston newsman inquired, "How did you escape the snare of the fowler?" She laughingly answered, "Well, I'm still on the wing."

Like most women, Evangeline had her own little vanities. Every summer at Lake George, she put on a diving exhibition before anyone else entered the water. Even at sixty-nine, according to spectators, when Evangeline stood on a high diving board she looked like someone who could have been in the Miss America pageant.

Throughout her life people flattered her. Colonel Bertram Rodda, who had known and worked with her for many years, recalled, "She loved flattery because she was human, but hated it because she had good judgment."

Evangeline's love for children is remembered by hundreds of retired officers who as children received the Commander's Christmas package. For many, the new dress or boy's shirts and trousers were the only new clothes they had had that year. She encouraged leaders at territorial and divisional centers to have an officers' kids' Christmas party for those in the area. The "OKs" looked forward to it for months. As Lieutenant Colonel Lyell Rader remembered, "It was always a big event, and we realized there was a throbbing human heart at the center of things instead of just an organization."

Mrs. J. Leonard LeViness, Evangeline's neighbor, remembered that the Commander personally distributed gifts to the pupils in the nearby Washington Avenue public school in Hartsdale.

The evidences of Evangeline's love for children and youth are endless—parents who received personal assurance of her prayers for a sick child, a check sent to help with extra expense because of a child's sickness, the way she encouraged children to participate in sports and then sometimes worried about them. For instance, she thought Kathleen Stretton's horse was too big for her and was afraid Kathleen might be thrown from it.[10]

When Clifford McIntyre made the cross-country team at Yale—the first time an officer's child had accomplished this—Evangeline sent him a bathrobe favored by athletes. On the card she wrote, *To the good, brave, and swift of foot.*

Always interested in recruiting someone for her Army, Evangeline encouraged teenagers to give their lives to Christ and become Salvationists. When Minnie Hokanson, a young Swedish girl, came to work as personal maid for the Jack W. Pagents, in Scarsdale, New York, she met the Commander at a corps supper in White Plains. Evangeline learned that Minnie wanted to be a missionary and asked Captain Victor Dimond to take Minnie to see the Army's school for officers' training. Later, she invited Minnie to visit her at Acadia and asked her to pray about becoming a Salvationist. Minnie finally became an officer because Evangeline "took time out of her busy life to acquaint a young girl with the possibilities for service in her Army."[11]

When the parents of Captain Louise Duerr were transferred back to Switzerland in 1933, Louise remained in the United States. She married Captain Paul Kaiser the next year, and they were amazed to receive a beautiful wedding gift from the Commander, with a note saying that since the bride's parents were too far away to be present, she wanted to give them her blessing. Years later, when Commissioner Kaiser became the national commander of the United States, he said, "The concept of Commander will never be the same as when she had it. The four territories are now coordinated by the national commander but it is not a command operation. Nevertheless, it will be a thrill to sit in the same office that she occupied."[12]

One of the reasons for Evangeline's outstanding success as an administrator was her ability to judge the capabilities of those who served her. She practiced the advice she gave to other Army leaders: "Surround yourself with the very best personnel you can." Often she used the single-talented person as much as the many-talented one, so long as that talent was dedicated to the Lord's service. Contrary to the beliefs of many, she respected those who differed with her although she seldom indicated this at the time.

When Colonel Walter Jenkins, her chief secretary for many years, opposed her in a conference discussion, Evangeline turned to him and said, "Jenkins, who wants your opinion?" Whereupon Colonel Jenkins said, "In that case, Commander, I beg to be excused," and walked out of the room.[13]

A similar incident occurred one summer at a commissioners' conference at Lake George. This time the dissident was Commissioner John McMillan. After the session was over, Evangeline said to George Russell (Colonel Griffith's assistant at the time), "Russell, there is a man of the future, a man who will not bow down to anyone. He has the courage of his convictions to say 'no,' and in this Army we've got to have more men who will stand on their feet and commit themselves. Never be afraid to stand on your feet so long as you think you are in the right."[14]

Since Evangeline was so positive in her orders, it took courage to oppose her. According to Lieutenant Colonel Blair Abrams, "If she decided, 'You are going to San Francisco,' you usually just put on your hat and went." As legal secretary, he found Evangeline forthright in expressing herself but not difficult to work with.[15]

Others have commented upon her tremendous ability to listen to a discussion, assess the situation, and make a wise decision. Captain Lillian Hansen, later Mrs. Colonel William Noble, took notes of an all-day property board meeting at the Chicago Evangeline Residence. "She was very erudite on boards and made useful comments. I had a notebook full and lost it somehow getting in and out of the car on a slushy, snowy day.

"After a fruitless search, I phoned the Commander at the hotel to tell her I had lost the day's notes. She was provoked, I'm sure, but graciously said, 'We've just finished it; I can do it over again.' She gave me the whole substance of those notes in a condensed form, which was much better because I would have had to do that. People said she was often gruff and imperious. Perhaps she was, but never with me."[16]

When Evangeline was speaking at a public meeting on one occasion, she stopped and asked, "Where's the *War Cry* editor? No more pictures." Clarence Hall, the editor at that time, sent the photographer home. When there were no pictures in the *War Cry,* she was upset. But Hall understood the great pressures under which she worked and spoke and was not disturbed when rebuked by her. He considered her "one of the great women of her era who used her dramatic ability as an evangelistic tool. The effect of her personality when speaking can scarcely be described with any other word than magical. I've seen reporters in her meetings converted from doubting Thomases to awed disciples."[17]

Evangeline always encouraged officers to make the most of every preaching opportunity. One day she had Captain Arthur Woodruff in her office. "Woodruff, what are you doing now?" she asked.

"Commander, I'm in a little corps—Dover, New Jersey."

"How are you making out?"

"All right, but I find it very difficult to preach. I'm not a preacher like you. You love it but I find it very, very hard."

"You must have a greater desire to preach, Woodruff. Preaching is the big job in the Army; it isn't sitting by a desk. It isn't delegating authority. It's the preaching. You've got to preach. You can make a sermon out of anything." On her desk she had pencils in a vase made from an empty World War I shell brought home by Colonel Barker. Pointing to the vase, she said, "Take this vase. At one time it was full of death and destruction. Now it's cleaned out and is giving useful service. This is what you must preach to people. They must be cleaned out, fixed up so that they can serve rather than waste their time. You see how this vase stands? It stands firm. Your people must stand firm."

Two weeks later, he was surprised to receive through the mail the shell from her desk. On it she had

had engraved, "To Woodruff from the General. Preach Him."[18]

Since Woodruff was married to Evangeline's adopted daughter Pearl, he knew how autocratic she could be. Nevertheless, he remembered her as a compassionate woman. So did Mrs. Commissioner Ernest Pugmire, who once witnessed a behind-the-scenes incident when Evangeline was in Chicago. "We were walking down the hotel hallway when an unknown woman came up to the General and began pouring out her troubles to her. The next thing we knew, General Evangeline and the woman were on their knees, Evangeline praying with her. Those are the kind of things she did."[19]

Officers account a variety of stories about her punctuality. When Lieutenant Eugene Rice was her aide-de-camp in California, he knocked on her hotel door at five minutes of two to let her know he was there when she was ready to leave.

"What time did I tell you to be here?" she asked.

"Two o'clock."

"I will be ready at two o'clock," she said and shut the door.[20]

Evangeline had a whirlwind round of farewells in the territorial centers at Chicago, San Francisco, and Atlanta. But the one to top them all was the National Tribute of Farewell in New York's Madison Square Garden on November 1, presided over by the Honorable Homer S. Cummings, U.S. Attorney General.

Reporting the occasion, Edwin C. Hill wrote, "As Evangeline Booth sat on that platform, surrounded by so many well-known influential people, a wistful memory must have come to her of another platform thirty-odd years before when she made her first appearance in America. The scene was not the Madison Square Garden; it was a hall in the slums, packed with a jeering antagonistic mob. To get into it, the young Englishwoman had to climb up a fire escape and crawl through a window."[21]

What a contrast to this night when Evangeline's close friend, Helen Keller, declared, "I am proud to stand beside Evangeline Booth. I love her dearly. . . . I cannot recall a woman to whom God has given a greater opportunity to serve mankind. . . . The whole world has heard the beat of her great heart . . . the spirit of love which is the spirit of Christ fills her soul. From my heart I salute Evangeline Booth and her valiant legions who speak the one language of brotherhood."[22] When Evangeline and Helen Keller embraced, the *New York Times* called it "a moving moment."[23]

General Evangeline left America on the highest crest of love and popularity she had ever known. She retained her American citizenship. She expected to be welcomed in Britain and taken to their hearts as they had done years before when she was their young Field Commissioner. Was she expecting too much?

24
The World for God

When the *Majestic* arrived at Southampton around the
latter part of November 1934, it was flying the red-
yellow-and-blue Salvation Army flag in honor of General
Evangeline, who was on board. The Chief of the Staff,
Commissioner Henry W. Mapp, and the British Commissioner, Charles Jeffries, met the General and noted
how fit she looked despite a rough passage.

Major Owen Culshaw, (later commissioner and assigned to many important positions at international
headquarters), wondering how he could get the forty-
four pieces of luggage for the General and her staff
through customs before the train left for London, went
to the chief customs officer. "We have General Booth on
board. Have you ever met Miss Booth?"

"No, I haven't but I would like to."

Culshaw introduced them and they walked along the
dock. When the customs officer asked, "General, do you
have anything of value to declare," she replied, "Sir, the
most valuable thing I've brought over to this country is
my Bible."

"That answer is good enough," he said. "Mark up all
the General's luggage and see that it gets onto the train,"[1]
he told one of his workers.

When they arrived in London, a newsman asked the
General, "Aren't the responsibilities you face going to be
too heavy for someone your age?" Although she would
be sixty-nine in a few weeks, she quipped, "I'm not old;
I'm brand new," and at a press interview she declared,
"I'm bubbling over with enthusiasm. I have taken up this
supreme responsibility because I feel it is God's will for
me. I am anxious to do anything and everything I can to
help the Army lead people to Christ. The North Atlantic
in November is not an easy place to work, but my staff
have been too busy to see much of the sea although they
have all felt it."[2]

Evangeline became General just five years after the
first High Council was held, when Edward J. Higgins
became the Army's first elected General. Her predecessor had spent most of his career in Great Britain and was
greatly loved. However, although referred to as a
"statesman" upon retirement, even General Higgins had
found himself confronted by difficulties during the years
when changes in Salvation Army structure were being
implemented.

General Evangeline came to Britain full of enthusiasm, anxious to make a worthwhile contribution to
her beloved Army. But she had been away from England
for thirty-eight years. For eight years in Canada and
thirty in America, she had led an Army that was constantly adjusting to the fast growth and changing needs
of young countries. Now she was back in traditional England. Salvationists in Great Britain felt they had already
achieved the kind of organization and methods of im-
plementing the Army's program of best suited to their
country.

Two generations of officers did not know her. Many
of this group had small administrative roles and would
not take kindly to abrupt changes. Some took a sort of

"wait and see" attitude. However, the commissioners and older officers who remembered "Miss Eva" accepted her wholeheartedly. And to the young captains and lieutenants, she was a legend come true. They liked her impetuous and unpredictable actions and readily marched behind her.[3]

Brindley Boon (later a colonel) remembered, "We were all intrigued when we knew The Salvation Army was going to have a lady General. We had attended the farewell meeting of General and Mrs. Higgins in Royal Albert Hall. That was the biggest occasion of its kind that the Army had had up to that time. We wondered how this could possibly be bettered at Evangeline Booth's welcome.

"But we immediately saw a glimpse of the spectacular as she marched through the arena from the back of the Royal Albert Hall to the acclaims of the people. The whole meeting was interesting but I especially remember that her new song 'The World for God'—written in the interim between her election and the taking of office— was presented in London in that meeting. She also announced 'The World for God' campaign for 1935."[4]

As the six hundred voices of the massed chorus sang "The world for God! The world for God! I give my heart; I will do my part," General Evangeline rose to her feet, making it her own pledge. After her message, as the voices repeated the refrain of her song, she seized the baton from the choral director and led the great crowd in singing the chorus again and again, making it "a dedicatory pledge by my soldiers of Great Britain." The Lord Chancellor joined the vast throng, declaring he was "putting in his part."[5]

Some who were present at that meeting remember how shocked they were that Evangeline would dare to take over the leading of her song, surrounded as she was by "a platform of dignitaries."

Behavior that had been considered dashing and audacious in a youthful Evangeline was sometimes criticized in her later years as being "too dramatic." Sensitive as she was, Evangeline must have realized that she was viewed critically by some—and that what had been acceptable in America might not always be understood by Salvationists in England. For instance, she was censured almost unanimously for the automobile she brought with her. "She knew British people and shouldn't have brought a Cadillac. Instead of riding around London in a car larger than royalty's, why didn't she ask the donors to let her buy a smaller car when she got to England?"

Others wondered why she brought so many of her staff to live in her home: Lieutenant Commissioner Richard Griffith, her private secretary of almost forty years; Gypsy, her companion since youth; Mrs. Colonel Minnie Brewer; Brigadier Florence Farrington; and Mrs. Major Mackness. Those who knew her best realized that she brought them because, through the years, they had become like a family to her.

Evangeline's appeal to the general public, however, came across with the same magnetism of leadership her father had possessed. Upon her, more than upon his other children, had fallen the mantle of his genius for striking fire in men's imaginations, of making them see visions and dream dreams, of inspiring them to not merely sit and think but to go and do something for the Lord.[6]

One officer who never adjusted to Evangeline's leadership was her chief of the staff, Commissioner Henry Mapp. When he differed with her—and they differed often—after hearing all he and others had to say on the subject, she would make up her mind and, as General, issue the necessary orders. She expected him, as her chief, to implement those orders.

Evangeline knew that at times her impatience was a

weakness but recognized that at other times this trait—
none of the Booths were known for their patience with
those who refused to move quickly under orders—was a
contributing factor to the Army's steady growth through
the years.[7] While some felt the brunt of her impatience,
many remember Evangeline for her kindness and
thoughtfulness. Colonel Catherine Baird (then a major),
former *Young Soldier* editor in Chicago, was transferred
to international headquarters shortly before Evangeline
became General. "When General Evangeline came over,
she sent for me one day and asked me to help her with
something very trivial. The next day she sent me the
money to buy an eiderdown. It was so nice and warm. I
hadn't said anything to her about being cold, but it was
the kind of thing she did for people."[8]

On her first Christmas day as General, Evangeline
took some of her staff and a dozen single bandsmen with
her to visit Salvation Army social centers in London. At
noon, they arrived at the Burn Street men's social hostel
in Marylebone, formerly the Great Western Hall where
she had been stationed as a newly commissioned
eighteen-year-old captain. The bandsmen played "Auld
Lang Syne" as the General came into the dining room
where hundreds of men had gathered for dinner.

After a short carol sing, Evangeline spoke briefly.
"What a lot of love there is in the world! Don't let anyone
make a fool of you over that! People sometimes say to me,
'Look at the news of crimes and sorrows spread over the
newspapers. Don't you think the world's love is growing
less?' Not on your life! There is still much love in the
world, and the greatest of all is the love of Christ."[9]

Christmas meant a twelve-hour stint for the
bandsmen, who had to walk home, because public transportation ended at four o'clock on Christmas afternoon.
But according to Brindley Boon, then the bandmaster of

the group, "It was all worthwhile. Before we parted, the General came to each of us, thanked us for our music, and gave us a box of chocolates to take home to our mothers or to our sweethearts."[10]

After launching the "World for God" campaign and being welcomed in cities throughout Great Britian, Evangeline left for Australia and New Zealand the following February to fulfill the engagement she had had to cancel the year before because of illness. On the way, the *Mooltan* stopped at Bombay, India, where the territorial commander, Colonel Alfred Barnett, had arranged for Evangeline to do a meeting.

Because of a smallpox scare, only Evangeline and her secretary were allowed to leave the ship. Evangeline's niece, Muriel Booth-Tucker, a young captain, was brought into Bombay to be the General's companion. Now a retired colonel, Muriel still remembers that outside meeting in Bombay. "Afterwards, all the officers went down to the docks to see the General off. Aunt Eva stood on the Captain's deck with Mrs. Major Mackness, and Lieutenant Colonels Walter Mabee and Griffith around her. As the ship moved away from shore, we heard Lieutenant Colonel Mabee's beautiful tenor voice singing " 'The World for God.' "[11]

When the ship neared western Australia, a steamer crowded with Salvationists sailed out to meet it and welcome the General. From the minute she landed at Fremantle, whether in crowded cities or traveling across the Australian desert, Evangeline was overwhelmed with the evidences of love from her officers and soldiers.

At the end of the Perth phase of her campaign, hundreds crowded the railway station to say good-bye. Police did their best to save the singing, shouting crowd from meeting with accidents. Railway employees caught the enthusiasm of Salvationists and joined in the farewells. As the bands played, the engineers of trains manipulated their whistles in time with the music, adding to the expressive din with which the General left Perth. Salvationists started home convinced that the brief campaign marked a high pinnacle in Army history, providing inspiration that would drive their forces forward.

At noon the next day, the train reached Kalgoorlie, in the gold-mining country, where officials asked Evangeline to plant a tree beside one her father had planted in 1905. As they continued across the arid wastes of the great Nallarbor Plain, the train stopped at remote stations where Salvationists waited to greet the General. At one point, 600 miles from the nearest corps, the Army flag was flying over a house where Salvationists, formerly from Scotland, lived. Dressed in full uniform, they came to salute the General and wept as she spoke to them and to their two children.[12]

Evangeline thanked God that, in both Australia and New Zealand, "Everything faded out but the call of the Cross. From the high galleries, from the back seats they came, husband bringing wife, wife going back to bring husband to the penitent-form. We heard of seekers around radio receivers, hundreds of miles away."[13]

In June, 4,000 young people welcomed Evangeline home at the Alexandria Palace in London. Groups scattered over the ground, picnicked, demonstrated gymnastics, put on small band and song concerts, and participated in competitive games and drills of all kinds. At sunset they all marched past the General—from slum children trundling soapbox wheelbarrows to trim, full-uniformed corps cadets marching with precision.[14]

That summer she conducted "World for God" congresses in Oslo and Stockholm.[15] Upon her return, Evangeline announced that in the fall she would do a thousand-mile motorcade throughout England and Wales, and in September the motorcade members—the British Commissioner, some bandsmen and soloists— assembled at Tottenham Citadel in North London. All wore their regulation Salvation Army uniforms, ready to start as soon as the General arrived. When Evangeline got out of her car, everyone was astonished to see her wearing, not her dark blue uniform and bonnet, but a pale gray uniform and shoes, a long red coat, and a bright red straw hat.

"She was dynamic; she was stunning," recalled Commissioner Alfred J. Gilliard, "But she was going to lead conservative British Salvationists! I was a reporter then, hanging around the edge of the crowd. Again and again, someone pulled my arm and asked, 'What's she wearin' that 'at for? 'Asn't she got a bonnet?' "[16]

Frederick Coutts (who later became the eighth General of the Army) was one of the bandsmen in that motorcade, and he tells the following: "When Evangeline asked bandsmen 'How do you like my hat?' they were too polite to express their opinion, realizing that she was the General and had already made up her mind to wear it whether they liked it or not."[17] She may have felt their disapproval, but since she had never been a traditionalist, she didn't let it bother her. As in previous motorcade speeches, she didn't use notes but spoke about things of local interest. For instance, "In the land of the potteries," said General Coutts, "she would begin with a teacup, a sign of fellowship. 'We sit down and share a cuppa.' From fellowship with each other, it was not a long step to talking about fellowship with the Savior, Jesus Christ."[18]

Commissioner Harold Orton recalled that at Bolton, Lancashire, when the mayor greeted the General, she responded, "The Lord Mayor is wearing his red robe and chain of office. My red coat is to keep me warm. Mr.

Mayor is wearing a chain, but when we get to heaven we won't have any chains—if we can only get there, Mr. Mayor, if we can only get there."[19]

One of Evangeline's most exciting and rewarding campaigns in 1935 was the Canadian congress. Many years had elapsed since she had been their enterprising Commissioner, and this was her first official visit to them since those early days.

General Arnold Brown, then a young corps officer, was assigned to take down verbatim every word Evangeline uttered in public. He has said, "I followed her everywhere, sat at her feet when she spoke, and worked all through the night, transcribing every word for posterity. She made a tremendous impression on everyone. I remember standing in the Royal York Hotel, waiting for further instructions from Army leaders.

"I saw her come out of her suite, surrounded by commissioners and top-ranking officers. She moved along that passage like royalty. What struck me was that these commissioners, for whom a young lieutenant had the most tremendous respect, admiration, and awe, seemed to be like courtiers, attendants. She just swept through—imperious, saying her piece as she went along, quite positive. I've never forgotten that and the impression made upon me. Then, of course, to see her in front of eighteen thousand people at the Maple Leaf Gardens, speaking on 'The World's Greatest Romance'—not a sound to be heard but her voice—is an amazing experience."[20]

It was the Army's first time to take over the Maple Leaf Gardens. When Evangeline came onto the platform that afternoon, she was accompanied by Ontario's Lieutenant-Governor, the Honorable Dr. Herbert Bruce and Mrs. Bruce, and Commissioner and Mrs. John McMillan. Officers present who had served under

Evangeline at the turn of the century remembered the rumors that Dr. Bruce had been enamored of her then and listened intently to his remarks that afternoon. "It would be difficult, indeed impossible," he said, "for me to express with what pleasure I accepted the kind invitation to preside on this occasion. The young lady who came to Toronto nearly four decades ago is with us again with the same tireless enthusiasm which has brought her the honor and acclaim of all nations and the gratitude of inarticulate millions of admiring men and women."[21]

General Clarence Wiseman and Mrs. Wiseman were then captains in charge of the Toronto Temple corps. "I can remember that when Evangeline rose to speak, there was something like an electric shock through the crowd," he said. "She commanded that audience. There was a certain charisma about her, and we were electrified by her message."[22] Another great crowd was there that night for the "battle for souls" in the salvation meeting. (Most of the other congress meetings were held in Massey Hall, where Evangeline had spoken so often when she commanded the Army's Canadian forces.)

During her first year as General, Evangeline sent officers to commence operations in Singapore and Malaysia and in Canton, South China.[23]

The summer of 1936, Evangeline conducted a second and even lengthier (ten-day) motorcade, starting at Land's End, the southern tip of the British Isles, and finishing at John O'Groats, Scotland. At St. Ives she unveiled a tablet commemorating her father's work there. At Torquay, the mayor recalled Evangeline's own conspicuous part in the Army's early battles.[24]

The Bertram Mills Family Circus was leaving Torquay just as the motorcade arrived. Colonel William Henry Charles, a motorcade member, recalled the excitement that swept through the huge crowd when Mills turned the circus around and marched them back to the meeting place. "Bertram Mills, who had become the 'circus king,' had been one of Evangeline's bandsmen at the Great Western Hall. She invited him to sit beside her and the internationally known circus artists mingled with the crowd."[25]

Later, when Evangeline visited Bertram Mills at his country home, he welcomed her on the steps. She looked around her and said, "Yes, Bertram Mills, you've done well for yourself, but are you really happy?" Tears came into his eyes and he told her, "General, I would give anything if I was as happy as I was when I played in your band."[26]

One of the highlights of every summer for Evangeline was the out-of-doors, all-day party at Boxmoor, Hertfordshire, for 1,500 children and 500 mothers from the poorest parts of London. Early in the morning the fifty-seven buses would begin to arrive at international headquarters, 101 Queen Victoria Street, with mothers and children from the Army's slum posts. This year a band of thirty to fifty members, selected from several Army bands, was already on the way to Boxmoor to furnish music throughout the day.

Evangeline was at the entrance to the grounds to greet her guests. As they swarmed over the grounds, she moved among them and joined in their games, laughing with them at Punch and sympathizing with Judy. She took scores of them for a ride in a horse-drawn vehicle. "Coo, this is better'n Christmus!" a little boy shouted.[27]

The mothers, many of them plump, loved to sing. One of their favorites was "Doing the Lambeth Walk," forming a ring and acting it out. Evangeline, who felt right at home with them, joined hands with them and glowed under their love.[28] She held a tiny baby while she talked to the mother. After Evangeline left, the baby's mother whispered to her, "That's somethin' for you to remember, Duckie. Miss Booth 'eld yer."[29]

That fall General Evangeline divided the Army's evangelical work of the British territory into four territories. Although The Salvation Army in Britain is very large, the country geographically is small. Nevertheless, the leading officers of that day agreed that four territories rather than one would prove beneficial to the Army. However, soon after she retired, the Army reverted to its previous structure, though Scotland continues to be a separate territory.[30]

By 1936 the demands of the Depression had taxed the Army's finances to the limit in the United States. In the Central territory, many mortgages were coming due without the funds to meet them. Commissioner McIntyre decided to take his acting financial secretary, Adjutant T. Herbert Martin, to London to seek the General's approval for a blanket mortgage scheme that would save the Army from many foreclosures and interest expense.

McIntyre and Martin discussed the plan with the General and top Salvation Army leaders, among them the chief of staff, the chancellor of the exchequer, and the international auditor. After further lengthy discussions, Evangeline gave McIntyre the go-ahead sign before he and Martin returned to Chicago. At those conferences, Martin felt he was given a close look at Evangeline's business acumen and administrative leadership.[31]

On September 19, 1936, the *London Times* announced that General Evangeline Booth would leave London in November for a world campaign, during which she would conduct meetings and inspect the work of The Salvation Army.

25
Grueling Schedules

Evangeline left for her four-month world campaign—physically, her most taxing tour—on November 10, 1936. Throughout India she traveled by train—a slow, dusty, noisy, hot (no air conditioning then) trip, or by cart, in blistering heat. She arrived in Anand after an all-night train ride but showed no sign of fatigue as she greeted the thousands who had gathered to welcome her.

Prior to taking her position for the salute and "march past" of 6,000 Salvationists, the General delighted everyone by heading up the procession on a huge elephant. The Indians noted, too, her interest in the banners, camels, and bullock carts, the Bhils with their bows and arrows, and the women with their brass water vessels.

Commissioner Arthur R. Blowers, the international secretary, who accompanied her, said, "General, I'm afraid you can't take this intense heat."

"So am I, but I'd rather die on this platform for these dear people than leave."[1]

When Evangeline's niece, Major Muriel Booth-Tucker, saw how the General suffered from the heat in her Army uniform, she asked, "Aunt Eva, why don't you wear one of my saris? You only need the minimum underneath. It's light, cool, and convenient."

"Oh, Muriel, do give me one of your saris!"

Muriel gave her a fine cotton one. In those days all Salvation Army women officers in India wore an orange sari—orange, the religious color of India—and a red cotton jacket. When the General appeared in their national dress, she was greeted with a roar of delight. From then on, she wore an Indian sari.[2]

Some people have wondered at the magnetic personality—the feeling of rapprochement—which Evangeline Booth was so adept at establishing between herself and an audience. When she visited India in 1936, the country was rising up under a great surge of nationalism, but everywhere she went, the crowds came literally by the thousands to hear her.

In one great meeting she said to the people, most of whom were "horny-handed sons of the soil," "I have come all the way from London to tell you I love you!" And this was a language they understood, for she had found a way to their hearts. "Love" was the magic word. Here was a general who had come halfway around the world to tell them of her love for her people in India. And when she began further to pour her heart out to them, telling of the love of God and His mighty power to save and renew, so immediate was the appeal that a great crowd surged forward to seek to know this God of love and mercy.

While in northern India, Evangeline inspected Emery Hospital, built with money donated by her American friends, the Thomas Emerys. She was especially interested, too, in the hospital at Nidubrolu because the patients were women and children.

On her last stop in the north, the General visited the Salvation Army's criminal tribes settlement at Stuartpuram. She stayed overnight in the compound, her guards some tall Indian men who had been murderers before their conversion. Now they were zealously watching their General. She never forgot the way 3,000 reformed criminals sang "The World for God" in her Sunday morning meeting.[3]

But it was the lepers she admired for their courage as they coped with their dread disease. At the Bapatla Leper Colony, she walked between a guard of honor—two long rows of men, women, and children disfigured and crippled by leprosy. At the conclusion of her meeting with the officers and patients, Evangeline with difficulty restrained the tears when ten little boys and girls—all lepers—sang for her in English the chorus of her song. She said afterward, "The Greatest compliment ever paid me was when those children sang, 'I give my heart; I will do my part.' "[4]

Shortly before her visit, the Army had taken charge of the Cochin State Leper Hospital at Koratty. The then Brigadier Dr. William Noble, senior medical officer at the Catherine Booth Hospital in Nagercoil with responsibility for the surrounding area, had arranged with the railroad authorities to stop the General's train from the north at a prepared spot near the leper hospital. When she alighted, 300 lepers waiting by the railroad tracks cheered and the children waved small flags as their brass band played the tune, "Always Cheerful."[5]

December 24 she traveled all day by cart, in terrible heat, with dust falling upon everything. At Puthencruz, she stopped for a wayside meeting. For an hour, under the shade of a great banyan tree, Evangeline talked "with sympathy and understanding, entering into their struggles and sorrows" with the 1,500 people gathered to hear their General.[6]

At noon she dedicated the Evangeline Booth Leper Hospital, opened only eleven months before. After a meeting with the staff and lepers, she left for Tiruvella, where she was to spend Christmas.[7]

Early Christmas morning, General Evangeline took

the salute as 10,000 Salvationists, led by a monster elephant, marched past her. Dressed in white, with flags, drums, fifes, and gaily colored paper umbrellas, they came singing, shouting, clapping, tears of joy streaming down their faces.

Following the march, she addressed the largest gathering of the tour. Twenty-two thousand sat on the ground, Indian fashion, under a huge pandal (a roof of palm leaves supported on bamboo poles for protection from the sun). General Evangeline spoke for an hour on "His Name Shall Be Called Wonderful." Although there was no available space for a penitent-form, at the General's invitation, 5,000 seekers lifted their voices in prayer, "the sound rising like the waves of a mighty sea."[8]

In all ten countries visited, in addition to inspecting Salvation Army operations and meeting with her troops, the General scheduled press interviews, lunches at service clubs, lectures in colleges, and meetings with heads of state.[9] But it was a boy with a sun-faded army flag, who promised to keep it high on the Australian parched wastes, who thrilled her heart.[10]

A month after she returned home, on April 13, 1937, General Evangeline welcomed her new chief of staff, Commissioner John McMillan.[11]

In May, the General appointed Colonel and Mrs. Alfred Lindvall to open the Army's work in the Philippines. On the eve of their departure from London, she gave them a flag with the inscription, "The Philippine Islands for Christ."[12] And she represented The Salvation Army at the coronation of George VI. In the midst of all the pageantry, she may have thought again, "It's a long route from working in London slums to sitting in Westminster Abbey."

In other parts of the world, war was inflicting havoc in many lives. Evangeline's heart went out to the Basque children, innocent victims of the civil war in Spain. She offered sanctuary at Salvation Army facilities for 1,400 children, part of 4,000 brought to England by the Spanish Central Relief Committee.[13]

At the same time, thousands were homeless in China as Japanese troops, in a war not officially declared until December 1941, occupied many Chinese seaports and cities.[14] The General called officers and soldiers to a day of prayer for Salvationists in China, who had written, "We shall remain here . . . doing all we can to serve the people." By January 1938, Salvationists were caring for 17,000 refugees in Shanghai.[15]

In England, Evangeline took time out from administrative duties to visit Salvation Army hospitals, slum settlements, and the crowded camps of hop pickers. As the chops sizzled and the kettle sang over a ground log fire, the hop pickers told her how they enjoyed the singsongs with the slum captain who had a hut in the camp. The children crowded around the General. When a boy told her his name was William, she said, "That was my father's name. There are many people who think that William Booth was a good man, but I'll tell you what he was: he was a good boy first!"[16]

In September Evangeline left on the *Berengaria* for the United States to conduct four territorial congresses, the first one in Atlanta to commemorate the Southern territory's tenth anniversary. At a soldiers' rally, she reminded people: "The Salvation Army did not start with a band, a uniform, or poor men's hotels or slum corps—we started with a penitent-form in the dark on Mile End Waste, London. The penitent-form is not merely one of the institutions of the Salvation Army—it is one of the *vitals* that can never change. It is our communion rail, our baptismal font, where the fire of the Holy Spirit falls upon our soldiers. It is at the foot of the Cross of Jesus

where the sinner lays down his burdens; it is our altar—
our *cornerstone*."[17]

In Mexican attire, Señor Alejandro Guzmán and a
party of Mexicans played their guitars and sang in that
meeting. The General had learned that the Mexicans
wanted to become Salvationists. She was so impressed
with their sincerity that in a surprise action she presented
Guzmán with a Salvation Army flag and charged him,
"Take this back to Mexico and start The Salvation Army
there."[18]

On the Sunday afternoon, an overflow crowd in
Atlanta's Georgian Theater heard the General speak on
"The March of Christianity." "Have no fear," she said.
"There's no enemy that can overtake Christianity. . . .
The wisdom of God has been the power of its disciples as
it has marched on through the ages."[19]

Back in London in January 1938, Evangeline
launched an international youth movement, the Torch-
bearers, to "not only seize upon every existing opportunity but to create new opportunities for capturing youth
for Christ and for service to humanity." Sunbury Court,
which had served as a men's social senior citizens' home,
was converted into a youths' conference and camping
center.

Young people in Britain, America, and around the
world responded enthusiastically to this new movement.
At an all-day rally at Clapton Congress Hall, when the
General stood to speak, they shouted a shattering "hallelujah" welcome. The General was now seventy-two, but
one man, speaking for many, said, "We love her because
of her position of course, but most of all because she is so
alive, and interested in *us*." During the prayer meeting
that evening, 414 young people knelt at the penitent-

form; 57 offered themselves for Salvation Army officership.[20]

No matter how busy she was, Evangeline always found time to talk to people. She established a warm friendship with the cleaning women at international headquarters. When she left the office after a late-night conference, she often walked among these cleaners who might comment to each other, "She looks a bit done up, an' no wonder!"

One evening she invited all of them to have tea with her in the building's lunchroom. Afterward, the General spoke to them informally. "What a lovely word 'cleaner' is. I am a cleaner! All my life I've been trying to make the world a cleaner place, cleaning up hearts, cleaning up homes, trying to sweep away some of the sin and misery."[21]

Lieutenant Colonel Ray Steadman-Allen, an office boy at that time, often took a tray of refreshments to the General when she worked late. "Sometimes she came out to get the tray herself and would say, 'It's time you were going home,' and give me half a crown, 'for your trouble.' She was marvelous; always showed her appreciation for any little service given to her."[22]

Gradually, Salvationists became accustomed to having the General suddenly change the order of a meeting. As one reporter said, "Try as they may to build up a nice, tight structure into which the General can fit and do her part, she *will* break through!" Like the Sunday at Luton Temple when the congregation was singing "Cleansing for Me." She stepped to the rail and said, "I ought to wait until I have been officially presented to you . . . but I want to begin right away and ask you to sing again with me:

"Lord, in Thy love and Thy power make me strong. . . . That's the word! Strong! What a world this would be if in a day of crisis all God's people were strong! What an Army we should have in Luton if every soldier was strong!" In a moment, the lilting song became a solemn prayer as the people sang it again.[23]

On September 19 the *London Times* reported, "On a site not far from where she began work as a London slum sister, General Evangeline Booth laid the foundation stone of The Salvation Army Goodwill Center at New North Road, Hoxton." The stone-laying ceremony of the multipurpose Hoxton Center took place at night. The General insisted upon this in order that the people mostly concerned with the center could be present after their day's work was over.[24]

She had no inkling on that joyous occasion that less than a month later she would suffer a great loss. In October, Evangeline went to Bristol with her personal and territorial staff for the Wales and Western territory to conduct meetings in the Colston Hall. As Commissioner Geoffrey Dalziel remembered, "I was a captain in the division and responsible for an officers' male party that would sing during the lecture the General would be giving. Before the afternoon meeting, Lieutenant Commissioner Griffith was giving me instructions about the cue board of colored lights." Frank Allum, then a major, who had driven the General to Bristol, was also there. "Commissioner Griffith then turned to me and said, 'It's time for you to go and fetch the General.' He started to run up the steps, but collapsed. We carried him to a side room and called for a doctor."

Commissioner Alfred Barnett went with Major Allum to pick up the General at the hotel. They tried to get her to go in the front door at the hall, but she said, "No, I'll go the back as always." As they stopped, she saw the ambulance and those who were bringing Griffith out on the stretcher. "When she saw the Commissioner, she knew he had gone and she went into the hall, obviously much affected by his death."[25]

The General did not give her lecture that afternoon.

Instead, Commissioner J. Evan Smith, the territorial commander, took her place, and Major Allum drove the General back to London.

Some thought the General should have appeared briefly to the people waiting for her at Colston Hall, asked them to excuse her because her armor bearer for forty years had been suddenly promoted to glory, and told them that Commissioner Smith would take her place. Others thought that if she had been urged by her associates to give her lecture, she would have had the stamina to do it. However, many felt that there was no need for her to make an appearance since, while the people were disappointed not to hear her, they would not expect her to speak under the circumstances.[26]

Major Allum also drove the General to Congress Hall the day of Griffith's funeral. "She did not go into the hall but stayed in the anteroom during the memorial service," he said. Commissioner George Langdon read the General's tribute. The body was interred in the Army plot at Kensico Cemetery, New York. Five weeks later, the *London Times* reported, "General Evangeline Booth spent some hours yesterday in her office at Salvation Army international headquarters for the first time since the death of her private secretary, the shock of which affected her health."[27]

Colonel Ernest Webb replaced Griffith at international headquarters as the General's executive secretary, while Captain Lily Bullard became secretary to Colonel Webb and at times took dictation from the General. The first time this happened, she said, "I was petrified, to put it mildly. But the General must have guessed how I felt. She was kind, looked at me with a twinkle in her eye, and talked slowly, enabling me to get the words down in spite of a trembling hand. As I got to know her better, I was at ease with her."[28]

Evangeline also sent for Major Gosta Blomberg,

whom she knew, to see if he would be suitable as her helper. After three months, he stayed on as her private secretary and traveled extensively with her.[29]

Several months before Griffith's death, Evangeline had decided, with the approval of leading officers, not to retire on her seventy-third birthday. In her 1938 Christmas note to Commissioner John McMillan, she wrote, "I have felt that you did not wish me to go on. Of course, had I known Dick would not be here, I should have yielded. Now I must finish! Have a happy Christmas."[30]

Her last year on active service was one of Evangeline's busiest. In February, she was the honored guest at a luncheon, presided over by the Lord Mayor of London, Sir Fran Bowater, in the Grocers' Hall, and in March she led the Army's Golden Jubilee congress in Belgium and presented her niece, Colonel Mary Booth, as the new territorial commander.

That spring her chief of staff, Commissioner John McMillan, became seriously ill. Worried about him, she wrote him from on board the *Aquitania* when she left for America in May, asking him to conserve his strength and reminding him, "In barely twelve days I shall be getting on board this old creaking ship again."[31] During those twelve days, she conducted meetings and interviews of all kinds and was decorated with the hood of an honorary Doctor of Laws by Nicholas Murray Butler, president of Columbia University.[32] She also commissioned the Dauntless Evangelists cadets in Toronto and New York.

Early that summer, she conducted North European campaigns and was received by the king of Norway, the king of Sweden, and Queen Wilhelmina of Holland. At the close of her meetings at The Hague, the people cheered and cheered, tears running down their faces, as they realized it would probably be their last time to see her.[33]

In July, Evangeline went to Buckingham Palace for an audience with the king,[34] and a short time later she was received by the Queen.[35]

Fifty-one territorial leaders came to London in August in response to a summons from the office of the chief of staff to serve on the High Council to elect the next General.[36] Evangeline welcomed them and the next day, when the officers posed for a picture, she told them, "I want my picture with the High Council." Someone reminded her that she was not a member, but she said, "I want my picture taken with my staff." Since she was still the General, the picture was taken with Evangeline Booth in the center of the first row, surrounded by her officers.[37] Commissioner George Lyndon Carpenter was elected General and was scheduled to take office November 1, 1939.

For months, war clouds had hovered over Europe. A gigantic farewell for General Evangeline had been scheduled for September 2 at Earls Court, but the event had to be canceled because war was imminent, young people were being evacuated, and the authorities discouraged such large gatherings.[38] And when war with Germany was actually declared, two days later, Evangeline called all Salvationists to "his or her post of duty, in whatever place, or whatever time, or whatever way, to prove yourselves soldiers of the Cross," telling women Salvationists to "put your knitting needles and sewing machines into service."[39]

September brought more personal grief to Evangeline with the promotion to glory of Commissioner John McMillan. She wrote his brother, Alex MacMillan, "Within the past year I have sustained the loss of two who perhaps stood nearer to me than anyone else in the world—first, Commissioner Griffith and now, Commissioner McMillan, my right hand, my ready helper, my Chief of the Staff. My loss in these two friends, for they were my intimate friends, is truly irreparable."[40]

One of Captain Lily Bullard's last tasks for General Evangeline was to go through the files in her office. Evangeline told her, "Destroy everything that has to do with officers and personalities; keep anything that has to do with Salvation Army constitution."[41]

Evangeline said good-bye to her home corps, Wimbledon, on October 14, urging Salvationists, "Be true to God. Teach that to your sons and daughters. Live it yourself. Let there be nothing between yourself and God."[42]

Instead of the spectacular Earls Court farewell, General Evangeline said good-bye to London, Sunday afternoon, October 22, at Regent Hall, which was packed with people long before starting time. She charged her troops, "The time for sacrifice has come. None of us is spared anxiety and sorrow. But neither sorrow, nor anxiety, nor fresh burdens can put our light under a bushel. My last word to you as your international leader is: 'Love one another!' Every sun that has gone down has strengthened my confidence in the power of love."

Through the *War Cry*, she spoke to all Salvationists:

> As General, my first charge to you was, *Preach the gospel of Jesus Christ!* My last word as your General is again, *Preach the gospel of Jesus Christ!* Let no man make you afraid. Preach Christ not merely as a gracious ornament of civilization, to be admired and accepted or not, at will, but as the Supreme Gift to a world lost without Him.[43]

Before Evangeline left England, she went to her father's boyhood home in Nottingham, and then to the Broad Street Wesleyan Methodist Chapel where William Booth had been converted, and told the crowded chapel, "The beginning of it all was *here*. He gave his all. But even that is not the whole secret. He gave all—and *he never took* it back." Then she went below to the schoolroom and unveiled a tablet in the floor which read:

HERE WILLIAM BOOTH GAVE HIS HEART AND LIFE TO
GOD, IN HIS FIFTEENTH YEAR, 1844.[44]

With England at war, Evangeline could not get passage to America until late November. Commissioners Charles T. Rich and David C. Lamb and Major Owen Culshaw accompanied her to Liverpool. Early the next morning before boarding the ship, Culshaw found the General in the hotel kitchen talking to the cook and his staff. The London officers were not allowed to wait until the ship sailed that night.[45]

For someone who had lived her whole life in the center of publicity, Evangeline now found herself in what one biographer termed "a vacuum . . . perhaps the hardest situation . . . she had ever had to face."[46]

General Carpenter asked Major Herbert S. Hodgson and his wife, on their way to the West Indies, to escort the General to America. As usual, Evangeline, a poor sailor, stayed in her cabin most of the time. Visits from the Hodgsons and Blombergs kept her aware of the ship's news. Every day she led a prayer meeting for the captain and his crew. Many of the passengers visited her in her cabin. Others told her staff, "We will make it safely. Evangeline Booth is on the ship."[47] But it was a rough trip, the ship battling a terrific storm in her zigzag course to avoid submarines.

The last day, the captain invited Evangeline up on the bridge. She stood with him as they approached the Statue of Liberty and thanked him for bringing the ship safely across the ocean. "No General," he said, "don't thank me. *We* thank *you* for our safety."[48] Then the gangplank was lowered, and Commissioner Ernest I. Pugmire and other American commissioners came aboard to welcome Evangeline home again.

26

Afterglow

After Evangeline returned to America to live in Hartsdale, she was out of the mainstream—another sat at her desk, the world was changing, as were the times, and the world made no pathway to her door. She no doubt expected to be consulted about major appointments and policy-making decisions, assuming that she would still be significantly involved in Army affairs. Instead, she was seldom consulted about anything of major importance. She once said, "It's stimulating to be shot at; killing to be ignored."[1] Although her personal household of many years still surrounded her at Acadia—Gypsy (Major Mary Welch), Brigadier Florence Farrington, Mrs. Major Mackness, and Major Gosta Blomberg and his family— she was lonely.

One of her closest friends, and perhaps the only one in her later years who called her Eva, was the second Mrs. Herbert Booth, who lived nearby in Yonkers. Evangeline often had someone drive her over there for a private chat.[2]

Still in demand as a speaker, she continued to draw large crowds wherever she went. Army leaders called upon her for special occasions. Shortly after General Carpenter instituted the Order of Distinguished Auxiliary Service in 1941 to mark the Army's appreciation of distinguished service rendered by non-Salvationists, Evangeline Booth made the first presentation in New York City to Henry W. Taft.[3]

She always responded gladly to invitations to speak to cadets. At the conclusion of a spiritual day at the School for Officers' Training, she told Major Mina Russell (later to retire as a lieutenant colonel), "It's a terrible thing, Russell, to be on the shelf, especially if the shelf is behind the door."[4]

Realizing that the General found it difficult to adjust to the afterglow years of retirement, the American commissioners asked her, "Why not write your autobiography?" She considered doing so and actually kept a publishing company expecting her manuscript for almost two years. Finally, she told Major Blomberg (later to retire as a commissioner), "I've never written about myself and I won't begin now. That decides it." She chose Philip Whitwell Wilson, for many years the religious news editor of the *New York Times*, to be her biographer and had Blomberg bundle up thousands of letters and papers and deliver them to Wilson, then retired in Westchester.[5]

As the possibility that the United States would enter World War II increased, Evangeline hoped her advice would be sought in planning how The Salvation Army could best serve the armed forces, but she was not consulted. Instead, she was shocked to learn in February 1941 that the Army had become a member of USO (United Service Organizations). She felt that the Army had rendered such good service in World War I that the government would finally have agreed to its serving in World War II as a separate entity. Feeling that in the USO the Army was not at liberty to conduct its own "brand" of programming, she often asked, "Why did we get involved?"[6] While many Salvationists, if asked, would have agreed with her, others—especially those who directed and worked in USO clubs—believed that the Army was meeting the spiritual as well as the social and physical needs of the military personnel through the overall USO program.

Advancing years did not keep Evangeline from expecting and demanding the best results possible from everyone. When a photographer who had taken her picture ten years earlier handed her some he had taken after her retirement, she was not pleased with them and told him so. Diplomatically, he answered, "But, General, I cannot take as good a photograph now as I did ten years ago. Remember, I was ten years younger then." She never said a word, but took the pictures and walked away.[7]

She was brought back briefly into the mainstream of Salvation Army life in November 1945 when she and General George C. Marshall, the United States Army's chief of staff, were guests of honor and principal speakers at the eightieth anniversary celebration of the founding of The Salvation Army in America. Salvationists from all parts of the country gathered in Kansas City, Missouri, to unite with Army friends for a series of meetings to thank God for His blessing upon their work through the years. Before the Honorable Alfred M. Landon presented Evangeline Booth, the Philharmonic Orchestra played her composition, "Streams in the Desert." When Evangeline caught the lilt of a harp, her favorite instrument, soaring above the great orchestra, her eyes brightened. Later, with quick wit, she responded, "Put the accent on the first syllable of Kansas City—it certainly *can* do things!"[8]

In her anniversary address, referring to the stormy beginnings of the Army and to her father's faith in God and love for men, Evangeline declared, "The ability to apply this faith and love to the needs of a sinning and sorrowing world is the Salvation Army's undergirding strength." In closing, she urged Salvationists and Christians of every denomination, "Keep on, jump into the struggle for right and truth, and love and justice. . . . I urge you to a swifter march. We must march on until sin, sorrow, and cruelty are swept before the tide of the love of Christ, and all nations of the earth recognize the Messiah, the Man of Nazareth, the Savior of the world!"

General Marshall paid his own tribute to Evangeline: "To me she has always represented the pinnacle of womanhood—of those who contribute to humanity. . . . Her charm and outstanding leadership have made her one of the great women of this country and of the world at large."

When Evangeline was asked to speak again at the large civic reception following the afternoon meeting, she turned to Mrs. Commissioner John McMillan and asked, "What shall I say? I didn't bring anything for this reception." Mrs. McMillan replied, "Give them the Lamplighter story, General."[9] It was one of Evangeline's favorite stories, and she told it with deep feeling.

"One night, after a strenuous day of speaking in motorcade meetings, an officer told me, 'There is a ninety-year-old man here who walked two miles to see you. He says he must talk to you.' I took the old gentleman aside and asked, 'What is it you wanted to tell me?'

" 'General, I was a boy, sixteen years old, when I saw a big tent over by the old Quaker cemetery. I slipped underneath it and when inside, I saw a tall man, with a black beard, preaching. That first night, I gave my heart to God. Night after night I listened to your father preach and finally begged, "Mr. Booth, let me do something for you." He said, "Well, my boy, if you want to do something, will you come down every day and take those little lamps all around this great tent, fill them with oil, cut the wicks off, and see that they are all lighted and burning every night?' "

"I listened to his story and told him that at sixteen he was lighting lamps that have never gone out but are shining today all over the world. You, who have honored us with your presence, are a part of the great procession of lamplighters, helping The Salvation Army lead thousands from darkness into the glorious light of God."

The next afternoon, General Evangeline was talking to her aide-de-camp, Cecil Briggs (at that time adjutant), about his family. When she learned that his oldest son, Walter, was a corps cadet, she said, "Tonight is the big soldiers' meeting. I want you to have Walter there because I am going to say something special for him."

As usual, the General preached a dynamic, soul-stirring sermon. She was conducting the prayer meeting when she turned around and asked Briggs, "Where is your son, Walter?"

"He's at the penitent-form, General."

"Go down and deal with him. You're the one that should be guiding your son. Then, when he is through praying, bring him up here. I want to say something to him."

Briggs prayed with his son and then brought Walter to the platform. Commissioner Allan stopped him, saying, "He's not allowed on the platform." But Evangeline said firmly, "Allan, I sent for this boy."

She drew Walter to one side and talked to him. "I don't really know what she told him," said Briggs, "but whatever it was, as he walked off the platform, he assured me, 'I'm going to be a Christian from now on.' From that day to the day he entered the School for Officers' Training, he studied to prepare himself for the ministry and Salvation Army work. We feel that whatever the General said, it had a definite bearing upon his life."[10]

Following the Kansas City meetings, Brigadier

Glenn Ryan (later a commissioner), divisional commander of Nebraska, had a meeting with the medical advisory
committee of the Omaha Booth Hospital. "Before we get
into business," said the chairman, "I want to tell you of an
experience I had in Kansas City last week. We saw in the
paper that The Salvation Army was having a big meeting,
with General Marshall and Evangeline Booth to be
present. Gentlemen, I've never seen anything like it. The
address of that woman—eighty years of age—it was a
tremendous experience. She enthralled that vast audience."[11]

On her way back to New York, Evangeline stopped
in Chicago for a few days. When she visited the School of
Officers' Training, Colonel Albert Pepper, the principal,
arranged for her to stay in a room on the second floor.
When Mrs. Pepper took the General a cup of tea,
Evangeline asked, "Can't I go down to the main floor
where the crowd is? You know, I'm often lonely since I
retired. I love to be where the people are." The Peppers
quickly fixed a room for her across from the principal's
office, and it became the center of activities for the rest of
the day.

That night when the Commissioners came to the
college for dinner, Evangeline sat at the head of the table
and guided the conversation, enjoying every minute of it.
After dinner the Commissioners went across the grounds
to the Peppers' home to listen to records of Evangeline's
messages. She asked Pepper, "Will you go over and listen
to them?"

When he came back, he told her, "General, your
voice came over wonderfully well."

"I'll believe that," Evangeline exclaimed. "Those fellows will come back and tell me that they sound good, but
I want to know if the records aren't good."[12]

The month after she returned from Kansas City,

Evangeline celebrated her eightieth birthday. In an interview for the *New York Times Magazine*, the reporter asked her, "What has been the controlling force in your life?" She replied, "I have one passion. It has eaten at my brain and at my heart. It has sapped all my physical resources. It has absorbed all thought, all plans, all desires. It has risen above blunders, lightened all troubles. It has held me back from a thousand errors and unctionized a thousand achievements. This controlling force has been a passion for God and goodness."[13]

Evangeline's interest in world affairs never diminished. When Winston Churchill visited New York in the forties, after he had been rejected as Prime Minister by the British people, she called upon him at the Waldorf Astoria and told him, "I feel that I am not in God's favor as once I was." He looked askance at her and she added, "Well, He's not answering my prayers or else you would have been Prime Minister."[14]

When receiving personal recognition of honors, Evangeline always realized that these came to her because, to the public, she *was* The Salvation Army. Accepting the 1945 Humanitarian Award of the Variety Clubs of America "in recognition of a noble life lived for others," Evangeline made an eloquent ten-minute speech on postwar human needs, especially among children, as seen by The Salvation Army.

Gradually, although reluctantly, Evangeline accepted her role as retired General, realizing that she could trust her beloved Army to the guidance of others whose lives were also dedicated to God's service through the organization's multifaceted programs. She concentrated more than ever on prayer, music composition, sermon preparation, and making opportunities to help people by letters and unheralded acts of kindness.

She was delighted when Captain Richard Holz (later

to become a Commissioner) told her in 1946 that one of his first postwar projects would be a musicians' homecoming rally at the New York Temple and that her music would be featured throughout the program, along with a march of Erik Leidzen's composition titled "ECB," Evangeline's initials. Because of her association with and love for music, Holz asked her to bring an inspirational address to this occasion. She looked forward to doing so, but shortly before the night of the festival she became seriously ill, and it was soon evident that she would not be able to attend. When Holz suggested that he bring a recorder to Acadia and record her message, she gladly assented.[15]

Tape recorders had not yet been perfected, but on a specified day Captain Holz, with his assistant, Alfred Swenarton, and Brigadier William Maltby, took the recorder to Acadia. Swenarton did not wear his Salvation Army uniform but, as the engineer, dressed in civilian clothes. Swenarton recalled:

"I sat before the machine with big padded earphones on and lights flashing red and green to record the General's message. Although still far from well, she was intrigued by the recorder. Several times her voice faltered or cracked. As soon as it did, she refused to proceed. Even a well person might find it difficult to speak seven or eight minutes without a catch or waver, but the General insisted that it had to be perfect.

"After we did it five or six times, both Maltby and Holz were getting edgy and worried that it might get worse. They tried to encourage her with 'That's fine, General.' She would say, 'Stop it. You know that isn't fine; you know that isn't excellent; you know that isn't as good as I can do. We'll do it again. What does Mr. Engineer say?' I said, 'We'll try it again, General.' And finally we finished a good recording."[16]

Until her eighty-first birthday, Evangeline was a familiar figure to neighbors as she rode her spirited horse, Goldenheart. Seated astride and as erect as a cavalry officer in her black coat, derby, jodhpurs, and well-shined boots, she cantered on nearby bridle paths. Colonel Richard Stretton once asked Commissioner Pugmire, "Don't you think we should persuade her to give up riding Golden? The last time she rode, the horse went down on its front legs. The General was thrown and could have been badly hurt." But no one could stop her from riding until Golden died during Christmas week 1946. Then she wrote her niece, Colonel Muriel Booth-Tucker, "My dear horse died but she was old and this, of course, to be expected although, like myself, she maintained her youthful spirit and good heart to the last."[17]

Notwithstanding her strong spirit and heart, Evangeline was growing weaker physically. One of her last public appearances was at the kickoff dinner meeting for a Salvation Army capital campaign at Syracuse, New York. Commissioner William Chamberlain, at that time the divisional commander, recalled how she "mesmerized seven hundred prominent citizens that night—not just with her personality, but she had a great story and a unique way of telling it."[18]

Every year that she could be there, Colonel Stretton invited Evangeline to be the speaker at the New England officers' retreat, held at the Army's camp at Sharon, Massachusetts. Mrs. Stretton recollected:

"She inspired the officers with her messages. Young officers who were discouraged and contemplating resigning would get up and say they no longer felt that way since listening to General Evangeline. She did her last meeting at Sharon when she was eighty-two. Evangeline walked into the building straight as a ramrod, with her cape thrown over her shoulder. That cape was a part of her and she was always perfectly groomed. No one could move a group of officers like Evangeline."[19]

Increasingly, Evangeline was confined to bed with long bouts of pain and nausea. Her staff, themselves all elderly women, hovered around her protectively, making it difficult for those who loved her to call, unless they were longtime personal friends. Even old friends sometimes found it difficult to get inside Acadia.

During one of her confinements to bed, Evangeline phoned Mrs. Commissioner John McMillan and asked her to come for a visit. Mrs. McMillan came on the next plane. Brigadier Farrington met her at the door and said, "The General is too sick to see anyone."

"I've come a long way. "Won't you give me a cup of tea?"

Evangeline heard their voices, came to the top of the stairs, and with outstretched arms welcomed her friend.[20]

As she suffered progressively severe pain, Evangeline sometimes phoned Commissioner Pugmire. One night he said, "General, will you go to the hospital and have X-rays to find out what is causing all this pain?" It wasn't easy to persuade her, but finally she went.[21] Major Arthur Woodruff drove her to the hospital, and after the X-rays and tests were over, she asked Woodruff to come and take her back to Acadia.[22]

When Commissioner Pugmire asked the doctor, "Is it cancer?" he replied, "You understand the confidence between patient and doctor, but I can tell you that if we live long enough, we all will die of cancer." The X-rays also revealed that Evangeline had an upside-down stomach, which was a revelation to those who knew how much she had suffered after meals for many years.[23]

However, Evangeline refused to succumb to her illness. In the afterglow of her potent, fruitful ministry, she continued to seek ways to make her life count for God. The year before she was promoted to glory, Captain Richard Holz returned to the office Monday morning from doing weekend meetings in New York State and found his phone ringing.

It was Commissioner Donald McMillan. "Where have you been, Holz? I've been trying to get you all night. General Evangeline has had an inspiration about a whole cantata. Get up to Hartsdale right away."

After phoning to say he was on the way, Holz took the train to Hartsdale. He found Evangeline in her dressing gown, walking around wringing her hands. Gypsy and some others were trying to calm her down. "Oh, Holz, if you had only been here. A great Easter cantata was just coming into focus last night. Now, all morning I've been trying to recall it, knowing you were coming up here, and I can hardly think of one thing."

Holz tried to encourage her, suggesting that if she relaxed it might come back. But all she could remember was the beginning of a song, "Mary Magdalene, why weepest thou?"

"It didn't come back," Holz said, "But right to the end she was still trying to do something worthwhile. She never rested on her laurels. Here was a woman unable now to preach or appear in public, suffering from a terminal illness, who still wanted to do something for the Lord."[24]

27
Battle's End

To the last, Evangeline wanted to preach. She told Frank
Guldenschuh (later a colonel), "I preached my first sermon as a child on 'the love of God' and I want to preach
just one more sermon on 'the love of God.' "[1] But she was
never again well enough. Her bold, bright spirit and
tireless body at last had to give in to death. Her adopted
daughter, Pearl Woodruff, and her niece, Mrs. Commissioner Hugh Sladen, were with Evangeline when she was
promoted to glory from her home on July 17, 1950. She
was hailed by newspapers in the United States and
around the world for her leadership, oratory, and administrative ability. Many referred to her as "friend of
the friendless"; others recalled that she had been known
as the "White Angel of the Slums." Close friends smiled
at this reference, remembering that she once said,
"Angels are very beautiful—in their own land, but they
are too good for earth. They fly too high. I try to keep my
feet on the ground."[2]

A reporter for the *British Weekly* wrote, "When I
heard her lecture in Manchester Free Trade Hall, I went
back to my news editor and begged to be allowed the high
privilege of writing her advance 'obit.' A strange compliment, perhaps; but one which newspapermen will understand.

"A decade ago, I claimed for her an eminence unchallenged by any but crowned heads and a few cabinet ministers, but I was wrong. From one standpoint, there is *no* exception. What empress ever inspired in so many millions in so many far-flung lands such heartfelt and spiritual loyalty as Evangeline Booth's sway over commissioner and commander and common Salvationist soldier?

"As I try to see her career in perspective, she seems a spiritual Boadicea and one whose chariots went into all the world."[3]

Her funeral, conducted by the national commander, Commissioner Pugmire, at the Salvation Army's Centennial Memorial Temple in New York City, was the first one attended by all American commissioners. Evangeline, with her love of the dramatic, would have approved of the Order of Service: the preliminary music by the New York Staff Band, the band that had traveled with her so often on evangelistic campaigns; the triumphant opening congregational song, "Sweeping Through the Gates of the New Jerusalem, Washed in the Blood of the Lamb."

Evangeline would also have appreciated the sincere tributes from those who had labored faithfully with her through the years. She would have been glad that her father's song, "O Boundless Salvation," was sung and that her niece, Mrs. Commissioner Sladen, spoke on behalf of the Booth family. She would have rejoiced also to see her nephew, Charles Brandon Booth, then general of the Volunteers of America, sitting with a large delegation of his officers in a section of the temple—evidence of the healed breach between herself and her brother Ballington.[4]

Most of all, she would have been happy to see a large number of poor and unknown people there. The homeless, wayward, and outcast from society to whom she had given her life grieved along with the elite and wealthy. A shabby but neatly dressed woman wiped away her tears and spoke for many when she whispered to a friend, "She truly loved us."[5]

Young Salvationists were there who had gone to General Evangeline for counsel in her retirement years. They thanked God for her influence upon their lives. The General had told one young officer, discouraged by the results of her work, "My dear, it is not so much what you do; what matters is how much you love."[6]

All who loved her could not get inside the temple that day. The great crowd that waited outside could hear the congregation singing Evangeline's song, "The Wounds of Christ Are Open." Some recalled that at other times when that song had been sung, the General had knelt and prayed with them at the penitent-form, helping them to know this Christ who had purchased their salvation.

In a casket draped with the Salvation Army flag, General Evangeline was carried out of the Temple on the shoulders of officers, while the band played her tribute to her father, "Fling Wide the Gates," written shortly after his death in 1912.

Along a prepublished route where thousands stood, the hundred-car cortege traveled with police escort from New York City to Valhalla, New York, the site of Kensico Cemetery. William Chamberlain and Paul Kaiser, accompanied by their wives, were in the last car. (Later, both Chamberlain and Kaiser would become national commander and occupy her former office.)

Unlike many personages of time, General Evangeline Booth left no "last words." However, a friend who was present at the great London gathering which bade her good-bye as she entered retirement, remembered having picked up, from her seat on the platform, an envelope on which the General had scribbled her last words spoken on that occasion:

"For the taper Thou hast always provided to make light my way in darkness, Lord, I thank Thee now.[7]"

Although she was naturally of a resilient and optimistic spirit, her pilgrimage had not always been easy. There had been heavy burdens, devastating griefs, and dark shadows. Yet as she moved on to what proved to be the loneliness of her last days, that light did not fail her until it became the eternal and everlasting light of the heavenly Kingdom.

At the close of the committal service, the poignant sound of "Taps," played by the now Lt. Commissioner William Parkins, echoed in the flower-scented air—the Salvation Army's final salute to General Evangeline Booth.[8]

As they listened, those who loved her could picture Evangeline—shoulders thrown back, head erect, eyes straight ahead, jubilantly marching through the gates of the new Jerusalem.[9]

Notes

1. ALL FLAGS WAVING

Documentation for the description of Evangeline Booth's arrival in New York on September 14, 1934 was obtained from the following sources: *The War Cry* (Central issue), October 29, 1934; New York newspapers, September 15, 1934; Wilson, *General Evangeline Booth*, p. 239; and a personal interview with Brigadier Christine McMillan.

2. GOD'S CHRISTMAS GIFT

1. Ervine, vol. I, p. 285.
2. *The War Cry* (Central issue), September 29, 1934, Clarence W. Hall, pp. 9, 10.
3. Ervine, vol. I, p. 283.
4. Wilson, p. 25, *General Evangeline Booth of The Salvation Army*, Scribners, 1948.

3. A GOODLY HERITAGE

1. Booth-Tucker, vol. I, pp. 292, 293.
2. Begbie, vol. I, p. 31.
3. Ibid., pp. 17, 28.
4. Ibid., pp. 40, 41.
5. Collier, p. 210; Wilson, p. 8.
6. Begbie, vol. I, p. 71.
7. Booth-Tucker, vol. I, p. 15.
8. Ibid., pp. 31, 32, 44, 45.
9. Begbie, vol. I, p. 114.
10. Begbie, vol. I, p. 236; Booth-Tucker, vol. I, pp. 82, 83.
11. Personal interview, Brigadier Christine McMillan.
12. Booth-Tucker, vol. I, pp. 98, 99.

13. Ibid., p. 111.
14. Ibid., pp. 189, 190.
15. Ervine, vol. I, p. 234.
16. Ibid., pp. 235-53; Begbie, vol. I, pp. 286-91; Collier, pp. 42, 43.
17. Watson, *The Artillery of Words*, p. 5.
18. Collier, p. 49; Wilson, p. 24.
19. Booth-Tucker, vol. I, p. 299.
20. Ibid., p. 302.

4. HALLELUJAHS AND AMENS

1. Catherine Bramwell-Booth, p. 319.
2. Ervine, vol. I, p. 269.
3. Ibid., p. 271.
4. Bramwell-Booth, p. 320.
5. Newspaper report, *New York World*, March 30, 1896.
6. Richard Collier, p. 57.
7. Ibid.
8. Letter from Mrs. Gayfer, who lived in villa of similar structure as one in which the Booths lived.
9. Booth—Tucker, vol. I, p. 305.
10. Ervine, vol. I, p. 299.
11. Begbie, vol. I, p. 317.
12. Watson, *Soldier Saint*, pp. 25, 76.
13. Begbie, vol. I, p. 317.
14. Ibid., p. 320.
15. Ibid., p. 323.
16. Ibid., p. 328.
17. Ibid., p. 329.
18. Wilson, p. 30.
19. Ibid., pp. 44, 45; personal interview, Commissioner Gosta Blomberg.
20. Begbie, vol. I, p. 321.
21. Wilson, p. 34.
22. Personal interview, Lt. Commander William J. Parkins.
23. Personal interview, Commissioner Gosta Blomberg.
24. *The War Cry*, April 9, 1938.
25. Collier, p. 56.
26. Personal interview, Commissioner Gosta Blomberg.
27. Wilson, p. 113.
28. Personal interview, Mrs. Colonel Hazel Stretton.
29. Wilson, p. 43.
30. Ibid.
31. *The Young Soldier* (British), December 22, 1934.
32. Wilson, p. 50.
33. Ibid.

5. GROWING PAINS

1. Ervine, vol. I, pp. 398, 399.
2. Richard Collier, p. 64.
3. Begbie, vol. I, pp. 404, 405.
4. Sandall, *History of The Salvation Army*, vol. I, p. 230.
5. Coutts, *No Discharge in This War*, p. 43.
6. Ibid., p. 39.
7. Wilson, p. 53.
8. Personal interview, Lt. Commissioner William J. Parkins.
9. Wilson, p. 42.
10. Sandall, vol. II, p. 67, 68.
11. Wilson, p. 113.
12. Watson, *Soldier Saint*, p. 45.
13. Wisbey, pp. 1, 2.
14. Watson, p. 64.
15. Article by Field Commissioner Eva Booth, "How to Sell the War Cry," in *The War Cry* (Canadian), October 1897, p. 7.
16. Wilson, p. 59.
17. Ibid., p. 60.
18. Article in *All the World* by Mahlah (Mother of Lt. Colonel M. Unsworth) titled "Staff Captain Eva Booth," December 1887.
19. Sandall, vol. II. pp. 97, 98; Commissioner A. G. Gilliard, tape of lecture to Chicago Cadets; personal interview, General Frederick Coutts.
20. Evangeline Booth's lecture "In Rags."
21. Sandall, vol. II, p. 98.
22. "Diary of a Slum Sister" in *The War Cry*, March 26, 1887.
23. Richard Collier, p. 186.
24. "Diary of a Slum Sister" in *The War Cry*, June 25, 1887.

6. ANGEL OF THE SLUMS

1. Catherine Bramwell-Booth, p. 395.
2. Wilson, pp. 62, 63.
3. Lecture, "Rags."
4. Ibid.
5. Ibid.
6. Wilson, p. 63.
7. Ibid., p. 64.
8. British *War Cry*, November 15, 1948, article by Commissioner Arch Wiggins.
9. Lecture, "Rags," *All the World,* December 1887.
10. Wilson, p. 75.
11. Ibid., p. 67.
12. Ibid.

13. *The War Cry*, February 26, 1887.
14. Ibid.
15. Wilson, p. 74.
16. Ibid., p. 75.
17. *The War Cry*, August 12, 1926.
18. *All the World*, December 1887, p. 392.
19. Personal interview, Lt. Colonel Arthur Woodruff.

7. SEND EVA

1. Begbie, vol. II, p. 443.
2. Coutts, *No Discharge in This War*, pp. 90, 91.
3. Wilson, p. 60.
4. Ibid., p. 61.
5. *Gipsy Smith, His Life and Work*, pp. 131-40.
6. Ibid., pp. 141-43.
7. Wilson, p. 62.
8. Mrs. General Frederick Coutts, personal interview.
9. Wilson, pp. 88, 89.
10. Ibid., p. 91.
11. Ibid.
12. Ibid., p. 93.
13. Ibid.
14. Ibid., p. 98.
15. Ibid., p. 102.
16. Personal interview, Mrs. General Frederick Coutts.
17. Wilson, pp. 103, 104.

8. DOUBLE DUTY

1. Booth-Tucker, vol. II, p. 319.
2. Ibid., p. 328.
3. Wilson, p. 110.
4. Personal interview, Colonel Frank Guldenschuh.
5. Wilson, p. 110.
6. Booth-Tucker, vol. II, p. 370.
7. Ibid., pp. 399-405; Wilson, p. 111.
8. Booth-Tucker, vol. II, pp. 406-13.
9. Article by Colonel Edward Joy in *The Officers' Review*, October 1942, p. 234.
10. Personal interview, Mrs. Commissioner Owen Culshaw.
11. Coutts, *No Discharge in This War*, p. 93.
12. *The Officers' Review*, February 1935, p. 34.
13. Personal interview with Lt. Colonel Miriam Richards, whose mother was a cadet under Eva Booth in 1894.

14. Personal interview, Lt. Colonel Miriam Richards; personal interview with Lt. Colonel Margery Joy, whose father was a cadet under Eva Booth.
15. *The War Cry*, October 15, 1927.
16. Book of Evangeline Booth's lectures to cadets.
17. Ibid.
18. Personal interview with Mrs. Lt. Colonel William (Alleyne) Devoto, whose mother was a cadet at the International Training College.
19. Personal interview, Colonel Emil Nelson.
20. Personal interview, Mrs. Commissioner Robert Hoggard.
21. *The Musician*, December 25, 1965, p. 864.
22. *The War Cry*, October 31, 1936, p. 6.
23. Personal interview, Lt. Colonel Ernest Parr.
24. Personal interview, Lt. Colonel Kenneth Rawlins.
25. Personal interview, Lt. Colonel Helen Purviance.

9. LOVE STORY

1. Ervine, vol. I, p. 548.
2. Sandall, vol. II, pp. 216, 217; Begbie, vol. II, p. 11.
3. Sandall, vol. II, pp. 217-20.
4. Ervine, vol. I, p. 550.
5. Wilson, p. 47; Lavine, p. 27.
6. *The War Cry*, November 3, 1886.
7. Personal interview, Colonel Ralph Miller.
8. Ibid.
9. Personal interview, Colonel Muriel Booth-Tucker.
10. Personal interview, Colonel Ralph Miller.
11. Wilson, pp. 47, 48.
12. Personal interview, Commissioner Gosta Blomberg.

10. CRISIS IN THE U.S.A.

1. Nicol, pp. 236-37.
2. Letter from Ballington and Maud Booth, January 31, 1896.
3. Letter from Bramwell Booth, February 15, 1896.
4. Wilson, p. 116.
5. Wisbey, p. 107.
6. Ibid., p. 109.
7. Ibid., p. 110.
8. Nicol, p. 235.
9. Letter to ECB from Herbert Booth, February 25, 1896.
10. Wisbey, p. 107.
11. Wilson, p. 116.
12. Wilson, p. 117; Nicol, pp. 242, 243.

13. Nicol, p. 244.
14. Wilson, p. 117.
15. Nicol, pp. 245-47.
16. Ibid., pp. 247-48.
17. Wilson, p. 117.
18. Nicol, p. 248.
19. *New York World*, March 2, 1896.
20. Ibid.
21. Wilson, p. 117.
22. *The War Cry*, June 13, 1896.
23. Nicol, p. 241.

11. MUSTERED TO CANADA

1. Wilson, p. 120.
2. Ervine, vol. II, pp. 754-55.
3. *The War Cry* (Canadian), July 4, 1896; (British), June 1896.
4. Herbert Booth's brief on Canada.
5. Ibid.
6. Ibid.
7. Ibid.
8. Brown, pp. 89-92.
9. Personal Interview with Dr. R. G. Moyles.
10. Ibid.
11. Ibid.
12. Ibid.
13. Ibid., p. 3.
14. Ibid., p. 6.
15. Wilson, p. 122.
16. Personal interview, Alex MacMillan.
17. Ibid.
18. *The War Cry* (Canadian), January 16, 1897.
19. Personal interview, General Arnold Brown
20. *Toronto Evening Star*, January 16, 1897, p. 2.
21. *The War Cry* (Canadian), January 30, 1897, p. 7.
22. Personal interview, Joy Miller, daughter of late Colonel Gideon Miller.
23. Personal Interview with Mrs. Major Norman Boyle.
24. *The War Cry* (Canadian), February 27, 1897, front page and two inside pages.
25. Ibid., April 18, 1903.
26. Ibid., July 3, 1897, pp. 7, 8, 9.
27. Ibid., p. 3.
28. Ibid., p. 7.
29. Personal interview, Alex MacMillan.
30. *The War Cry* (Canadian), December 10, 1904, p. 6.

31. *The War Cry* (Canadian), Christmas 1897.
32. Moyles, *Blood and Fire in Canada*, p. 99.

12. THE GAMBLER AND THE LADY

1. Troutt, *Decision* Magazine, July 1965, pp. 10, 12.
2. *The War Cry* (Canadian), July 2, 1898, p. 7.
3. Colonel Chester Taylor's manuscript; *The War Cry* (Canadian), July 2, 1898, p. 3; Moyles, *Blood and Fire in Canada*, p. 102.
4. Troutt, *Decision* Magazine, July 1965, Sources for article: Wilson, *General Evangeline Booth of The Salvation Army*, p. 127; Brown, *What Hath God Wrought?*; Wickersham, James, *Old Yukon*; W. R. Collier and E. V. Westrate, *The Reign of Soapy Smith*. Files of *The War Cry* (Canadian).
5. *The War Cry* (Canadian), December 8, 1898, p. 5.
6. Moyles, *Blood and Fire in Canada*, p. 113.
7. Brown, p. 109.
8. Personal interview, Commissioner Glenn Ryan.
9. Begbie, vol. II, p. 200.
10. Wilson, p. 138.
11. Begbie, vol. II, p. 230.
12. Wilson, p. 138.
13. Ibid., pp. 130-31.
14. Personal interview, Alex MacMillan.
15. Ibid, *Songs of the Evangel*, pp. 26, 27.
16. Brown, p. 113.
17. *The War Cry* (Canadian), December 10, 1904, p. 16.
18. Personal interview, Gordon Moyles.
19. Moyles, pp. 151, 152.
20. Personal interviews, Alex MacMillan and Joy Miller.
21. Personal interview, Commissioner Owen Culshaw.
22. Brown, p. 114.
23. Ervine, vol. II, p. 785.
24. Wilson, p. 141.
25. Begbie, vol. II, p. 284, 285.
26. Brown, p. 114.
27. *The War Cry* (Canadian), October 29, 1904, p. 9.
28. Ibid., p. 16.

13. MARCH ON

1. *The War Cry*, November 17, 1934.
2. *The Story of America*, pp. 342-44.
3. *200 Years—A Bicentennial Illustrating History of the United States*, pp. 104, 105.
4. *The War Cry*, December, 1904.
5. Ibid., January 14, 1905.

6. Records secured from Lt. Colonel E. MacLachlan.
7. Wilson, pp. 147, 148.
8. Ibid., p. 26.
9. Letter from William Booth to Evangeline.
10. Personal interviews.
11. Personal interview, Lt. Commissioner Llewellyn Cowan.
12. Personal interview.
13. Ibid.
14. Wilson, p. 148.
15. *The War Cry*, January 21, 1905.
16. Ibid., January 28, 1905, p. 9.
17. Wisbey, pp. 150, 151.
18. Collier, pp. 216, 217.
19. Bramwell Booth, *These Fifty Years*, pp. 234, 235.
20. Collier, pp. 226, 227; Wisbey, pp. 152, 153.
21. Wilson, pp. 85, 86.
22. *The War Cry*, May, 1906; Wisbey, p. 153.
23. Newspaper report, South Framingham.
24. Letter from Mrs. Brigadier John (Mildred) Fahey.
25. Wisbey, p. 143.
26. Letters between Evangeline and Herbert.
27. Wisbey, p. 144.
28. Begbie, vol. II, p. 356.
29. Wisbey, pp. 144, 145.
30. Personal interviews, Commissioner Richard E. Holz and Commissoner Glenn Ryan.
31. Wilson, p. 149.
32. Ibid., p. 146.
33. Hall, *Out of the Depths*, p. 109.
34. Ibid., p. 110.
35. Ibid., p. 59.
36. Ibid., pp. 101-6.
37. Ibid., pp. 120, 21.
38. Ibid., pp. 124-29.
39. Wisbey, p. 151.
40. Hall, p. 107.
41. Ibid., p. 108.
42. Wilson, p. 164.

14. AT HOME

1. Personal interviews, Lt. Commissioner William J. Parkins and Brigadier Muriel Creighton.
2. Letter from J. Leonard LeViness.
3. Personal interview, Brigadier Muriel Creighton.
4. Ibid.
5. Personal interview, Lt. Colonel Lyell Rader.

6. Personal interview, Lt. Commissioner William J. Parkins.
7. Personal interview, Brigadier Muriel Creighton.
8. *The Young Soldier*, May 6, 1944.
9. Personal interview, Lt. Commissioner William J. Parkins.
10. Personal interview, Colonel T. Raymond Gabrielsen.
11. Personal interview, Brigadier Muriel Creighton.
12. Ibid.
13. Personal interviews, Mrs. Colonel Marian Evans and Colonel Charles Bearchell.
14. Personal interview, Lt. Colonel George Russell.
15. Ibid.
16. Personal interview, Lt. Commissioner William J. Parkins.
17. Personal interview, Brigadier Muriel Creighton.
18. Personal interview, Mrs. Colonel Marian Evans.
19. Personal interviews; Wilson, p. 162.
20. Personal interview, Colonel Bertram Rodda.
21. Personal interview, Lt. Commissioner William J. Parkins.
22. Personal interviews, Mrs. Colonel Marian Evans and Mrs. Lt. Colonel John (Elspeth) Busby.
23. Personal interview, Commissioner H. French.
24. Personal interview, Brigadier Christine McMillan.
25. Personal interview and letters.
26. Personal interview, Brigadier Ernest Newton.

15. A NEW ERA

1. Begbie, vol. II, pp. 375-77.
2. Ibid., pp. 394-97.
3. Ibid., p. 410.
4. Ibid., p. 415.
5. Personal interview, Commissioner Gosta Blomberg.
6. Begbie, vol. II, p. 432.
7. Ibid., p. 420.
8. Ibid., p. 422.
9. Ibid., p. 423.
10. Ibid., p. 431.
11. Ibid., p. 429.
12. Wiggins, vol. V, p. 238. Begbie, vol. II, p. 431.
13. Ervine, vol. II, p. 815.
14. Wiggins, p. 244.
15. Wilson, pp. 168-69.
16. Personal interview, Mrs. Commissioner Glenn Ryan.
17. Wisbey, p. 154.
18. (International) *War Cry*, July 4, 1914.
19. Ibid.

20. Wilson, p. 171.
21. Wisbey, p. 155.
22. Personal interview, Colonel William Ware.

16. DOUGHBOYS AND DOUGHNUTS

1. Personal interview, Mrs. Lt. Colonel William (Alleyne) Devoto.
2. Wisbey, p. 156.
3. Ibid., pp. 158, 159.
4. *War Service Report of The Salvation Army 1917-19*, p. 1.
5. Ibid.
6. Personal interview, Mrs. Brigadier Keitha Holz.
7. Booth and Hill, *The War Romance of The Salvation Army*; Wilson, p. 177.
8. Personal interview, Commissioner Paul S. Kaiser—quote of Evangeline Booth from talk given to officers.
9. Hill, pp. 45-47.
10. Ibid., pp. 48-50.
11. Ibid., p. 52.
12. Wisbey, p. 161; Hill, p. 82.
13. Wisbey, p. 161.
14. Wilson, p. 174.
15. Wisbey, p. 162.
16. *The War Cry*, August 25, 1917, p. 9.
17. Personal interview, Lt. Colonel Helen Purviance.
18. Personal interview, Colonel Florence Turkington.
19. Hill, p. 55.
20. Ibid., p. 51.
21. Personal interview, Lt. Colonel Helen Purviance.
22. Ibid.
23. Personal interviews, Colonel T. Raymond Gabrielsen, Lt. Colonel H. Purviance
24. Hill, p. 257.
25. Ibid., pp. 178-85.
26. *The War Cry*, March 9, 1918, p. 16; March 16, 1918, p. 13.
27. Personal interview with officer who survived the fire.
28. *The War Cry*, March 16, 1918, p. 9.
29. Wisbey, p. 167.
30. Agnew, pp. 4, 5.
31. Ibid.
32. Personal interview, Lt. Colonel Helen Purviance.
33. Ibid.
34. Hill, pp. 260, 261.
    War Service Herald, September, 1919.
    Gangplank News, June 25, 1919, p. 69.

35. Wilson, p. 187.
36. Wisbey, p. 169.
37. *War Service Report of The Salvation Army 1917-19*, p. 7.

17. MUSIC MAKER

1. Wilson, p. 37.
2. Ibid.
3. Personal interview, Commissioner Paul S. Kaiser.
4. Wilson, p. 37.
5. *War Cry* article, Lt. Colonel Cyril Barnes: Series on "Words of Catherine Booth."
6. Booth, *Songs of the Evangel*, p. 43.
7. Ibid., p. 39.
8. Personal interview, Mrs. Colonel Hazel Stretton.
9. *Songs of the Evangel*, p. 27.
10. Ibid., p. 7.
11. Personal interview, Commissioner Richard E. Holz.
12. Personal interview, Commissioner Gosta Blomberg.
13. *Songs of the Evangel*, p. 8.
14. Personal interview, Commissioner Gosta Blomberg.
15. Ibid.
16. Personal interviews, Commissioner Gosta Blomberg and Brigadier Muriel Creighton.
17. Wilson, p. 135.
18. Personal interview, Brigadier Muriel Creighton.
19. Ibid.
20. *The Musician*, July 11, 1936.
21. Personal interview, Commissioner Gosta Blomberg.
22. Personal interview, Lt. Colonel Lyell Rader.
23. Personal interview, Colonel Douglas E. Norris.
24. Personal interview, Bandsman Russell Crowell.
25. Personal interview, Colonel William Slater.
26. Personal interview, Colonel Emil Nelson.
27. Personal interview, Colonel William Maltby.
28. Personal interview, Lt. Colonel William E. Bearchell.
29. Personal interview, Brigadier Muriel Creighton.
30. Letter to Captain Ernest Newton, June 9, 1932.
31. Personal interview, Lt. Commissioner William J. Parkins.
32. Notes on Miss Eva, from S/Major Mrs. Rae McMahon.
33. *The War Cry*, April 16, 1977, pp. 12, 13.
34. Ibid.
35. Personal interviews, Lt. Commissioner William J. Parkins and Lt. Colonel William E. Bearchell.
36. Personal interview, Lt. Commissioner William J. Parkins.
37. Ibid.

38. Fossey, *This Man Leidzen.*
39. Ibid., p. 72.
40. Personal interview, Colonel Douglas E. Norris.
41. Personal interview, Colonel William Maltby.
42. Ibid.
43. *The Musician,* July 29, 1950, p. 236.
44. *The War Cry,* July 4, 1946, p. 8.
45. Personal interview, Brigadier Bramwell Darbyshire.
46. *The Musician,* December 25, 1965, p. 864.
47. Ibid., October 28, 1939, p. 674.

18. THE WORLD'S GREATEST ROMANCE

1. *Toronto Daily Mail and Empire,* November 22, 1897.
2. Lavine, p. 56.
3. Lecture, "In Rags."
4. *The Officer,* article by Commissioner Edward J. Parker, November-December 1950, p. 353.
5. Mrs. Brigadier John (Mildred) Fahey, Commissioner Parker's daughter. Pottsville newspaper, March 10, 1931.
6. Personal interview, Colonel William Maltby.
7. Personal interview, Colonel Tom Gabrielsen.
8. Personal interview, Lt. Colonel Lyell Rader.
9. Personal interview, Lt. Colonel Helen Purviance.
10. Personal interview, Mrs. Colonel Hazel Stretton.
11. Personal interview, Colonel Emil Nelson.
12. Personal interview, Colonel Charles Bearchell.
13. Personal interview, Colonel Emil Nelson.
14. Personal interview, Colonel Albert Pepper.
15. Personal interview, Mrs. Brigadier Keitha Holz.
16. Personal interview, Mrs. Commissioner Paul S. Kaiser.
17. Personal interview, Lt. Commissioner William J. Parkins.
18. Personal interview, Commissioner Richard E. Holz, Jr.
19. Personal interview, Lt. Commissioner William J. Parkins.
20. Personal interview, Commissioner Paul S. Kaiser.
21. Personal interview, Commissioner Claude E. Bates.
22. Personal interviews, Commissioner Glenn Ryan; Colonel Albert Pepper; Colonel Douglas E. Norris.
23. Personal interview, Colonel William Maltby.
24. Ibid.
25. Personal interview, Commissioner Catherine Bramwell Booth.
26. Personal interviews, Bandmaster Alfred Swenerton; Brigadier Earl Lord; Commissioner Richard E. Holz; Lt. Colonel William E. Bearchell.

19. FULL STEAM AHEAD

1. Wilson, p. 186.
2. Wisbey, p. 170.
3. *New York American* February 23, 1919.
4. *War Service Herald*, April 1919.
5. Wilson, p. 186.
6. Personal interview, Lt. Commissioner Llewellyn Cowan.
7. Wilson, p. 186.
8. *The War Cry*, June 12, 1919, p. 9.
9. Ibid., October 25, 1919, p. 8.
10. Personal interview, Lt. Colonel Arthur Woodruff.
11. Wisbey, p. 172.
12. Salvation Army Year Book, 1921.
13. "Shall America Go Back?" paper read at WCTU Convention in Philadelphia 1922.
14. Ibid.
15. *The American*, New Jersey edition, April 22, 1922.
16. Message to the Senate Judiciary Committee, 1926.
17. *The American*, New Jersey edition, April 22, 1922.
18. Personal interview, Lt. Commissioner Llewellyn Cowan.
19. Wilson, p. 165.
20. Ibid., p. 160.
21. Miller manuscript.
22. Chesham, pp. 128, 175.
23. Personal interview, Lt. Colonel Fritz Nelson.
24. *War Cry*, February 1 and 23, 1924; March 1, 8, 15, 1924.
25. Personal interview, Mrs. Lt. Colonel John (Elspeth) Busby.
26. Personal interview, Colonel Ray Gabrielsen; Lt. Colonel William E. Bearchell.
27. *The War Cry*, October 1926.
28. Personal interview, Colonel Ray Gabrielsen.
29. Jacket of book *On We March* by Mrs. Colonel Lillian Noble.
30. *The War Cry*, March 19, 1927.
31. Personal interview, Mrs. Colonel Lillian Noble.
32. *The Officer*, November-December 1950, p. 356.
33. Letter and recollections of ECB from Lt. Colonel Edward Laity.
34. *San Francisco Examiner*, December 12, 1929.
35. Personal interview, Mrs. Commissioner Ernest I. Pugmire.
36. Wilson, p. 236.
37. Personal interview, Mrs. Commissioner Ernest I. Pugmire.
38. *The War Cry*, January 4, 1930.
39. Ibid.
40. Personal interview, Mrs. Commissioner Ernest I. Pugmire.
41. *San Francisco Examiner*, December 12, 1929.

20. STORMY WEATHER

1. Personal interviews.
2. Wilson, pp. 194, 195.
3. Ibid., pp. 196, 197.
4. 1916 *Year Book*, p. 13.
5. Wilson, p. 200; Wisbey, p. 179.
6. Wilson, p. 200.
7. Wisbey, p. 181.
8. Wilson, p. 202.
9. Wisbey, p. 181.
10. Wilson, pp. 202, 203.
11. Personal interview, Lt. Colonel Fritz Nelson.
12. Personal interviews.
13. Ervine, vol. II, p. 895.
14. *The War Cry*, October 15, 1927.
15. Ervine, vol. II, p. 902.
16. Personal interview, Colonel Tom Gabrielsen.
17. Personal interviews, Colonel Tom Gabrielsen and Lt. Colonel Fritz Nelson.
18. *The War Cry*, October 15, 1927.
19. ECB's Notes for Interview with the General, October 11, 1927.
20. Memorandum to ECB from Bramwell, November 24, 1927.
21. Ibid.
22. Wilson, p. 207.
23. Ibid.
24. Catherine Bramwell-Booth, *Bramwell Booth,* p. 500; Ervine, vol. II, pp. 923, 924.
25. Catherine Bramwell-Booth, p. 501; Ervine, vol. II, p. 926.
26. Catherine Bramwell-Booth, p. 503; Ervine, vol. II, p. 930.
27. Catherine Bramwell-Booth, p. 309, 510; Ervine, vol. II, pp. 934-36.
28. Coutts, *The Better Fight*, p. 81.
29. Catherine Bramwell-Booth, p. 518.
30. Coutts, p. 83.
31. Ibid., p. 84.
32. Catherine Bramwell-Booth, pp. 520-21; Wilson, p. 211.
33. Commissioner Brengle's letter, January 14, 1929.
34. *The War Cry*, February 2, 1929.
35. Wilson, p. 216.
36. Coutts. *The Better Fight*, p. 91.
37. Letter from ECB to Walter F. Jenkins, February 3, 1929.
38. *London Daily Mirror*, February 19, 1929.

21. THE GREAT DEPRESSION

1. *John Markle, Representative American*; *The War Cry*, November 3, 1928.
2. St. Johns, p. 238.
3. Personal interview, Colonel Bertram Rodda.
4. *New York Times*, November 27, 1930.
5. Personal interview, Lt. Commissioner Llewellyn Cowan.
6. McCollum and Pearson, p. 211.
7. Personal interview, Lt. Commissioner Llewellyn Cowan.
8. Personal interviews, Lt. Commissioner Llewellyn Cowan and Mrs. Colonel Hazel Stretton.
9. *The War Cry*, December 13, 1930.
10. Letter from Betty Gedney, General Foods Corporation, March 6, 1978.
11. *The War Cry* and personal interviews.
12. Personal interview, Lt. Commissioner Llewellyn Cowan.
13. Chesham, p. 206.
14. From interview of William S. Hedges with John F. Royal, August 24, 1964.
15. Personal interview, Lt. Commissioner Llewellyn Cowan.
16. Interview of William S. Hedges with John F. Royal, August 24, 1964.
17. Personal interview, Lt. Commissioner Llewellyn Cowan.
18. Letter from Adela Rogers St. Johns, April 21, 1978.
19. St. Johns, *The Honeycomb*, p. 254.
20. Wisbey, p. 190.
21. *The Story of America*, p. 289.
22. *The War Cry*, August 5, 1933.

22. OUT OF THE CLOUD

1. *The War Cry*, June 7, 1930.
2. Brindley Boon, "Play the Music, Play."
3. Personal interview, Colonel Douglas E. Norris.
4. *The War Cry*, June 7, 1930.
5. *The War Cry*, June 28, 1930.
6. Coutts, *The Better Fight*, p. 95.
7. Ibid., p. 98.
8. General Higgins's letter, August 24, 1930.
9. Personal interview, Lt. Colonel George Russell.
10. *New York Times*, November 28, 1930.
11. Ibid., November 20, 1930.
12. Coutts, *The Better Fight*, p. 101.
13. Personal interview, Colonel Brindley Boon.
14. *New York Times*, November 28, 1930.

15. Wilson, p. 225.
16. Personal interviews, Lt. Commissioner William J. Parkins and Colonel Emil Nelson.
17. *The War Cry*, October 24, 1931.
18. Evangeline Booth's Christmas letter, 1931.
19. Personal interview, Colonel Tom Gabrielsen.
20. *The War Cry*, July 9, 1932.
21. *Chicago Tribune*, June 27, 1932.
22. *The War Cry*, September 3, 1932.
23. *The War Cry*, July 8, 1933.
24. Personal interview, Commissioner J. Clyde Cox.
25. *The War Cry*, September 8, 1934.
26. Personal interview, Brigadier Christine McMillan.
27. Coutts, *The Better Fight*, p. 127.

23. GENERAL EVANGELINE

1. *London News Chronicle*, September 4, 1934.
2. *London Daily Herald*, September 4, 1934.
3. *London News Chronicle*, September 4, 1934.
4. *New York Times*, September 4, 1934.
5. 1965 *Year Book*, p. 34.
6. Personal interview, Brigadier Christine McMillan.
7. Personal interview, Lt. Commissioner William J. Parkins.
8. Personal interview, Lt. Colonel Charles Overstake.
9. *The Officers' Review*, February 1935, p. 37.
10. Personal interview, Mrs. Colonel Charles Bearchell.
11. Personal interview, Mrs. S/Major Lawrence Hall.
12. Personal interview, Commissioner and Mrs. Paul S. Kaiser.
13. Personal interview, Mrs. Colonel Bertram Rodda.
14. Personal interview, Lt. Colonel George Russell.
15. Personal interview, Lt. Colonel Gus Blair Abrams.
16. Personal interview, Mrs. Colonel William (Lillian) Noble.
17. Personal interview, Clarence Hall.
18. Personal interview, Lt. Colonel Arthur Woodruff.
19. Personal interview, Mrs. Commissioner Ernest I. Pugmire.
20. Personal interview, Lt. Colonel R. Eugene Rice.
21. Edwin C. Hill, 1934 King Features Syndicate, Inc.
22. *The War Cry*, November 17, 1934.
23. *New York Times*, November 2, 1934.

24. THE WORLD FOR GOD

1. Personal interview, Commissioner Owen Culshaw.
2. *The War Cry* (International), December 8, 1934.
3. Personal interviews with officers.

4. Personal interview, Colonel Brindley Boon.
5. *The War Cry* (International), December 8, 1934.
6. Personal interviews with officers.
7. Personal interview, Commissioner Gosta Blomberg.
8. Personal interview, Colonel Catherine Baird.
9. *The War Cry*, January 5, 1935.
10. Personal interview, Colonel Brindley Boon.
11. Personal interview, Colonel Muriel Booth-Tucker.
12. *The War Cry*, March 30, 1934.
13. Ibid., June 22, 1935.
14. Ibid., June 29, 1935.
15. Coutts, *The Better Fight*, p. 134.
16. Lecture to cadets by Commissioner A. J. Gilliard.
17. Personal interview, General Frederick Coutts.
18. Ibid.
19. Phone interview, Commissioner Harold Orton.
20. Personal interview, General Arnold Brown.
21. *The War Cry* (Canadian), October 19, 1935.
22. Personal interview, General Clarence Wiseman.
23. Coutts, *The Better Fight*, pp. 135, 137.
24. *The War Cry*, July 11, 1936.
25. Personal interview, Colonel William Henry Charles.
26. Personal interview, Colonel Brindley Boon.
27. *The War Cry*, August 8, 1936.
28. Personal interview, Colonel Catherine Baird.
29. *Young Soldier*, August 8, 1936.
30. Coutts, *The Better Fight*, p. 140.
31. Letter from Colonel T. Herbert Martin, June 16, 1978.

25. GRUELING SCHEDULES

1. Commissioner A. R. Blowers, report on tour.
2. Personal interview, Colonel Muriel Booth-Tucker.
3. Commissioner Blower's report.
4. Personal interview, Commissioner Gosta Blomberg.
5. Personal interview, Colonel (Dr.) William Noble.
6. Ibid.
7. *The War Cry* (International), February 20, 1937.
8. Commissioner Blower's report.
9. Ibid.
10. *The Young Soldier*, October 21, 1939.
11. Coutts, *The Better Fight*, p. 141.
12. Ibid., pp. 138, 139.
13. Personal interview, Colonel Catherine Baird.
14. Coutts, *The Better Fight*, p. 146.
15. *The War Cry*, October 2, 1937, and January 22, 1938.

16. Ibid., September 11, 1937.
17. *War Cry* (Southern U.S. Edition), September 18, 1937.
18. Personal interview, Commissioner Glenn Ryan, and letter from Brigadier Ivy Waterworth.
19. *Atlanta Georgian*, October 4, 1937.
20. *The War Cry* (International), March 26, 1938.
21. Ibid., February 19, 1938.
22. Phone interview, Lt. Colonel Ray Steadman-Allen.
23. *The War Cry* (International), February 26, 1938.
24. Ibid., September 24, 1938.
25. Personal interviews, Commissioner Geoffrey Dalziel and Lt Colonel Frank Allum.
26. Personal interviews with officers.
27. *London Times*, November 11, 1938.
28. Letter from Mrs. Lt. Colonel Bramwell Sylvester (née Lily Bullard).
29. Personal interview, Commissioner Gosta Blomberg.
30. Letter to Commissioner John McMillan, December 22, 1938.
31. Letter from ECB to Commissioner John McMillan, May 29, 1939.
32. Personal interview, Commissioner Gosta Blomberg.
33. Personal interview, Commissioner Gosta Blomberg, and letter from ECB July 17, 1939, to Commissioner William Arnold.
34. *London Times*, July 28, 1939.
35. Ibid., October 28, 1939.
36. Coutts, The Better Fight, pp. 155-58.
37. Personal interview, Lt. Commissioner Herbert S. Hodgson.
38. Letter from Commissioner Edgar Grinsted, April 19, 1977.
39. *The War Cry*, September 9, 1939, and October 14, 1939.
40. Letter from ECB to Alex MacMillan, September 28, 1939.
41. Letter from Mrs. Lt. Colonel Bramwell (Lily) Sylvester, November 4, 1977.
42. *The War Cry*, October 21, 1939, p. 7.
43. Ibid., October 28, 1939, p. 9.
44. Ibid., November 4, 1939, p. 7.
45. Personal interview, Commissioner Owen Culshaw.
46. Wilson, p. 248.
47. Personal interviews, Lt. Commissioner Herbert S. Hodgson and Commissioner Gosta Blomberg.
48. Personal interview, Commissioner Gosta Blomberg.

26. AFTERGLOW

1. Personal interviews.
2. Personal interview, Commissioner Gosta Blomberg.
3. 1942 *Year Book*.
4. Letter from Lt. Colonel Mina Russell, June 29, 1977.

5. Personal interview, Commissioner Gosta Blomberg.
6. Personal interview, Lt. Commissioner William J. Parkins.
7. Personal interview, Commissioner Gosta Blomberg.
8. *The War Cry*, December 8, 1945.
9. Personal interview, Colonel Albert Pepper.
10. Personal interview, Brigadier Cecil Briggs.
11. Personal interview, Commissioner Glenn Ryan.
12. Personal interview, Colonel Albert Pepper.
13. *New York Times Magazine*, December 23, 1945.
14. Personal interview, Lt. Commissioner William J. Parkins.
15. Personal interview, Commissioner Richard E. Holz.
16. Personal interview, Bandmaster Alfred Swenarton.
17. Letter to Colonel Muriel Booth-Tucker, 1947.
18. Personal interview, Commissioner William Chamberlain.
19. Personal interview, Mrs. Colonel Hazel Stretton.
20. Personal interview, Brigadier Christine McMillan.
21. Personal interview, Mrs. Commissioner Ernest I. Pugmire.
22. Personal interview, Lt. Colonel Arthur Woodruff.
23. Personal interview, Mrs. Commissioner Ernest I. Pugmire.
24. Personal interview, Commissioner Richard E. Holz.

27. BATTLE'S END

1. Personal interview, Colonel Frank Guldenschuh
2. *The War Cry*, August 12, 1950.
3. *British Weekly*, July 27, 1950.
4. Personal interview, Lt. Commissioner William J. Parkins
5. Personal interviews with officers
6. General Eva by Fred Brown, St. Albans, England: Salvationist Publishing and Supplies.
7. *The War Cry*, July 11, 1964, article by Mrs. Commissioner John McMillan
8. Order of service program, and interviews with officers.
9. Personal interviews with officers.

Bibliography

NEWSPAPERS AND PERIODICALS

All the World
Atlanta Georgian
British Weekly
Chicago Tribune
Des Moines Register &
  Tribune
The Field Officer
Gangplank News
London Daily Herald
London Daily Mirror
London New Chronicle
London Pall Mall Gazette
London Times
The Musician
New York American
New York Recorder
New York Times

New York Times Magazine
New York World
The Officer
The Officers' Review
San Francisco Examiner
Toronto Daily Mail and
  Empire
Toronto Evening Star
Toronto Globe
The War Cry (British,
  Canadian, and
  American Issues)
War Service Herald
Washington Herald
The Year Book
The Young Soldier

PRINTED AND MANUSCRIPT SOURCES

Agnew, Fletcher, *History of The Salvation Army Central Territory Prior to 1920.*

Anderson, Arthur E., *The Life of Evangeline Booth*. Moline, Ill: Strombeck Press, 1951.

Baird, Catherine, *God's Harvester*. London: The Salvation Army, 1948.

Begbie, Harold, *Life of William Booth, Founder of the Salvation Army* (2 vols.). New York: Macmillan, 1920.

Bishop, Edward, *Blood and Fire*. Chicago: Moody Press, 1965.

Blowers, A. R., "Visit of General Evangeline Booth to India, Ceylon, Singapore, and Netherlands Indies" (manuscript). London: 1937.

Booth, Bramwell, *These Fifty Years*. London: Cassell, 1929.

Booth, Catherine, *Female Ministry*. London: The Salvation Army, 1859; reprinted, New York, 1975.

Booth, Evangeline, "Book of Lectures to Cadets" (hand written). 1892—94.

———, *Poems*. New York: The Salvation Army.

———, *Woman*. New York: Revell.

———, *Songs of the Evangel*. New York: The Salvation Army, 1927.

Booth, Evangeline, and Grace Livingston Hill: *The War Romance of The Salvation Army*. Philadelphia: Lippincott, 1919.

Booth, William, *In Darkest England and the Way Out*. England: 1890; Reprinted in United States, Tyler and Co., 1942.

Booth-Tucker, F. de L., *The Life of Catherine Booth* (2 vols.). London: The Salvation Army, 1924 (3rd printing).

Bramwell-Booth, Catherine, *Bramwell Booth*. London: Rich & Cowan, 1933.

———, *Catherine Booth*, London: Hodder & Stoughton, 1970.

Brown, Arnold, *What Hath God Wrought?* Toronto: The Salvation Army, 1952.

Burrows, William, *With Colours Waving*. London: The Salvation Army, 1957.

Carpenter, Minnie Lindsay, *William Booth*. London: Epworth Press, 1942.

Chesham, Sallie, *Born to Battle*, Chicago: Rand McNally & Co., 1965.

Collier, Richard, *The General Next to God*. London: Collins, 1965.

Collier, W. R., and E. V. Westrate, *The Reign of Soapy Smith*. New York: Doubleday, 1935.

Coutts, Frederick, *The Better Fight*. London: Hodder & Stoughton, 1973; reprinted, The Salvation Army, 1977.

————, *No Discharge in This War*. London: Hodder & Stoughton, 1975.

Duff, Mildred, *Catherine Booth*. London: The Salvation Army, 1914.

Ervine, St. John, *God's Soldier: General William Booth* (2 vols.). New York: Macmillan, 1935.

Fosey, Leslie, *This Man Leidzen*. London: The Salvation Army, 1966.

Hall, Clarence W., *Out of the Depths*. New York: The Salvation Army, 1935.

————, *Samuel Logan Brengle*. New York: The Salvation Army, 1933.

Hansen, Lillian E., *The Double Yoke*. New York: Citadel Press, 1968.

Keating, Peter, *Into Unknown England*. London: Fontana/Collins, 1976.

Larsson, Flora, *My Best Men are Women*. New York: The Salvation Army, 1974.

Lavine, Sigmund A., *Evangeline Booth, Daughter of Salvation*. New York: Dodd, Mead & Co., 1970.

Ludwig, Charles, *The Lady General*. Grand Rapids, Mich.: Baker Book House, 1962.

Lunn, Brian, *Salvation Dynasty*. London: Wm. Hodge & Co., 1936.

Mackenzie, F. A., *The Clash of the Cymbals*. New York: Brentano's, 1929.

McCollum, John, and Charles H. Pearson, *College Football USA*. Greenwich, Connecticut: Hall of Fame Publications (published for National Football Foundation).

Miller, Ernest, "Let Your Light So Shine" (manuscript).

Moyles, R. G., *The Blood and Fire in Canada*. Toronto: Peter Martin Assoc., Ltd., 1977.

Neal, Harry Edward, *The Hallelujah Army*. Philadelphia: Chilton, 1961.

Nicol, A. M., *General Booth and The Salvation Army*. London: Herbert & Daniel, 1911.

Nygaard, Norman E., *Trumpet of Salvation*. Grand Rapids, Mich.: Zondervan, 1961.

Ottman, Ford C., *Herbert Booth*. London: Jarrolds, 1928.

Palmer, Agnes L., *Twenty-two*. New York: The Salvation Army. 1926.

Parker, Edward J., *My 58 Years*. New York: The Salvation Army, 1943.

St. Johns, Adela Rogers, *The Honeycomb*. Garden City, N.Y.: Doubleday, 1969.

Sandall, Robert, *History of The Salvation Army*, Vols. I-III. London and New York: Thomas Nelson & Sons, 1947—55.

Smith, Gipsy. *His Life and Work*. New York: Revell, 1901.

Spence, Robert J., ed., *John Markle, Representative American*. New York: Leonard Scott Publishing Company, 1929.

Story of America, The, Edited by Carroll C. Calkins. The Reader's Digest Association, 1975.

Strachey, Lytton, *Queen Victoria*. New York: Harcourt, Brace, 1921.

Strahan, James, *The Marechale* (23rd edition). London: Morgan and Scott, 1921.

200 Years—A Bicentennial Illustrated History of the United States. Published by U.S. News & World Report, 1975.

Watson, Bernard, *A Hundred Years War*. London: Hodder & Stoughton, 1964.

————, *The Artillery of Words*. London: The Salvation Army, 1968.

————, *Soldier Saint*. London: Hodder & Stoughton, 1970.

Wickersham, James, *Old Yukon*. Washington, D.C.: Washington Law Book Co., 1938.

Wiggins, Arch R., *History of The Salvation Army*, vols. IV, V. London: Thomas Nelson, 1964, 1968.

Wilson, P. Whitwell, *General Evangeline Booth*. New York: Revell, 1935.

————, *General Evangeline Booth of The Salvation Army*. New York: Scribner's, 1948.

Wisbey, Herbert A., Jr., *Soldiers Without Swords*. New York: Macmillan, 1956.

The Booth Family

WILLIAM BOOTH

"The Founder"

Born: April 10, 1829
Parents: Samuel Booth and Mary Moss Booth
General: 1878–1912
Died—Promoted to Glory: August 20, 1912

CATHERINE BOOTH (MRS. WILLIAM BOOTH)

"The Army Mother"

Born (Catherine Mumford): January 17, 1829
Parents: John Mumford and Sarah Milward Mumford
Married William Booth: June 16, 1855
Died—Promoted to Glory: October 4, 1890

WILLIAM BRAMWELL BOOTH

Born: March 8, 1856
Married Florence Soper: October 12, 1882
Chief of the Staff: 1881–1912
Served as General: August 21, 1912, to January 17, 1929
Died—Promoted to Glory: June 16, 1929

BALLINGTON BOOTH

"The Marshal"

Born: July 28, 1857
Married Maud Charlsworth: September 17, 1886
National Commander of the United States: 1887–1896
Resigned from The Salvation Army: January 31, 1896
Died—Promoted to Glory: October 5, 1940

CATHERINE BOOTH (MRS. ARTHUR BOOTH-CLIBBORN)

"The Marechale"

Born: September 18, 1858
Married Arthur Sydney Clibborn: February 8, 1887
The Marechale (Marshal) France and Switzerland: 1881–1896
Belgium and Holland: 1896–1902
Resigned from The Salvation Army: January 10, 1902
Widowed: February 20, 1939
Died—Promoted to Glory: May 9, 1955

EMMA MOSS BOOTH (MRS. FREDERICK DE LAUTOUR BOOTH-TUCKER)

"The Consul"

Born: January 8, 1860
Married Frederick St. George de Lautour Tucker: April 10, 1888
Consul in India: 1888–1896
Co-Commander in the United States: 1896–1903
Died—Promoted to Glory (railway accident): October 28, 1903

HERBERT HENRY (HOWARD) BOOTH

"The Commandant"

Born: August 26, 1862
Married Cornelie Ida Ernestine Schoch: September 18, 1890
Commandant in Canada: 1892–1895
Commandant in the United States: 1896–1902
Resigned from The Salvation Army: February 3, 1902
Bereaved of his wife: 1919
Married Annie Lane: November 26, 1923
Died—Promoted to Glory: September 25, 1926

MARIAN (MARIE) BILLUPS BOOTH

Born: May 19, 1864
Staff Captain, but little leadership activity because of physical limitations
Died—Promoted to Glory: January 5, 1937

EVANGELINE (EVELYNE, EVELINE, EVALINE) CORY BOOTH

"The Commander"

Born: December 25, 1865
Commander in Canada: 1896–1904
Commander in the United States: 1904–1934
Served as General: 1934–1939
Died—Promoted to Glory: July 17, 1950

LUCY MILWARD BOOTH (MRS. EMANUEL BOOTH-HELLBERG)

Born: April 28, 1868
Married Emanuel Daniel Hellberg: October 18, 1894

Leader in India: 1894–1896
Commander in France and Switzerland: 1896–1904
Commander in Denmark: 1910–1919
Commander in Norway: 1920–1928
Commander in South America: 1929–1934
Retired: 1934
Widowed: June 5, 1909
Died—Promoted to Glory: July 18, 1953

Index

Abney, Park, 66
Acadia, 132-136, 273, 284
Adams, Blair, 244
Addams, Jane, 116
Agnew, Fletcher, 161
Alaska, 104, 107, 108
Albert of Belgium, King, 192
Allan, John, 277
Allum, Frank, 267, 268
America, 11, 12, 35, 36, 65, 82,
    84, 120, 149, 151, 190, 247,
    265, 273
Aquitania, S.S., 269
Archibald, W. P., 111, 112
Armenians, 97, 98
Arnold, William, 101, 140
Ashbourne, Derbyshire, 20
Astor, John Jacob, 116
Atlanta, 198, 246, 264
Australia, S.S., 36
Aylesworth, Deke, 221

Baird, Catherine, 240, 252
Ball, Eric, 72, 170, 177, 178
Barker, William S., 154-157, 160,
    245
Barnett, Alfred, 253, 267

Bearchell, Charles, 137, 172
Bell, Graham, 185
Berengaria, S.S., 264
Berlin, Irving, 222
Bernhardt, Sarah, 182
Billups, Mary Coutts, 26
Blaine, James, 195
Blind Beggar (public house), 16,
    22
Blomberg, Gosta, 170, 268, 273,
    274
Bloss, Fred, 108
Blowers, Arthur R., 260
Blurton, Annie, 149, 150
Boon, Brindley, 230, 250, 252
Booth, Ballington, 25, 35, 68,
    81-85, 87, 88, 90, 115, 125,
    197, 203, 285
Booth, Mrs. Ballington (Maude
    Charlesworth), 82-84, 115
Booth, Bramwell, 17, 24, 33, 57,
    65, 68, 81, 82, 88, 103, 127,
    146-148, 150, 154, 193,
    203-206, 207-215, 227
Booth, Mrs. Bramwell (Florence
    Soper), 211, 227, 230
Booth, Catherine: childhood, 20;

meets Booth, 20; love and marriage, 21; women's rights, 20, 21; encourages William to leave Methodists, 22; birth of Salvation Army, 18, 19; birth of Evangeline, 16, 17; illness, 23, 26; education of children, 24, 29, 30; flags for America, 36; learns she has terminal cancer, 64; last public appearance, 65; death and funeral, 66

Booth, Catherine (Kate), 25, 77, 90, 125, 198

Booth, Charles Brandon, 285

Booth, Emma, 17, 25, 35, 38, 64, 68, 77, 84, 89, 109, 113, 124

Booth, Evangeline: birth, 15-17; childhood "Papa's favorite," 25; family life, 25-29; first sermon, 30; conversion, 31; enthusiastic soldier, 34-36, 38; sent with Cadman to preach, 38; to Training Home with Emma, 38; part of the Cellar, Gutter, and Garret brigade, 39; active in Army's purity crusade, 41; sent to Great Western Hall, 41; becomes known as "White Angel of the Slums," 41-53; farewells from Great Western Hall and ill for several months, 54; sent to trouble spots in England, 56-63; becomes Field Commissioner, 63; lives at home while mother is ill and dying, 64, 65; cares for London waifs, 67; becomes International Training Home principal, 68; asks permission of father to marry, 75-79; sent to the United States to persuade Ballington to accept transfer orders, 82-88; sent as Field Commissioner to Canada, 89-102, 103-114; spiritual campaigns, 99-101, 111; Klondike expedition, 103-107; prison work and men and women's social programs expanded, 111-113; parole system, 111, 112; immigration program, 112; Emma's death, 113; becomes Commander of Army's forces in United States, 114-122; San Francisco earthquake, 122, 123; Boozers' Day meetings, 128-131; at home, 132-137; working vacations at Lake George, 137-143; and father's eye surgery, 144, 145; visits Booth in England, 145, 146; Booth's death, 147; and Bramwell as General, 148; youth programs expanded, 148; international congress of 1914, 149-151; in World War I, 152-164; musician and composer, 165-178; lecturer and preacher, 179-189; puts Salvation Army in U.S. on sounder financial footing, 190-192; U.S. divided into three territories, 194; fights attempt to repeal 18th Amendment, 194-196; sets up Advisory Boards, 196; creates Southern terri-

Booth, Evangeline (*cont.*)
tory, 198; initiates Commissioners' conference, 199; visit to Japan, 200-202; and Bramwell's visit to U.S., 204; told of transfer from U.S., 205; orders canceled, 205, 206; as honored guest of American Legion at Paris convention, 207, 208; confers in London with General Bramwell, 209; 1929 High Council, 211-215; in the Great Depression, 217-224; at Golden Jubilee Congress, 225-227; motorcades, 230-232, 255-258; elected General, 236; returns to U.S. as General-elect, 11-14; personality, 237-247; visits Australia and New Zealand, 253, 254; at Canadian congress, 256, 257; visits India, 260-263; conducts European, American, and Canadian congresses, 264, 265, 269; farewell meeting canceled because of World War II, 270; retirement, 273-283; death, 284-287

Booth, Herbert, 34, 68, 83, 84, 89-91, 109, 110, 125, 197, 203

Booth, Mrs. Herbert (Annie Lane), 273

Booth, Lucy, 23, 26, 68, 77, 90, 146, 214, 235, 236

Booth, Marian (Marie), 24, 28, 68, 76

Booth, Mary, 208, 214

Booth, Mary Moss, 19

Booth, Samuel, 19

Booth, William: childhood and youth, 19; conversion and evangelism, 19, 20; meets Catherine, 20; courtship and marriage, 20, 21; with Methodist Reformers, 20; with Methodist New Connexion, 21; resigns from Methodist New Connexion, 22; finds his destiny, 18, 19; family life, 24, 26, 29, 30; turns Christian Mission to The Salvation Army, 33; encourages Eva to sell War Crys and preach, 37, 38; sends Eva to Great Western Hall, 41; sends Eva to trouble spots, 56-63; promotes Eva to Field Commissioner, 63; and Catherine's illness, death, and funeral, 64-66; refuses Eva permission to marry, 78, 79; learns of Ballington's resignation, 82; visits W. E. Gladstone, 109; and Kate and Herbert's resignation, 109; visits Eva in Canada, 110, 111; and Emma's death, 113; sends Evangeline to United States, 114; visits U.S., 124-126; blindness, 144-147; visit from Evangeline, 145, 146; death, 147

Booth-Clibborn, Arthur Sydney, 109

Booth-Tucker, Frederick St. George de Latour, 84, 90, 117

Booth-Tucker, Muriel, 253, 260, 261, 281

Boozers' Day, 128-131

Bowarter, Sir Frank, Lord Mayor
of London, 269
Bowes, Major Edward, 221
Boyle, Mrs. Norman, 99
Bramwell-Booth, Catherine,
187, 210, 212, 214, 227, 229,
230, 236
Brengle, Samuel, L., 212-213,
219, 230
Brewer, Minnie, 251
Briggs, Cecil, 277
Briggs, Walter, 277
Bright, John, 50
British Weekly, 284
Broad Street Wesleyan
Methodist Chapel, 19, 271
Broughton, William, 171
Brown, Arnold, 93, 98, 256
Bruce, Dr. Herbert, 79, 256, 257
Bryan, William Jennings, 187
Bullard, Lily, 268, 271
Busby, Mrs. John (Elsbeth), 140
Butler, Nicholas Murray, 269
Byrd, Richard E., 198, 199

Cadman, Elijah, 33, 38
Cairns, Earl, 50
Camp Cory, 138-140
Canada, 71, 89-115, 119, 148,
166, 179, 256-257
Carnegie, Andrew, 116
Carnegie Hall, 82, 115, 116, 226
Carpenter, George Lyndon, 270,
273
Carr, Hannah, 66, 238
Castle Garden, 12, 36
Cellar, Gutter, and Garret
Brigade, 39, 68
Chamberlain, William, 281, 286
Chapman, J. Wilbur, 80
Charles, William Henry, 257
Chicago, 69, 87, 153, 161, 183,

186, 194, 220, 246, 278
Chicago Tribune, 232
Choate, Joseph C., 123
Christian Mission, 30, 33
Christian Mission Magazine, 34
Christmas Day, 14, 16, 27, 28,
121, 144, 230, 237, 252, 253
Christmas Eve, 15, 121
Churchill, Winston, 279
City Temple, Holborn, 64
Clapton Common, 35
Clapton Congress Hall, 67, 69,
87, 88, 216, 235, 237, 265,
268
Clark, Mrs. Samuel Adams, 221
Clemenceau, Georges, 208
Coles, Bramwell, 170
Collins, Dr. Edward Treacher,
146
Cooke, Dr. William, 21, 22
Coolidge, Calvin, 198
Coutts, Frederick, 255
Cowan, Llewellyn, 191, 192
Cox, Blanche B., 39
Cox, Fred, 110
Cox, J. Clyde, 233, 234
Creighton, Muriel, 134, 136, 169
Crofts, Dr. Henry, 21, 22
Crosby, Bing, 221
Crowell, Russell, 171
Culshaw, Owen, 112, 248, 272
Culshaw, Mrs. Owen (Eva), 67
Cummings, Homer S., 246

Daily Chronicle, The, 74
Daily Herald, The, 237
Daily Telegraph, The, 66
Dalziel, Geoffrey, 267
Damon, Alex M., 126
Darbyshire, Bramwell, 177
Dawson City, 104, 108
Depew, Chauncey M., 82

Dimond, Victor, 242
Doumergue, Gaston, 208
Dowie, John Alexander, 109
Duerr, Louise, 243

Eastbourne, 67, 68, 81
East London Christian Mission, 15
Edward, Prince of Wales, 192
Emory, Thomas (hospital), 261
Empress of Ireland, S.S., 149
Espagne, S.S., 156
Estill, Thomas, 153, 161, 194
Evans, William, 119, 126, 199

Farrington, Florence, 251, 273, 282
Ferdinand, Archduke Francis, 151
Foch, Ferdinand, 208
Ford, Henry, 115
Fowler, Bill, 63
Fowler, Frank, 171
Fowler, Henry H., 63
France, 152, 154-157, 164
French, George, 122
French, Holland, 141
Frost, William, 148, 211
Fuller, George, 49

Gabrielsen, Tom, 232
Gabrielsen, T. Raymond, 135
Galitzin, Prince, 79, 80
George VI, King of Britain, 263, 270
Gershwin, George, 222
Gifford, Adam, 119, 126, 194, 199
Gilliard, Alfred J., 255
Gladstone, W. E., 109, 203, 204
Globe, The, 94

Goldenheart, 134, 171, 281
Goldman, Edwin Franco, 174
Grace Hospital (Canada), 113
Grand Rapids, Michigan, 149
Great Western Hall, Marylebone, 40, 41, 46, 47, 49, 53, 68, 77, 89
Greene, Wilfred, 214
Griffith, Richard, 119, 133-135, 138, 141, 169, 175, 228, 236, 251, 253, 267-270
Gustav, King of Sweden, 233
Guildford, 56
Guldenschuh, Frank, 65, 284
Guzman, Alejandro, 265
Gypsy, *see* Welch, Mary

Hackney, 23, 35
Hadleigh, 112
Haines, William, 212, 214
Hall, Clarence, 244, 245
Hanley, 56, 57
Hansen, Lillian, 244
Hartsdale, N.Y., 132, 196, 273, 283
Hay, James, 212
Hearst, William Randolph, 222
Hearst, Mrs. William Randolph, 221
Higgins, Dr. Charles, 146
Higgins, Edward J., 119, 211, 215, 216, 227-231, 235, 249, 250
High Council, 88, 204, 210-216, 235, 236, 249, 270
Hill, Edwin C., 246
Hirohito, Emperor, 200
Hodgson, Herbert S., 272
Hoggard, Mrs. Commissioner Robert (Mary Martin), 72
Holz, Ernest, 161, 184

Holz, Richard E. (grandfather of present Commissioner Richard E. Holz), 119, 126, 127, 199

Holz, Richard E., 161, 168, 170, 176, 279, 280, 283

Hokanson, Minnie, 242

House of Commons, 63

Howard, Railton, 177

Hurley, Patrick, 219

Hurren, Samuel, 236

Hutton, E. J., 220-222

India, 168, 253, 260-263

International Congress, 113, 149-151

International Training College (formerly International Training Home), 68, 69, 87

International Headquarters, 77, 147

Jacobs, Clement, 95

Jeffries, Charles, 248

Jenkins, Walter F., 194, 206, 212, 243

Jowitt, William, K.C., 213, 215

Joy, Edward, 67

Kaiser, Paul, 165, 243, 286

Kappel, Frederick, 138

Keller, Helen, 135, 247

Kern, Jerome, 222

Kilbey, George, 118

Kirkton, Mary, 23, 26

Kitching, Wilfred, 170

Klondike, 103-107, 115, 148

Ladlow, Fred, 172

LaGuardia, Fiorello H., 11-13

Laity, Edward, 199

Lake George, N.Y., 137-143

Lamb, David C., 236, 272

Lancaster (jail), 65

Landon, Alfred M., 275

Langdon, George, 268

Leidzen, Erik, 168, 170, 174-176, 280

Leopold of Belgium, Prince, 192

Leviathan, S.S., 11, 12, 235

LeViness, J. Leonard, 132, 133, 242

Lindvall, Alfred, 263

London, 20, 22, 23, 38, 63, 67, 75, 83, 87, 113, 120, 180, 235, 248-250, 259, 269

London Daily Mirror, 216

London News Chronicle, 238

London Times, 151, 259, 267-268

Lord, Herbert, 67

Lundgren, Olof, 173

Luther, Martin, 166

Mabee, Walter, 171, 175, 177, 198, 253

MacFadden, Bernarr, 139

MacMillan, Alex, 96, 97, 101, 102, 110

Mackness, Mrs., 251, 253, 273

Majestic, S.S., 248

Maltby, William, 172, 177, 187, 280

Mapp, Henry W., 236, 248, 251

Margetts, Myrtle, 153

Markle, John, 217, 218

Marshall, George C., 275, 276, 278

Marshall, Norman S., 161

Martin, T. Herbert, 259

Marylebone, 41, 50, 51, 54, 59, 68

Massey Hall, 98, 99, 103, 114, 115, 179, 257

McArthur, Douglas, 220

McBride, Warren, 201

McElroy, Henry F., 234

McElroy, Mary, 234

McGee, Walter, 234

McGill, Tom, 108

McIntyre, Clifford, 242

McIntyre, William A., 119, 126, 128, 194, 198, 199, 240, 259

McKie, Thomas, 75-79, 90, 148, 193

McMillan, Christine, 235, 236, 239

McMillan, Donald, 283

McMillan, John, 141, 173, 174, 186, 199, 244, 256, 263, 269, 270

McMillan, Mrs. John, 141, 256, 276, 282

McNab, John L., 201

Methodist New Connexion, 21, 22

Methodist Reformers, 20

Milans, Henry F., 129, 130

Miller, Joy, 99

Mills, Bertram, 50, 257, 258

Mooltan, S.S., 253

Morning Advertiser, The, 87

Morris, Arthur, 101

Moyles, Dr. R. G., 94

Musician, The, 170

Nelson, Emil, 71, 171

Newton, Ernest, 142, 172, 173

New York, 11, 13, 36, 37, 115, 119, 120, 123, 124, 126, 128, 149, 152, 160, 162, 181, 191, 193, 195, 196, 207, 217, 220, 225, 227, 246, 269, 286

New York American, 190

New York Daily Tribune, 85

New York Mercury, 129

New York Recorder, 86

New York Sun, 82

New York Memorial Temple Corps, 173, 174, 226, 285

New York Times, 137, 196, 218, 219, 229, 238, 274

New York Times Magazine, 279

New York World, 117, 205

Nice, Mrs. Edith, 220

Nichols, Ruth, 12

Nicol, Alex M., 82-85, 88

Noble, Dr. William, 262

Norris, Albert, 226

Norris, Douglas, 171

Nottingham, 19, 271

Ochs, Adolph, 137

Old Grecian corps (was Grecian theatre), 74-76

Oliphant, William Elwin, 76

Olympic, S.S., 150

O'Neil, Fred, 137

Onslow, Lord, 50

Orton, Harold, 255

Ostby, Klaus, 168

Overstake, Charles, 240

Pagents, Jack W., 242

Paget, Sir James, 64, 89

Pall Mall Gazette, 60

Park, Guy, 233, 234

Parker, Edward J., 119, 124, 180, 181, 199, 233

Parkins, William J., 140, 174-176, 187, 188, 287

Parkins, Mrs. William J. (Eva), 239

Parr, Ernest, 73

Peacock, Thomas, 99

Peacock, Walter, 101

Peart, William, 119, 194

Pease, Carrie, 92, 101

Pepper, Albert, 278
Pershing, John J., 79, 154-156, 208
Philadelphia, 35-37, 87, 126
Philpott, Peter, 93, 94
Piccadilly Circus, 43
Porter, Melville, 56
Pratt, (Admiral) W. B., 220
Pugmire, Ernest I, 201, 272, 281, 282, 285
Pugmire, Mrs. Ernest I. (Grace), 201, 246
Purviance, Helen, 158, 159, 162, 241

Queen Victoria Saint (International Headquarters), 77, 147

Rader, Lyell, 73, 134, 186, 242
Rader, Paul, 161
Railton. George Scott, 12, 26, 33, 35-37, 79
Ranger, Dr. Alfred, 148
Rapee, Erno, 221
Rawlins, Kenneth, 73
Red Knights of the Cross, 99, 110
Redwood, Hugh, 11
Regent, Hall, 69, 271
Reinhardsen, G. S., 142, 143, 206
Renton, Ethel, 220
Rice, Eugene, 246
Rich, Charles T., 272
Ripley, Robert, 108
Riverside (launch), 11
Rodda, Bertram, 154, 241
Rogers, Will, 223
Romberg, Sigmund, 222
Roosevelt, Franklin Delano, 223
Roosevelt, Mrs. Franklin Delano (Eleanor), 221, 226

Roosevelt, Quentin, 160
Roosevelt, Theodore, 116, 150
Rotherhithe, 43, 66, 67
Royal, John F., 221
Russell, George, 228, 229, 244
Russell, Sir George, 63
Russell, Mina, 274
Ryan, Glenn, 108, 277, 278

St. Johns, Adela Rogers, 222
St. Louis, Mo., 37
Salvationist, The, 34
San Francisco, 122-123, 194, 201, 246
Sankey, Ira D., 169
Sarajevo, 151
Seagate (launch), 12
Seige, The, 99, 111, 121
Shaftesbury, Earl of, 50
Sharp, William G., 154
Shaw, George Bernard, 121, 122
Sheldon, Margaret, 158
Sheppard, Stanley, 171
Shirley, Amos and Anna, 35, 37
Shirley, Eliza, 35, 37
Short, Jane, 26-28
Skagway, 104-106, 108
Skeleton Army, 48, 49, 55, 56, 68
Sladen, Mrs. Hugh (Motee), 284, 285
Slater, William, 171
Smiles, Alma, 70, 71
Smith, J. Evan, 268
Smith, Jefferson Randolph (Soapy), 104-107
Smith, Rodney (Gipsy), 56, 57
Sneath, Frederick, 227
Sousa, John Philip, 226
Speyer, James, 195
Stanyon, Thomas, 101
Steadman-Allen, Ray, 266
Stretton, Richard, 281

Stretton, Mrs. Richard (Hazel), 167, 281, 282
Strong, William L., 82
Swenarton, Alfred, 280

Taft, Henry W., 274
Taylor, Chester, 104
Tees, S.S., 104, 105
Texter, George Clinton, 138
Tlingit Indians, 108, 110
Toronto, 94, 97, 103, 107, 114, 257, 269
Toronto Daily Mail & Empire, 179
Toronto Evening Star, 98, 103
Toronto Globe, 95
Torquay, 58-63, 208, 233, 257
Torquay Harbour Bill, 63
Torquay Times, 59
Tucker, Frederick St. George de Latour, 64
Tumulty, Joseph P., 154
Turkington, Florence, 156, 240

Uncle Tom's Cabin, 17
USO (United Service Organizations), 274, 275
United States, 36, 71, 81-83, 86, 87, 90, 93, 108, 109, 114, 115, 116, 117, 125, 127, 144, 149, 155, 160, 166, 171, 179, 180, 190, 205, 264

Vanderbilt, Cornelius, 191
Van Norden, Emma, 87
Van Norden, Warner, 162
Victoria, Queen, 34, 58, 109
Volunteers of America, 86, 125, 197, 285

Voorsanger, L. M., 201

Wald, Lillian, 116
Walker, James E., 132
Walker, Jimmy, 218, 219
Wanamaker, John, 79, 126, 185
Wanamaker, Rodman, 192
War Cry, The, 34, 37, 38, 41, 43, 76, 82, 102, 117, 152, 153, 211, 244, 271
Ware, William, 151
Watson, Adjutant, 94
Watts, Isaac, 169
Webb, Ernest, 268
Welch, Mary (Gypsy), 71, 92, 110, 119, 133, 251, 273, 283
Wesley, Samuel, 169
Westbrook, Emma, 30, 36, 37
Westminster, Palace of, 63
Whalen, Grover A., 219
Whitchurch, 56
White Angel of the Slums, 43
Whitechapel, 15, 27, 36
Whitman, Charles S., 191
Whittaker, Etta, 101
Wilhelmina of Holland, Queen, 269
Willard, Frances Elizabeth, 118
Wilson, Philip Whitwell, 57, 205, 274
Wilson, Woodrow, 152, 153, 159, 163
Wiseman, Clarence, 257
Wolverhampton, 63
Woodruff, Arthur, 193, 245, 246, 282
Woodruff, Pearl, 284
World, The, 86
World War I, 152-164, 203, 208, 274

World War II, 200, 274
Wrigley, William J., Jr., 220

Young, Alleyne, 153

Young, Mrs. Robert (Alma), 71
Young Soldier, The, 252

Zuber, Braxton, 159